A DIVIDED KINGDOM

THE SPANISH MONARCHY
from Isabel to Juan Carlos

JOHN VAN DER KISTE

SUTTON PUBLISHING

First published in the United Kingdom in 2007 by
Sutton Publishing Limited · Phoenix Mill
Thrupp · Stroud · Gloucestershire · GL5 2BU

British Library Cataloguing in Publication Data
A catalogue record for this book is available from the British Library.

Hardback ISBN 978-0-7509-3789-4
Paperback ISBN 978-0-7509-3814-3

Typeset in Sabon.
Typesetting and origination by
Sutton Publishing Limited.
Printed and bound in England.

Recent titles by John Van der Kiste
published by Sutton

The Romanovs 1818–1959: Alexander II of Russia and his family (1998)
Kaiser Wilhelm II: Germany's last Emperor (1999)
The Georgian Princesses (2000)
Gilbert & Sullivan's Christmas (2000)
*Dearest Vicky, Darling Fritz: Queen Victoria's eldest daughter and the German
Emperor* (2001)
Once a Grand Duchess: Xenia, sister of Nicholas II
[with Coryne Hall] (2002)
William and Mary (2003)
*Emperor Francis Joseph: Life, death and the fall of the Austro-Hungarian
Empire* (2005)
Sons, Servants and Statesmen: The men in Queen Victoria's life (2006)
Devon Murders (2006)

Contents

The House of Bourbon

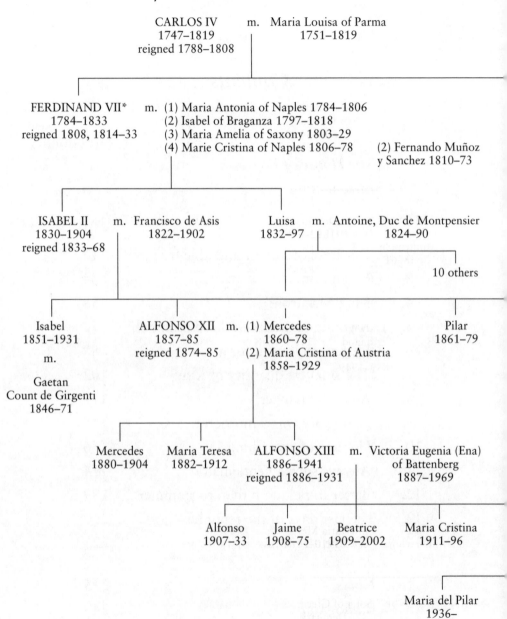

CARLOS IV   m.   Maria Louisa of Parma
1747–1819   1751–1819
reigned 1788–1808

FERDINAND VII*   m.   (1) Maria Antonia of Naples 1784–1806
1784–1833   (2) Isabel of Braganza 1797–1818
reigned 1808, 1814–33   (3) Maria Amelia of Saxony 1803–29
                       (4) Marie Cristina of Naples 1806–78   (2) Fernando Muñoz
                                                       y Sanchez 1810–73

ISABEL II   m.   Francisco de Asis   Luisa   m.   Antoine, Duc de Montpensier
1830–1904   1822–1902   1832–97   1824–90
reigned 1833–68

                                                                              10 others

Isabel   ALFONSO XII   m.   (1) Mercedes   Pilar
1851–1931   1857–85   1860–78   1861–79
m.   reigned 1874–85   (2) Maria Cristina of Austria
                                                1858–1929
Gaetan
Count de Girgenti
1846–71

Mercedes   Maria Teresa   ALFONSO XIII   m.   Victoria Eugenia (Ena)
1880–1904   1882–1912   1886–1941   of Battenberg
                             reigned 1886–1931   1887–1969

Alfonso   Jaime   Beatrice   Maria Cristina
1907–33   1908–75   1909–2002   1911–96

                                                                    Maria del Pilar
                                                                      1936–

* Ferdinand's first three marriages left no surviving issue.
** Carlos V, VI and VII were pretenders to the Spanish throne.

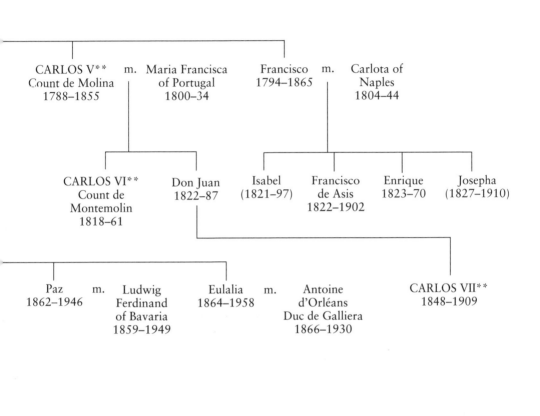

CARLOS V** m. Maria Francisca Francisco m. Carlota of
Count de Molina of Portugal 1794–1865 Naples
1788–1855 1800–34 1804–44

CARLOS VI** Don Juan Isabel Francisco Enrique Josepha
Count de 1822–87 (1821–97) de Asis 1823–70 (1827–1910)
Montemolin 1822–1902
1818–61

Paz m. Ludwig Eulalia m. Antoine CARLOS VII**
1862–1946 Ferdinand 1864–1958 d'Orléans 1848–1909
of Bavaria Duc de Galliera
1859–1949 1866–1930

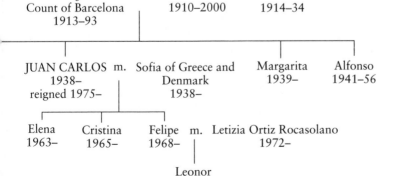

Don Juan m. Maria Mercedes Gonzalo
Count of Barcelona 1910–2000 1914–34
1913–93

JUAN CARLOS m. Sofia of Greece and Margarita Alfonso
1938– Denmark 1939– 1941–56
reigned 1975– 1938–

Elena Cristina Felipe m. Letizia Ortiz Rocasolano
1963– 1965– 1968– 1972–

Leonor
2005–

Introduction

Early in 1931 King Alfonso XIII of Spain asked his Prime Minister, Admiral Aznar, to form a government and prepare the country for new municipal and parliamentary elections. He then went to England for a short holiday. As a cousin by marriage of King George V of England, he was part of the family network of monarchs who could claim a close connection with Queen Victoria and King Edward VII as the grandmother and uncle of Europe respectively.

Spain had recently been through difficult times. Parliamentary government under General Primo de Rivera ('my Mussolini', as the King had called him with admiration) had been suspended for several years, and though the largely benevolent despotic regime had brought considerable economic benefits to the nation, it had been unpopular, and culminated in the ailing General's resignation and death soon afterwards.

The King had hoped to prepare the way for a peaceful return to constitutional government and a reign lasting many more years. When the elections held in April 1931, soon after his return to Spain, showed an unexpected swing towards the socialist and republican parties, especially in the large cities, he was unnerved. It was, he remarked sadly, as if he had gone to make a visit to a friend, and on arriving at the house found that he was dead. Believing that anti-monarchist fervour would soon subside, he decided to leave Spain for a while, and consented to a suspension of his powers, while insisting that he would not abdicate.

It was yet another twist in the remarkable saga of the Spanish Bourbons, who had reigned with one brief interruption since the beginning of the eighteenth century. King Alfonso XIII's grand-mother, Queen Isabel, had been driven from the kingdom some sixty years earlier, and a short interregnum had given way to the far from unanimous election of a King from the House of Savoy, followed by the establishment of a republic and the subsequent recall of Isabel's son, who reigned as King Alfonso XII.

Uniquely among the nations of Europe, King Alfonso XIII's departure left Spain a republic – or more accurately, as would be confirmed some years later, a monarchy without a king. Some thirty-eight years after the King and Queen went into exile, their grandson was chosen as king-in-waiting, thereby and somewhat controversially bypassing his father who was still alive and in good health, to wait in the wings and succeed General Franco, the head of state, on the latter's death. After a republican interval of forty-four years, in November 1975 Spain was once again a kingdom.

The aim of this book is to trace the family vicissitudes from the Napoleonic era onwards, through the lives, characters and reigns of the kings, queens and their consorts who reigned over the country and, notwithstanding their faults, never completely forfeited the love and respect of an often volatile but fundamentally generous and forgiving country that always as a whole held the historical tradition of monarchy in high regard.

The names of Spanish royalty require some explanation. Members are not princes or princesses, apart from the heir to the throne, who is Prince or Princess of Asturias; the others are Infantes or Infantas. The title Prince of Asturias, the Spanish Crown Prince, was created in the fourteenth century by King Juan I of Castile. The style of Infante or Infanta or 'grace' can be granted by the Spanish monarch to close family members, or members of foreign dynasties who marry into the family.

*   *   *

I wish to acknowledge the gracious permission of Her Majesty The Queen to publish material from the Royal Archives, Windsor. For permission to quote an unpublished letter, I am grateful to Ian

Shapiro of Argyll Etkin Ltd. For regular advice, support and the loan of various materials I would like to thank Sue and Mike Woolmans, Coryne Hall, Karen Roth, Robin Piguet, Ricardo Mateo Sainz de Medrano and Art Beéche; and for access to their collections I am indebted to the staff at Kensington and Chelsea Public Libraries. Last but not least, my thanks as ever go to my wife Kim, my mother Kate and my stepdaughter Laura for their constant encouragement and reading through the draft manuscript; and to my editors at Sutton Publishing, Jaqueline Mitchell and Anne Bennett for all their hard work in seeing the project through to completion.

This book is respectfully dedicated to the memory of Gracie Cole Geldard.

ONE

A child queen

By 1808 the star of Napoleon Bonaparte, self-proclaimed Emperor of the French whose mastery over much of Europe had been virtually unchallenged, was beginning to wane. It was the year that he sent troops into Spain, and the British government responded by sending an army into the Iberian peninsula in order to encourage Portuguese and Spanish resistance. In March an uprising in Spain led to the abdication of King Carlos IV, and the throne passed to his son, who ascended as King Ferdinand VII. Within the week Carlos had retracted his abdication, claiming it had been made under duress. Nevertheless Ferdinand was still regarded as the rightful sovereign, until he was forced to abdicate by Napoleon in May, and Carlos was again King. Almost at once Carlos abdicated a second time, surrendering his throne to Napoleon, who proclaimed his brother Joseph King of Spain as José I a month later. Early French victories in the war soon gave way to defeat; after the battle of Vittoria in June 1813 Napoleon was driven out of Spain, and in December that year the Bourbon monarchy was restored with Ferdinand on the throne a second time. With the death of his father in January 1819 he could consider himself secure on the throne at last.

In 1829 Ferdinand lost his third wife, Queen Maria Amelia, born a princess of Saxony. His second wife Isabel, a Portuguese princess, had died in childbirth in 1818, leaving a daughter who lived for only four months. Neither of his first two marriages had produced any surviving children. If he died without issue, the throne would pass to his younger brother Don Carlos. Ferdinand's cruelty, religious intolerance and despotism had made him unpopular, but

1

his brother was disliked even more. Don Carlos, the Spaniards said, was more Catholic than the Pope, and more royalist than the King.

Nevertheless Carlos had his positive qualities. It was said that he was always honest, the only member of the royal family who never broke his word and always paid his bills, and there were many in Spain who would have liked him to succeed Ferdinand on the throne. In 1825 there was a small but unsuccessful rising in his favour, and two years later a body calling itself the Federation of Pure Royalists issued their own manifesto, calling on him to become King. He kept his distance, letting nobody doubt his loyalty to the Spanish crown, if not to his brother. Perhaps he assumed that as his brother's heir, he would inherit the throne before long. With a forceful wife who saw herself as the next Queen of Spain, and three young sons, they would surely see that the Bourbon dynasty remained in safe hands.

At forty-four King Ferdinand was in poor health, and seemed older than his years. Nevertheless he was urged to marry a fourth time in order to produce an heir. In December 1829 he married Princess Maria Cristina of Naples, who was some twenty years younger than him. Like most other royal marriages of the time, it was a strictly dynastic arrangement, for neither partner was really in love with the other. She had already lost her heart to Don Fernando Muñoz y Sanchez, a handsome young officer in the Garde du Corps, who had been in the suite which escorted her to Madrid. Nevertheless by spring the next year she was known to be *enceinte*, and on 10 October 1830 she gave birth to a daughter. When told that the Queen had just produced 'a robust infanta', the King turned pale.

As next in succession to the throne the baby was accordingly created Princess of Asturias. Christened Maria Isabel Luisa, she was always known in the family by the second name. Any hopes that a baby brother would soon arrive and thus displace her were dashed with the appearance of another girl, Luisa, born in 1832.

In failing health and increasing pain, King Ferdinand knew he was unlikely to have any more children. Determined to ensure that his elder daughter would assume the throne, in June 1833 he first induced the Cortes to set aside the Salic Law which would have debarred her – and any infanta – from the succession, and then to stage a ceremony at the Church of San Jeronimo in Madrid, at which each member would take an oath of allegiance to her as heiress apparent. The proceedings were boycotted by Don Carlos, who saw it as a personal insult as well as the ultimate frustration of his personal ambitions.

Nobody, least of all the ailing monarch himself, had any doubt that the throne would soon change hands. Though only 48, the consumptive King Ferdinand was becoming progressively weaker. On 29 September 1833, with Queen Maria Cristina beside him, he died after a severe stroke. Three days later his last will and testament was read. The Infanta was immediately proclaimed Queen, and the widowed Queen Maria Cristina was appointed Regent. Queen Isabel II was recognised as the rightful sovereign by the courts of England and France, while at home her supporters included the government in Madrid, the Liberals in the Cortes, and those in the south and centre of Spain. In the meantime her uncle, Don Carlos, was proclaimed Carlos V, King of Spain, and recognised as sovereign by Russia, Austria and the Vatican.

At home his most fervent partisans were to be found in the north of Spain. The family itself was divided, for among those who regarded him as the true monarch were the Regent's own brother Ferdinand II, King of Naples, who sent him an envoy acknowledging his sovereignty. An uprising in his favour was followed by several small revolts against Queen Isabel throughout the northern provinces. It marked the start of the Carlist wars, which would destabilise the Spanish monarchy for several decades. The First Carlist War lasted over seven years and fighting spanned most of the country at one time or another, although the main conflict centred around the Carlist homelands of the Basque country and Aragon.

In political terms the Spanish Bourbons had split into two opposing factions. The Carlists were the absolutist, legitimist branch, who denied the validity of the Pragmatic Sanction that had abolished the Salic Law; while the Cristinos, the reigning branch, were the constitutional, liberal branch headed by the Queen and her mother. The term liberal, however, was relative, and the Queen's governments

3

were generally just as reactionary as their opponents. As a constitutional monarch, she was obliged to put her trust in whoever headed her government. Even so, the legitimists would see themselves as liberals, with the Carlists staking their claim as the embodiment of conservative values and an adherence to the traditions of the past. George Villiers, a British minister in Madrid, believed that most of the Spanish people were Carlists at heart, ready to embrace absolutism, and haters of liberal governments and institutions. Queen Isabel's position was maintained largely through the support of the army, the Cortes, Liberals and Progressives.

Within a few years politicians would regroup into two broad parties, the progresista (progressive) and the moderados (moderate) parties. As their names suggested, the former were more liberal, even radical, and sometimes hostile to the Church, though not republican apart from a few individuals, while the latter were more conservative, comprising largely the landowners and the aristocracy who feared any threat to the established hierarchy.

On 28 December 1833, three months after the death of King Ferdinand, Queen Maria Cristina and Muñoz went through a secret ceremony of marriage, performed by a village priest who was a friend of the groom. The witnesses at the ceremony were afterwards sent away to different parts of the kingdom, with instructions not to reveal what had taken place. Loath to lose Muñoz, yet with too much respect for the sanctity of marriage to take him as a lover, the widowed Queen was intent on marrying him. Having done her duty in taking, or in letting herself be taken by, a husband who needed a wife solely for reasons of state, she felt she deserved some happiness. Nevertheless, under Spanish law she was required to remain a widow in order to retain guardianship of her daughters during their minority. It was therefore imperative for her to keep her second marriage a closely guarded secret, for otherwise she would forfeit her position as Queen Regent, her allowance and her daughters by her first husband.

Muñoz lived in the palace, ostensibly as the Regent's groom of the bedchamber, and the little white lie of her widowhood was thus maintained. He was also given the title Duke of Riansares. During the next few years two more daughters and two sons were born to

4

the couple, but kept firmly away from the public gaze. All the same, when news of the Regent's marital union to the low-ranking soldier became public, her standing in Spain diminished accordingly; it undermined her position as Regent and gave rise to concerns that she was not genuinely supportive of her liberal ministers and their policies. Eventually the army, the backbone of Queen Isabel's support, and the liberal leadership in the Cortes made a joint demand that she should relinquish her position, and in 1840 the army commander-in-chief, General Baldomero Espartero, replaced her as Regent. He was regarded as something of a progressive in political terms, though at the same time incorrigibly lazy. If anything went wrong, said friends and opponents alike, he took to his bed and stayed there; bed was his answer to every crisis.[1]

After she had made an abortive attempt to reclaim power, Maria Christina retired permanently to exile in France after 1844, and France remained her primary residence for the rest of her life. Espartero remained Regent for only two years, for in 1843 he was turned out by a military and political *pronunciamento* led by Generals O'Donnell and Narvaez. They formed a cabinet led by Joaquin Maria Lopez, and the government persuaded the Cortes to declare Isabel Queen.

In personality Queen Isabel was a good-natured young girl, precocious in manner if not very clever, impetuous and wilful. Untidy and lazy in general, her table manners were almost non-existent, and she regularly spilt food down the front of her clothes. As she could scarcely be bothered to dress or undress herself, it took four servants to dress her every morning, a process which normally took over an hour. She could barely read and showed no interest in books, her handwriting was appalling, and her education had been lacking; as her mother once complained, those around her made no effort to induce her to study, lest they should lose her favour.[2] It was said that she only liked toys and dogs.[3] With her lack of interest in exercise she rapidly put on weight, and from early childhood she suffered from ichthyosis, a skin disease that resulted in her body, especially her head and limbs, being covered with dry, scaly, fish-like skin. It was an affliction which never ceased to trouble her.

All the same, early in life she cultivated an air of queenly dignity, inherited from her mother who impressed on her the importance of deportment. She had a warm smile and a ready laugh which often disarmed people; she was warmhearted and generous by nature, and as she had no idea of the value of money she could be impulsively generous to those in need.

To supervise her and her sister Luisa during their adolescent years and in their mother's absence, Espartero appointed a governess, Countess Espoz y Mina. Agustin Arguelles became the Queen's official guardian, and Quintana her tutor. Mina was impressed by the girls' 'confiding openness' and their affectionate nature. Quintana became very fond of them as well, though he found them very young for their age, as nothing had ever occurred to train their attention to any specific subject. They were too easily distracted, he saw; even so, they learned to read and write, and to do simple arithmetic, and could speak, translate and write French to a reasonable standard. They also acquired a rudimentary knowledge of music and geography. 'Their understanding is clear and unimpeded, without any vice or fault in their faculties; so that when they seek to fix attention, and give their interest to showing what they have really learnt, there is no exercise in which they do not succeed marvellously. But the lack of attention and interest is a grave inconvenience with which we have to struggle at all times.'[4]

During the first months of Espoz's appointment occurred what the young Queen would always refer to as 'that awful night', 7 October 1841. She was having a singing lesson with her master Valldemosa at the Palacio Real when their peace and quiet was disturbed by the noise of shouting, clashing steel and then a volley of shots from the outer courtyard. Her ladies immediately got up and bolted all the doors and windows of the royal suite. As Countess Espoz ran towards the young sovereign's apartments, she saw a gang of armed men moving upstairs to attack the police guard drawn up on the landing. Further shots rang out before she reached the apartments where she found the girls, still very upset and bewildered, wanting to know whether the men were rebels, and Queen Isabel screaming, 'Do they want *me*?' After further shooting the commotion died down, as the palace guard managed to hold out against the rebels, who fled during the night.

The man responsible was General Diego de Leon, a partisan of Queen Maria Cristina. An adversary of Espartero, he had decided to kidnap Queen Isabel. There had recently been an uprising in northern Spain on behalf of Queen Maria, and a junta, or political council, had been established in Bilbao in her name. Leon had intended to take the young Queen away to the protection of the junta, and probably to demand the return to Spain of Queen Maria Cristina. He and several of his fellow conspirators were condemned to death, leaving the Regent shocked and in tears. She refused to say whether she had been implicated in the move or not. Leon's wife, the Marquesa de Zambrano, personally came to see Queen Isabel and begged her to spare her husband's life. The Queen asked her not to cry, 'or you will make me cry too', and assured her that he would be saved. Dismissing the woman, she then sent for Arguelles and asked him to persuade Espartero to pardon Leon. But it was to no avail, for he and five other officers had been shot the previous day.

Espartero was sure that Queen Maria Cristina had been behind the conspiracy. She had already bribed General Narvaez to raise Andalusia against Espartero, but as the rising was a failure he returned her money. When Don Salustiano Olozaga, the Spanish ambassador in Paris, called on the Dowager Queen a few days later and she innocently asked him what was happening in Spain at the time, he told her that he found the question very strange, as he thought that Her Majesty was better informed than anyone else.

In order to strengthen his authority, particularly against those who were still agitating for the Regent's return, Espartero decided he ought to appear in public more often with the Queen. In 1843 he asked her to open the new session of the Cortes for the first time. She did not make a good impression. Spectators considered that she looked rather gauche, and lacked grace; her movements were too abrupt. She made a less favourable impression than her younger sister, whose smile seemed warmer and less forced, and whose curtsy was far more graceful. Thus Espartero's position was still vulnerable. After further revolts and instability he decided to dissolve the

Cortes, and General Narvaez landed at Valencia with a small force and proceeded to march on Madrid. Espartero fled to England, leaving the way clear for the General.

Nevertheless the people decided that they did not want a military dictatorship. Instead, the Cortes decided to declare Isabel legally of age. On 8 November 1843 the 13-year-old Queen was driven in state to her assembly, and seated on the throne. The President of the Cortes brought her the Bible, and the text of the royal oath. Placing her right hand on the book, she swore by God and the Holy Gospel 'to preserve the constitution, and cause it to be observed'. It was hardly surprising that at her tender age she looked a little puzzled as she repeated the words, 'If I should act contrary to what I have sworn, or to any part of it, I ought not to be obeyed.'[5]

Those who had expected that such action would usher in a period of stability in Spain were to be disappointed. Olozaga was appointed Prime Minister. He shared Espartero's liberal politics, and was resented by the conservative courtiers surrounding the young Queen. Encouraged by General Narvaez, they decided that Olozaga would have to go. Seven weeks after Isabel had been declared of age, Olozaga decided to dissolve the Cortes. He had foreseen that the conservatives would not look kindly on his programme of reforms. In secret he prepared a decree for the dissolution, and on 28 November he took it to the palace for the Queen to sign. He entered into her presence, she received him alone, and he only stayed for fifteen minutes. According to the halberdiers who saw him leave, when he reappeared he looked rather pleased with himself as he closed the door behind him.

Next morning the Marquesa de Santa Cruz asked the Queen what decrees she had signed the previous night. The Queen replied that she did not remember exactly, but thought it was a decree dissolving the Cortes. With horror, the Marquesa told her that she had just signed the death sentence of the monarchy. The Queen was thoroughly frightened, as the Marquesa went to tell the partisans of Narvaez what had happened. When Olozaga heard that his political enemies were making their way to the palace, he went there too and asked a gentleman-in-waiting, the Duke of Osuna, to send the Queen word

8

that he was bringing her some important despatches. The Duke kept him waiting, then came back to say that the Queen refused to see him. While he waited in the antechamber, he overheard some of the other gentlemen there discussing in a hushed voice what he took to be some interesting rumour, so he told the Duke that it was vital he should be able to see the Queen as a matter of urgency. The Duke left and returned a few minutes later with the message that Her Majesty had just dismissed him as Prime Minister. If he returned to the ministry, he would find her signed decree confirming the matter. He was also asked to return the decree of dissolution she had signed for him the previous night.

However, when Olozaga returned to the ministry he found no such decree, nor indeed any documents from the palace demanding his resignation. He then summoned the cabinet, and was with his ministers when a despatch arrived from the palace, signed by the Queen, stating that she was relieving him from all his duties 'for grave personal reasons'. When he asked the reasons for his dismissal, he was accused of having obtained her signature by force, and was told that he would be placed on trial. He agreed to submit to such proceedings, but refused to surrender the decree.

At a public enquiry in the middle of December the new Prime Minister read out a statement that had been made by the Queen in the presence of several witnesses. In it, she claimed that Olozaga had presented himself to her with a decree dissolving the Cortes which he wanted her to sign. She told him she was unwilling to sign as the Cortes had declared her of age, but he insisted and she again refused. She turned to the door on the left of her desk and tried to leave the room, but he placed himself between her and the door, which he then bolted. When she tried to leave by another, he did the same once again. Then he took hold of her by her dress, forced her into a chair, took her hand in his and guided it over the document so she had no choice but to sign. After extracting a promise from her never to mention the incident to anyone else, he left.

In the seventeen-day trial he questioned this version of events. He maintained that the Queen's firm, clear signature on the paper did not look as though it had been obtained by coercion, and he swore that there were no bolts on the doors through which she had tried to leave. But he could hardly accuse his sovereign of lying, though his allies were ready to accuse him of doing so. The most convincing explanation he could provide was that he told her it was her duty as a constitutional monarch to sign the document, and that her disapproving or jealous courtiers, whose political sympathies diverged considerably from his, were using this as an opportunity to force him out of office.

Whatever the truth of the matter, it would hardly do for any politician to dare to hint that his sovereign was wrong, or even that she might have been ill-advised. The proceedings against him were dropped, but he was ordered to leave the country and went to settle in Portugal. Four years later his friends asked Queen Isabel to pardon him, to which she replied that she could not forgive him since he had not offended her. She was never one to hold a grudge and it was said that she forgot easily. Moreover, she was still little more than a child of barely average intelligence. Trying to act the role of a constitutional sovereign while surrounded by unscrupulous self-seeking politicians, unable to trust anybody in her family to tell her the truth about anything or anyone, the best she could do was to try to be as pleasant as possible to those she had to work with. As they were not over-anxious to treat her with respect, it was probably more than they deserved.

In the spring of 1844, soon after Olozaga's flight, Maria Cristina returned in triumph. The liberals and progressives in the Cortes demanded that she must repay the large sums of money she had taken with her when she left Spain after her abdication as Regent, but this was circumvented when she requested the arrears of her pension, which had been stopped by Espartero after Diego de Leon's abortive kidnap attempt. A royal decree was passed whereby the arrears of her pension were to be paid, and this proved considerably more than the repayment for which she was being asked.

She was given an enthusiastic reception on her return. As Washington Irving noted, somewhat bemused, when she left the kingdom in 1840 'the whole world seemed to be roused against her, and she was followed by clamour and execrations'. What a contrast it was with the scene four years later, when 'the cities that were then almost in arms against her now receive her with fêtes and rejoicings. Arches of triumph are erected in the streets; *Te Deums* are chanted in the cathedrals; processions issue forth to escort her; the streets ring with shouts and acclamations; homage and adulation meet her at every step; the meanest village has its ceremonial of respect, and a speech of loyalty from its alcalde.'[6]

Near the Palace of Aranjuez a large tent had been erected, where Queen Isabel and the Infanta Luisa awaited her arrival, and it was an emotional moment for all three as her carriage drew up, escorted by squadrons of lancers. A decree was drawn up to legitimise the marriage between Queen Maria Cristina and Muñoz, and to dispel any doubts about its validity they went through another wedding ceremony in the palace chapel, conducted by the Bishop of Cordoba.

Maria Cristina's return brought a new sparkle to the royal court. Almost at once there were magnificent balls, receptions and banquets. Queen Isabel threw herself into this lavish social life with gusto. Still an immature young woman desperately unsure of herself and her sovereign duties, she welcomed the return of her mother, who could not only provide her with some kind of reassuring presence, but would also take a lead in providing the court with enough colour to make it the envy of other countries. It was said that she attended the balls with the gaiety and enthusiasm of a schoolgirl, which in effect was all she really was at heart.

* * *

As a sovereign regnant, the unmarried Queen Isabel would soon be perhaps the most eligible woman in Europe for any prince seeking a royal bride. By the time she was fifteen, the time was right for her to find a husband – or to have one found for her. Queen Maria Cristina was keen for both her daughters to marry French princes, a scheme strongly opposed by the British government on the grounds that it contravened the Treaty of Utrecht, which included a clause stating that the crowns of France and Spain could never be united in one person. That both countries had reigning monarchs at that time whose thrones were not based upon the principle of legitimacy made no difference. Any attempt to carry out the Regent's wishes would meet with opposition from Britain, though it was unlikely that British interests would be supported by any other country, as the other powers did not have the same interest in Spain. Isabel was eager to marry, and as François Guizot told his master King Louis Philippe of France, there was something in the physical exuberance of Spanish infantas that made it possible for them to have an heir before they had a husband. An early marriage for Her Majesty was obviously the only way of preventing such an outcome.

In March 1842 M. de Sainte-Aulaire, French ambassador at the court of St James's, wrote to Guizot informing him that his emissary M. Pageot, Chargé d'Affaires at Madrid, had arrived in London. They called jointly on Lord Aberdeen at the Foreign Office to assure him that King Louis Philippe intended to withdraw his country's claims for the hand of the Queen of Spain for one of his own sons. He was well aware that a powerful party in Spain was keen for this union, but at the same time he knew that such a marriage would have 'exclusive advantages for France'. Nevertheless he expected that the crown of Spain would not go to any prince outside the Bourbon family. There were several branches of that house and several members in each branch, and the Queen's husband should be chosen from one of them. The King 'recommends or excludes none of them'.[7] He was aware that England was keen for Isabel to marry a prince of the house of Saxe-Coburg, and that Austria would be equally keen to press the claims of a Habsburg archduke.

Aberdeen said he did not understand the declaration, and could not see what right France had to intervene. Was it not up to the Queen of Spain to make her own choice of husband? Sainte-Aulaire replied that he knew perfectly well it would not be the Queen who would decide on such a matter, but her government. Aberdeen insisted that, in the view of the British government, it was a purely domestic matter and did not propose to interfere. In reply Pageot said he would tell the King that, should the Queen want to marry her cousin the Duc d'Aumale, His Majesty's fourth son, Aberdeen himself would make no objection.

In September 1845 Queen Victoria of England and her husband Prince Albert visited Louis Philippe at the Chateau d'Eu, accompanied by Lord Aberdeen, while King Louis Philippe was attended by Guizot. The question of the Spanish marriage was discussed, as the Queen and Albert wished Isabel to marry one of the Catholic Coburgs, Leopold, the younger brother of Ferdinand who had married the Queen of Portugal. However, Ferdinand's tyrannical methods had been met with revolution in the country, and prospects of a Catholic Coburg prince for the young sovereign's hand were not encouraging.

Of all the potential candidates for Isabel's hand only two were now left, namely Francisco, Duke of Cadiz, and his brother Enrique, Duke of Seville, both children of Francisco, the youngest son of Carlos IV. The British government favoured the Duke of Seville, who was regarded as more liberal than his reactionary brother, and also physically stronger. Aberdeen reported to Sir Robert Peel, the British Prime Minister, that until Queen Isabel was married and had children, they should veto any French marriage for the Infanta Luisa, whom they knew King Louis Philippe regarded as a likely bride for his son the Duc de Montpensier. If the Queen remained childless, her sister Luisa would inherit the Spanish throne, and therefore any children born to her and Montpensier after her death would do likewise. This would be contrary to the Treaty of Utrecht, signed in 1713, which forbade the union of France and Spain, and also debarred the heirs of the Orleans dynasty from ever succeeding to the Spanish throne. As a result, the British and French ministers at Eu agreed that until Queen Isabel had children, her sister should not marry a French prince. At the same time Guizot made it clear that France would oppose a Coburg on the Spanish throne, and Aberdeen was at pains to assure Guizot that despite Queen Victoria's personal preferences, the British government would not support a Coburg candidature.

When he returned to Paris, Guizot felt he had not done enough to safeguard his country's interests. On 27 February 1846 he drafted a memorandum including a statement to the effect that if the marriage of Queen Isabel with Prince Leopold of the Belgians (the future King

Leopold II), or with any prince other than a descendant of Philip V, became probable, the French government would consider itself free of all its obligations, and thus justified in demanding the hand of the Queen or the Infanta for the Duc de Montpensier. Aberdeen was advised of this, but he could not accept the view that any agreement concerning the Queen's marriage producing children before the Infanta could marry should be dependent on dismissing the Coburg candidature altogether. All he had consented to was that the British government would not support a Coburg prince, but it could not interfere with Queen Victoria's freedom to recommend one if she or Prince Albert (actively encouraged by the wily King Leopold of the Belgians) chose to do so.

In June the British Tory government of Sir Robert Peel was defeated, to be succeeded by a Liberal administration with Lord John Russell as Prime Minister and Lord Palmerston as Foreign Secretary. King Louis Philippe and Guizot were convinced that Palmerston intended to place a Coburg prince on the throne of Spain. They were right, for in July the new Foreign Secretary sent the British minister in Spain a despatch in which he denounced the tyranny of conservative rule in Spain, and also recommended that Leopold should be reinstated as a possible husband for Queen Isabel. King Louis Philippe and Guizot both felt they were being tricked by Queen Victoria and her government, and thus felt themselves no longer bound by any of the provisions of the agreement made at Eu the previous year.

Without further discussion the French and Spanish ministers at Madrid arranged matters their own way. On 8 September Queen Marie Amélie of France announced the marriage of her son with the Infanta Luisa in a letter to Queen Victoria. The British sovereign replied civilly enough, saying that it could only cause 'surprise and very keen regret'. She was more forthright to Palmerston, writing that 'really the French have behaved so very unhandsomely and unfairly about this – to say the least',[8] while to her uncle Leopold, King of the Belgians, she denounced the settlement of the marriage as 'infamous'.[9]

After protracted negotiations for a suitable candidate, on 10 October 1846 Isabel married one of her Spanish Bourbon cousins,

Don Maria Ferdinand Francisco de Asis, a nephew of Carlos V. It was a double wedding ceremony, for that same day Luisa married Antoine, Duc de Montpensier, a son of King Louis Philippe. Britain was furious that Spain had reneged on the agreement by not waiting until the Queen had borne any children before her sister's marriage.

Don Francisco was small and slight, with a shrill voice. In an age when princes were generally expected to be dashing soldiers and incorrigible philistines, he was a peace-loving devotee of the arts. He was also a hopeless hypochondriac who refused to give audiences to anyone suffering from a cold. Throughout the courts of Europe he was known as 'Paquita', which translated into English as 'Fanny'. It was said that when in uniform he looked just like a young girl dressed up as a general.

If Queen Isabel had been looking for a husband who was the personification of manliness, then she was to be sorely disappointed. He was believed to have little interest in consummating their marriage, even if he was capable of doing so. If he did not provide the Queen with any children, the crown of Spain would pass to the descendants of her sister Luisa. To Leopold, King of the Belgians, Queen Victoria railed bitterly about 'this truly unfortunate and painful Spanish business', saying that her 'feelings were and are *deeply* wounded at the unhandsome and secret manner (so totally, in letter and in meaning, contrary to an entente cordiale) in which this affair was settled, and in which the two marriages were incorporated'.[10]

The wedding ceremonies were performed in the palace. Queen Isabel wore a white moiré dress covered with diamonds, and the groom the uniform of captain-general. Both burst into tears of emotion when declared husband and wife. An eyewitness at the wedding said that Francisco was neither handsome nor tall, and he did not appear to look healthy. 'When he was still a student in Paris he had more presence than now. He looks embittered.'[11] Nevertheless the celebrations lasted ten days, with bullfights and gala performances at the theatre, a dinner at the palace and a ball given by Bresson at the French academy. On his marriage, the Queen granted her husband the courtesy title of King.

Magnificent as the ceremonies were, few believed that these weddings would bring happiness for the brides and grooms, or security for Spain in her relations with other countries. In London *The Times* guardedly offered its best wishes, 'if not our most joyful congratulations' to the Spanish people. The Queen, it said, was 'united to a native Prince, who brings in his train no elements of discord, and offers no stormy prospects as the price of his alliance'. He would introduce 'no foreign influence to injure or insult the people of his country, and his descendants will not be liable to the jealous intervention of neighbouring powers as the unlawful heirs of a forbidden birthright, nor will Spain be taught to regard them as debarred by right from a succession to which they are introduced by blood'.

It was a different matter entirely where the Infanta's marriage to Montpensier was concerned. In this case the bridegroom was arriving 'among a people whose detestations of his pretensions can hardly be drowned in the purchased acclamations of noisy crowds well trained and carefully posted on his road'. They would see through the scheming of his family, and know the extent to which he was disqualified by solemn engagements for the position as husband to the heir apparent which he was expected to fill. He was thrust upon them with a deep purpose or with none. If it was the latter, his intrusion was a gratuitous insult to Spain and the Spanish, endangering their relations with friendly Powers which, perhaps less than any other country in Europe, they could ill afford to imperil, and creating nothing but suspicion and discontent. If it was the former, 'Spain is condemned to a perpetual dread of a detested influence, and to the reflection that the descent of her crown will entail war and bloodshed upon unknown generations'.[12]

They would prove prophetic words. The Spanish marriages, planned if not connived at in such detail beyond the borders of Spain, would create more problems for those involved than they had solved.

T W O

'Destitute of honest and able friends'

Now sixteen and newly married, Queen Isabel was developing into a more graceful and assured if not exactly pretty woman. She was never physically attractive, and not even the finest clothes could conceal what the American writer Washington Irving called her 'rough and somewhat mealy look'. Yet with maturity, the childhood surliness of expression had given way to a greater affability. The pressures of growing up as a child-sovereign, unloved and a stranger to affection, still only a schoolgirl yet in theory the most powerful woman in the kingdom, who must be obeyed by everyone as she was the Queen, were starting to ease. Most observers thought she seemed more self-confident, less petulant, appropriately regal when the occasion demanded, but equally spontaneous and good-humoured. A few were critical enough to consider her self-willed, frivolous, even impossible, but in the case of a young woman who had had no chance to grow up under a normal upbringing, it was perhaps only to be expected. However, even Irving admitted that she conducted herself with 'dignified yet simple grace'.[1]

Isabel's love of social events was legendary. She had discovered the diversions of a life of pleasure, and after a miserable childhood she could hardly be blamed for finding some form of release from the formality which her status demanded of her. For her there would be no drudgery of early to bed and early to rise; her balls at court lasted well into the early hours of the morning, before she retired to bed at around dawn and got up in the middle of the afternoon. After a very late breakfast, still wearing her nightclothes and slippers, she would give audiences to diplomats, listen to music, look at the newspapers, paying particular attention to any reports of proceedings of the Cortes, and perhaps have a game of shuttlecock with her ministers or maids of honour. At about 5 p.m. she would dress and go for a drive in the Pardo in her small pony phaeton, accompanied by her cousin Infanta Josepha and her uncle Don Francisco de Paula, never attended by a full military escort, only an outrider and one or two servants. She would alight from her carriage and walk for up to an hour, leaning on the arm of her uncle or her cousin, followed at some distance by the servant in royal livery, in the midst of her people. They would return to the palace between 7 and 7.30 for dinner, after which she would spend two or three hours dancing. On nights when she was not hosting a ball, she would generally go to the theatre, this being followed by supper in the private room of one of the capital's finest restaurants.

The King would wait until after she was gone from the palace before he himself left, generally in a closed carriage. He would go in the opposite direction to the Pardo, and return about an hour later. That their routines diverged so much, and that they seemed determined to lead separate lives, did not go unnoticed. It was evident that they disliked each other, and that they had been incompatible from the start. As *The Times* commented, 'Where the parties most interested in each others' happiness were originally unblamable – where neither was in fault – what terms ought to be applied to the unprincipled and heartless men who have made them miserable for life?'[2]

Isabel was unfailingly generous, though such a characteristic was by no means rare among royalty who had no idea of the value of money. Often she visited the sick, gave large sums of money to the Church, and would climb down from her carriage so that her place might be taken by a priest taking the sacrament to a man dying in the slums. She flung herself enthusiastically into Spanish ceremonies such as the washing of the feet of the poor at Easter. Sometimes she would remove the bracelets from her arms to hand to beggars at the palace gates. When the daughters of ministers or generals were betrothed, she would present them with magnificent dowries.

Had she been no more than an idle pleasure-loving monarch, she might have been deeply resented by her subjects. But with her legendary love of the good life being matched by her innate kindness, she was liked if not adored. On at least one of her drives in Madrid she was shot at but uninjured, and the next time her carriage was seen in the streets, her courage and defiance were applauded.

* * *

Forced into the most transparent of arranged marriages at the age of sixteen, Queen Isabel was prepared to take this thoroughly unsuitable husband in her stride. What, she would remark with a shrug of her shoulders, was there to say of a man who on his wedding night wore more lace than she did?[3] She had been a pawn in the hands of an avaricious mother, power-mad Spanish politicians and heartless European courts, who rarely if ever stopped to consider her personal interests and happiness. Had her elders if not betters procured her a more virile young man, maybe she would not have found it necessary to seek her gratification elsewhere.

Some consideration needs to be given to the assumption that King Francisco was homosexual or bisexual. His effeminate manner was remarked on by several contemporaries, and for years his homo-sexuality was taken for granted, though not always spoken of too openly. More recent schools of thought have suggested that this was an over-simplification, and that he may have been one of those reserved men who found it difficult to show his wife much passion, or perhaps he found her too ardent and hot-blooded a lover. It is all too tempting to conjure up comic visions of a nervous young gentleman taking to his heels in terror from the embraces of an oversexed bride (perhaps the reverse of those tales of innocent virgin brides fleeing from their virile husbands), but in this case such a story might contain more than a germ of truth.

Perhaps he resembled in personality his contemporary and fellow-consort, Prince Albert of Saxe-Coburg Gotha, husband of Queen Victoria of England. Victoria and Albert had nine children, but Albert had been psychologically scarred by his parents' divorce and, unlike his brother Ernest, was the one puritan in a family which had more than its fair share of rakes and philanderers. His attitude towards sex was that it was a duty to procreate, but certainly not recreational – a view which contrasted with that of his fun-loving wife and her Hanoverian forebears, something which even the heavily censored version of her journals which survives today cannot entirely conceal.

If Francisco and Albert had certain characteristics in common, so did Isabel and Victoria. Both princesses had lost their fathers when they were very small, and both were passionate, high-spirited characters who needed firm, steady guidance as well as affection. Victoria was extremely fortunate in her mentors throughout adolescence, not least her Prime Minister Lord Melbourne, whose superior knowledge and years of experience she had the common sense to respect and learn from. She was even more felicitous in her marriage, to a cousin who became her best friend and political adviser as well as husband. Isabel had no such advantages. A sovereign from childhood, she was constantly at the mercy of opposing bitter factions in Spanish politics, poorly educated, surrounded by flatterers instead of disinterested, sensible advisers, and forced into an unsuitable marriage while still a child with a cousin who eventually became a friend but could never become her lover. If she was a bad Queen, it was because she had little chance to become a good one. Her morals may have been open to question, but this did not make her a bad woman.

If Francisco de Asis, King of Spain, was unable or unwilling to consummate the marriage and provide her with children, said the cynics, she would undoubtedly find others who could. She seemed to think, or was led to believe, that her husband would be happy enough with the title of King Consort and a generous allowance from the civil list for his own use. She was soon informed otherwise. Her husband declared his intention to control her private life, and to assume what he considered a fitting role in the government of the country.

Despising and disregarding her husband, Isabel soon found what she wanted in the arms of other men. One of the first was General Francisco Serrano y Dominguez, a handsome dashing courtier whom she had known before her marriage. Twenty-two years older than the Queen, he had followed a military career and rose in rank from captain to brigadier-general in the Carlist wars, then went into politics and became a member of the Cortes. In 1840 he had helped Espartero to overthrow Queen Maria Cristina, and for his efforts was rewarded with the post of minister for war in Olozaga's government.

Queen Maria Cristina held strong views on the sanctity of marriage, and would probably have briskly dispelled any notions her pleasure-loving elder daughter might have had about allowing the General to share her bed. Yet Isabel was now confident enough to refuse to be dictated to by her mother, and within a few weeks of her wedding it was an open secret that Serrano was her lover.

If Francisco was forced to accept this state of affairs – and if he was less fond of women than men, his being excused from marital duties to such a full-blooded woman as Queen Isabel may have come as a relief – then he would find compensations of a different kind. She was the most powerful woman in Spain, and as her husband he was surely the most powerful man. Some of her more reactionary courtiers, ready to curry favour, began to attach themselves to him. They doubtless suspected that should there be a palace coup on his behalf against her, they would be poised to reap the reward. Others were probably motivated more by hatred of Serrano, whom they might have seen as a king in all but name.

Francisco resented Serrano, not as a rival for his wife's attentions and voracious sexual appetite, but as someone who would easily supplant his own influence. When he spoke sharply to the Queen about the over-mighty General, she told him sharply that it was none of his business. He asked the Prime Minister to convene a council to order an inquiry into her infidelities, but the wily politician refused. To do otherwise would have meant instant dismissal by the Queen, and he probably took the common-sense view that there was no point in wasting time enquiring into something which was common know-ledge. Much as she privately sympathised with her young son-in-law, Queen Maria Cristina had little patience with this washing of dirty linen in public. She told Francisco indignantly, with a sense of irony that doubtless escaped her, that he was not worthy to lie in her daughter's bed. In fact Francisco had his own separate bed. It had been put in the Queen's bedchamber, but he so disliked even sharing the room with her that he had it taken to another room in the palace.

Weary of a situation which she was powerless to control, the former Regent took herself back to France. Freed from her mother's censorious gaze, Queen Isabel flaunted her liaison even less shamelessly. Her affection for Serrano was an open secret throughout Madrid. In the theatre he usually sat in a box opposite the royal box, and she never took her eyes off him. After the play was over she met him secretly in a private room in a nearby restaurant. Meanwhile her husband asked Pacheco, the new Prime Minister, to do something about Serrano. The King's friends had suggested he take a pistol to the man, but he thought better of it and preferred to deal with the situation by more legal means. Pacheco persuaded Serrano to leave Madrid, but he went only as far as Aranjuez, where the Queen soon joined him and there they spent the summer of 1847.

While leaving for her new temporary home in a phaeton, the Queen experienced the first attempt on her life, when Angel de la Riva, a journalist and lawyer, fired a pistol at her. Nobody was hurt and the would-be assassin was arrested and sentenced to death; Isabel, however, commuted the penalty to four years' exclusion from Madrid, Aranjuez and the other royal residences. Meanwhile Francisco settled at the palace of El Pardo.

Within six months of their wedding it was common knowledge that the Queen and her King Consort thoroughly disliked each other. Sir Henry Bulwer, who had been British ambassador at Madrid since 1843, feared it was only a matter of time before the Queen's marriage was over. In the last week of April one of Francisco's friends (exactly who was never revealed) asked him to resume friendly relations with the Queen. He agreed to do so, on condition that he would be allowed a separate establishment, a voice in affairs of state and the right to intervene in matters of government. An ultimatum was sent to the Queen, Francisco warning her that if she refused to accede to his terms, he might appeal to the sympathies of the army and also issue a manifesto to the nation. As he was far less popular in the country than his wife, he would almost certainly have met with little response, but the fact that he was prepared to make such threats alarmed the ministers.

When his conditions were presented to her, she was furious. She summoned an attendant and demanded that the Chamberlain of the Palace should be sent to her at once. When he told her that the King had gone out for a drive, she demanded that the man should move His Majesty's furniture, books and other possessions out of her apartments and take them to those of the Duc de Montpensier. When the Chamberlain asked respectfully if she should wait until the King returned, she retorted that this was her house and she was its mistress; she would be obeyed. He withdrew, muttering sadly to himself, 'Revolution, revolution in the kingdom, in the Cortes, in the Cabinet, and, worse than all, in His Majesty's furniture! The very chairs, tables, and consoles have become Progresistas!'

To the messenger who had brought the King's conditions, she said that the King was partial to French advisers. If he appealed to the army or issued a manifesto, she would order her horse to be saddled, would mount it and would put herself at the head of the first battalion she met in the streets, 'and, alone and unattended, call on them as loyal subjects to rally round their Queen, and as Spaniards and *caballeros* to protect a defenceless young woman! God help me, I am surrounded by spies, and unaided by those whose duty it is to support me. Where can I look for aid, or whom shall I ask for counsel?'[4]

When Francisco returned, he found his apartments in total confusion. His furniture, books and various other belongings had been moved to Montpensier's wing of the palace, and the King demanded an explanation for these upheavals which was accordingly given him. Realising that the Queen's mind was made up and she would not be swayed, he agreed to listen to her advisers. He refused to see his own counsellors, who were anxiously awaiting to see what effect there might have been on the Queen after his threat to demand the army's support to help him get his own way if necessary. Instead he sent a message to declare his sincere repentance of everything that had passed, and his readiness to submit to all Her Majesty wanted. He would make no conditions, he said, and his only desire was to be reconciled to his wife and his Queen.

She was so irritated by his talk of appealing to the army, which she knew came not from Francisco himself so much as from his advisers, whom she did not trust, that she refused to receive the messenger. Francisco told him to persist, but she proved obdurate, and at length he knew he would have to try to see her himself. He went to her private apartments and after some delay was admitted. Duly penitent, he said he was prepared to accept her terms without making any conditions of his own, while she herself was all firmness and dignity. Sobs and weeping, presumably hers, were heard through the closed door by courtiers, and after some time the King and Queen came out of the apartment together, she leaning fondly on his arm.

Those who did not expect the reconciliation to last were soon proved right. In the third week of May the Queen told her ministers that they should consider the question of her divorce. If the government or any other power put any obstacles in her way, she told them, she was determined to renounce her crown and even go into exile, rather than live in bonds she longed to break, married to a man she had always loathed but never more than at the present moment. Within the next twenty-four hours they must decide whether they were prepared to sanction her divorce or quit their posts. If they would not do one or the other, she would appoint a cabinet that would maintain her in her appeal to the nation, to all Europe, to its chivalry and its manhood, to sympathise with her and protect her against those who betrayed her and 'the tyrants who oppressed and bullied her into a hateful marriage'.[5]

Nobody was in any doubt as to her refusal to compromise. Nevertheless the ministers tried to assure her that there was one way to cut short the scandal that had become too public for comfort, and that was by Her Majesty leaving Aranjuez and returning to the Palace at Madrid. To this she reiterated that she would not listen to any proposition short of separating herself for ever from a man whom she hated, and by whom she herself was hated. She would sooner lay down her crown than continue to be the wife of Don Francisco.

The ministers spent an anxious morning deliberating the situation. They were evenly divided, with two or three in favour of the Queen divorcing, two or three against it, and one undecided. The situation had to be resolved as soon as possible. Already there were rumours of a conspiracy at Aranjuez, with troops prepared to march against the Queen, probably encouraged if not actively instigated by French agents. It was also said that the officers of the Madrid garrison were meeting to decide whether they should side with the Queen or the King, and that like the ministers with regard to the divorce question they were thoroughly split on the issue. When informed, Isabel repeated that she would dress herself in the uniform of her own regiment, ride out on horseback in the streets and put herself at the head of the first battalion she met.

Francisco now resolutely denied having given his free consent to his marriage with the Queen. He declared that he had been forced to marry her, and that he disliked her as much as she did him. To add to the general confusion, the press in Spain announced that the Queen was 'in a condition likely to give an heir to the throne'. Nobody believed there was the remotest possibility of her being with child. When she was told about it at an interview with Bulwer, initially she treated it as an absurd joke and laughed, but then said she did not know 'how to put an end to it'. There is no evidence that she was genuinely pregnant at the time; she may have had a brief pregnancy which ended in a miscarriage. Perhaps she made one or two teasing remarks to that effect which quickly spread by word of mouth and were accepted as fact.

On one thing most parties were agreed – that France was trying hard to bring about civil war in Spain, either between the Queen and her husband's partisans, or between her and any other faction, with the object of stepping in and intervening by arms.

Concerned for the good name of the crown of Spain, if not that of her daughter as well, Queen Maria Cristina wrote from Paris, asking Queen Isabel to return to her husband. The Pope also told her to go back, saying that he was hesitant about letting his nuncio present letters of credence until she was reconciled with her husband, and long-delayed discussions on the Concordat could not start until a better state of affairs prevailed at the royal palace. It was said that Queen Maria Cristina was going to Italy in order to persuade the Vatican to persist in its refusal to sanction her daughter's divorce.

By the end of May La Presse, a leading Parisian journal, was accusing Bulwer of a Machiavellian policy, namely replacing the faithful attendants of Queen Isabel with his own creatures, by causing her to regard herself as a victim sacrificed to the ambitions of a foreign prince, King Louis Philippe, whom she believed was determined on her dethronement so that he could place the crown on the head of his daughter-in-law, her sister. The English ambassador was pressing her to seek a divorce, said the paper, and if the Pope refused to cooperate, Bulwer would advise her to take the initiative in dissolving her marriage, as King Henry VIII of England had done some three hundred years earlier, and declare the divorce herself. Should this happen, England would thus have avenged herself on France for her defeat in the Montpensier marriage matter, by creating a schism in the Catholic Church which would benefit Protestantism in Spain, and at the same time establishing British commercial and political supremacy in Spain. Guizot, now French premier, was said to have acted foolishly by withdrawing the French minister, Conte Bresson, from the embassy in Madrid and thus abandoning the field to Bulwer, enabling him freely to carry out the schemes of the British government.

Bulwer said that the dissolution of Isabel's marriage would provide the only chance for 'her happy life and creditable reign', conveniently overlooking the fact that England (and France) had been largely responsible for the meddling and therefore the ill-starred marriage. He added that the Spaniards were a very decorous nation, and that some very well-respected men 'discussed very gravely the propriety of putting the King quietly out of the way by a cup of coffee; but the scandal of a divorce shocked them'.[6]

If the Pope refused to gratify the wishes of England by dissolving the marriage of Queen Isabel, *La Presse* declared,

England would urge the Queen to divorce herself despite the wishes of the Vatican. Double profit for England! A divorce! and with a divorce schism and Protestantism in Spain! The religious propaganda of the Anglican Sectarians triumphing in Spain at the same time with the political and commercial propaganda of England! Is not this a pleasant dream? To plunge Queen Isabel into

26

the excesses of which the reign of Henry VIII offers the most perfect model – to renew between the Holy See and the Sovereign of a Catholic nation the odious contest which caused Protestantism to triumph in England – to complete a second time the separation of which she has given the example to the world – to revenge herself on France, and at the same time to satisfy her political interests and her religious passions – is not that a plan worthy of British diplomacy?[7]

Early in July there were plans suggested for a conspiracy in Paris for the 'enforced abdication' of the Queen. Several members of the Spanish cabinet, previously loyal friends of the sovereign but opponents of Narvaez, were suspected of having passed over to the Montpensier party. Narvaez, then Spanish ambassador in Paris, was said to be waiting for orders to proceed to Madrid and prepare for the accession of Montpensier to the Spanish throne. Conspirators were said to be ready to enter the apartments of Isabel's uncle Don Francisco de Paula, which had a connecting door with those of the Queen; two fellow conspirators were to strike the first blows and Don Francisco the third, but he was so impatient to start that he confided his intentions to those around him. The alarmed ministers were ready to have him arrested and interrogated, and then send him to France under escort. In future the Queen would wear armour in order to forestall attempts on her life, especially if her uncle and father-in-law were to be accomplices in such underhand behaviour. There was little truth in these allegations, but such was the state of excitement among the people of Madrid that they were all too readily believed.

By the beginning of August the situation seemed to be going from bad to worse. England was as suspicious as ever of French motives, and positive that Queen Isabel had been 'coerced into these ill-omened nuptials' and that Queen Victoria had been duped by one who professed to be her nearest ally. The course of policy followed by Queen Cristina and King Louis Philippe since the marriage, said *The Times*, 'convicts them of one of the basest and most odious conspiracies which was ever matured by the Bourbon family'. The spoils of an empire, it went on, 'and the possession of a throne will never efface the infamy of such a violation of the laws of nature, of honour, and of duty.' Their aim, and that of the French government, had been to make the accession of the Duchesse de Montpensier as Queen and her husband as King consort inevitable. By giving sanctuary to many of the Carlist leaders in France, they were also keeping alive the insurrection in Catalonia and other Spanish provinces, for whenever it suited the policy of the Tuileries to aggravate the state of affairs in Madrid by this kind of secret hostility. Such a state of affairs could not continue. Those at court could not agree among themselves; even if the Queen had as much experience and judgement as she was said to have courage and spirit, she was 'encompassed with snares and destitute of honest and able friends'. A catastrophe, in the form of divorce or abdication or both, would surely be the eventual outcome.[8]

It was no wonder that the Queen felt isolated, abandoned, insulted and deceived to the point where she seriously contemplated retiring into private life, and would surely do so if only she could be sure of preventing her father's crown from passing into the hands of her worst enemies. For her own sake, but still more for that of her country, the paper remarked, 'we earnestly trust she will have the courage to persevere in the arduous duty of reigning over the Spanish nation. The independence of Spain, and perhaps the peace of Europe, rest upon her firmness and decision, and she deserves to earn the loyal attachment of her subjects and the respect of Europe if she holds her ground with resolution and dignity against all the dangers and intrigues which surround her path.'[9]

On 8 August Señor Benavides, Minister of the Interior, was chosen by his fellow-ministers to go to the Pardo and tell Francisco that the separation could not go on indefinitely, as it was to the advantage of neither the Queen nor himself. In the course of a two-hour interview the King agreed; he said he had gone into the marriage fully aware of the potential problems. He knew that Isabel did not love him, and he forgave her for that as their marriage took place for reasons of state 'and not inclination'. There was no mutual affection, he agreed; he was 'all the more tolerant' as he had no love for her either. He tried to keep up appearances, never wanted a final rupture, but she had 'less delicacy' than him, she was 'more violent, did not want to play her part, and refused to make the sacrifice the nation demanded'. Maybe she was more frank or more passionate than him, but even so she was 'unable to fulfil this hypocritical duty as a sacrifice for the good of the nation'. He married 'because I ought to marry, and because I was flattered with the idea of being King'.[10] He did not credit the tales being circulated about the Queen's character, and said that such stories should not and did not in themselves prevent him from returning to the society of his consort.

While he had done his best to be magnanimous, he particularly resented the rudeness of Serrano. The General's presence would not have mattered if only he had tried to make himself agreeable. Favourites, he said, were all very well as long as conventions were observed. As Serrano had been neither pleasant nor deferential, and had persistently insulted him by calling him rude names, Francisco would not tolerate him. Only when Serrano was removed from Madrid and sent out of the country, along with all those who were supposed to have obtained places near the person of the Queen through his influence or that of his friends, would Francisco return. An outrage had been committed against his marital dignity, and it was grossly unfair as he had always asked for so little.

Though he did not mention the matter, Francisco might have believed in the rumours of his wife's apparent pregnancy. In later years he would come to accept her (not necessarily their) children as part of the family, but as a newly married husband he must have felt humiliated by the idea that she had been carrying another man's child.

Benavides felt Francisco's demands were impractical, as they would result in the dismissal of most if not all of the servants and ministers. Such a matter had to be referred to the Queen, which would make reconciliation even more unlikely. As the King and Queen so disliked one another, separation was well nigh inevitable.

Pacheco planned to reconvene the Cortes and lay before all members the steps taken to settle the 'Palace Question'. If the Queen refused to live with her consort, they proposed, she should be declared incompetent to reign and a Regent should be named, the most obvious candidate being her sister the Duchesse de Montpensier. Some members of the Cortes said that the Regent should be the King Consort, citing an article in the constitution which established that the person called to exercise the office of Regent should be at least twenty years old, 'that party, besides, being the nearest relative of the Sovereign declared incompetent, and not labouring under exclusion from the throne'.[11]

On the next day, 16 August, the Queen was asked to send Serrano away from Madrid, but she refused. As a compromise she was prepared to let the King return to the palace, on condition that they had their own apartments, took their meals separately and only appeared together in public. Everyone thought that she was resisting attempts at a further reconciliation as she was secretly trying to obtain a divorce. The general opinion was that 'the unhappy and desolate girl was bullied by Bresson and his accomplices into a detested marriage'[12] from which she was desperate to escape.

A week later Narvaez left Paris and returned to Madrid. Some thought that he had the consent of King Louis Philippe and Queen Maria Cristina to begin divorce proceedings between the King and the Queen, and that he intended to send Bulwer away, maybe even have Serrano shot. Unknown to everyone else, the fickle Queen Isabel was beginning to tire of Serrano. A young opera singer, José Mirall, had been spending much time at the palace, ostensibly on the grounds that he was giving the Queen singing lessons. On 6 September the Cabinet Council in Madrid decided that a bill should be presented to the Cortes for the dissolution of the Queen's marriage, as well as a bill to change the succession to the throne after the death of Queen Isabel, reverting to the Salic Law and excluding women from the throne. After the Council broke up, General Linages was sent to London with an invitation to General Espartero to hurry back to Madrid, as ministers believed him to be the only person capable of carrying the Queen's desires into effect.

On 24 September a decree was issued prohibiting the entry into Spain of any member of the royal family without the previous consent of Queen Isabel. This was thought to be directed especially against Queen Maria Cristina. Nevertheless, early the following month it was rumoured that the Queen's mother and her husband were leaving secretly for Madrid, without any official announcement beforehand, in order to surprise her daughter. Queen Cristina still might have some influence over the wayward young sovereign; she was keen to bring about another reconciliation between the unhappy married couple, and she wanted to prevent her enemies from putting any obstacles in her way. She and Muñoz arrived in Madrid early in October, though by this time their imminent appearance had become common knowledge. Simultaneously it was announced that Serrano had left the capital. He was aware that his fortunes were bound to change, and it was thought that he was responsible for recalling Narvaez from Paris in order to safeguard his position and to keep on the right side of him. Rewarded for his loyalty with the captain-generalship of Granada, he left court with good grace.

Narvaez continued to work hard for a royal reconciliation, and spoke in turn to the Queen, to Francisco and then to Maria Cristina. In October he and the papal nuncio, Monsignor Brunelli, closeted themselves with Francisco, who eventually agreed to return to his wife. At first Brunelli only succeeded in persuading him to address a letter of congratulation to the Queen on her birthday, but he persevered in his efforts to make the King go a little further.

The stage was therefore carefully set for a grand reconciliation at the palace on 13 October. Francisco entered Madrid in one of the royal coaches with Brunelli by his side, and Narvaez sitting in front. A group of dignitaries including the Captain-General of Madrid and the Military Governor joined them, and with their respective escorts they went to the palace, where Francisco was received with full honours by the guard on duty. Queen Isabel, accompanied by her cousin the Duchess of Sessa, was waiting for them, and stood watching their arrival from her balcony. The atmosphere was almost akin to that of the entrance of a conquering hero – perhaps the papal nuncio saw himself as one – with eager faces watching from the windows of nearby houses and some people holding out hand-kerchiefs to flutter in welcome. As the carriage drove to the foot of the grand staircase, halberdiers were drawn up to receive the King, while ministers in full uniform were present to conduct him to the Queen's apartments. Brunelli wanted to go with them and had to be dissuaded by Narvaez, who asked him to let the young couple sob and kiss alone; 'these things come easier without witnesses'.[13] The couple embraced eagerly, and remained alone for about half an hour, after which the President of the Council was summoned and the King retired to the quarter of the palace set apart for him. Later he went off to their private apartments.

Yet nobody believed that this grand display of courtliness had been any more successful than the attempts to persuade them to bury their differences earlier in the year. Lord Canning wrote to Lord Malmesbury that he should not believe a word in the reconciliation on either side, as it was one thing to take a horse to water and another to make him drink, 'especially if he should happen to have the hydrophobia'.[14] Palmerston reported to Queen Victoria that Queen Isabel's position was 'as forlorn as can well be imagined'. She was surrounded by spies, traitors and enemies, 'a prisoner at large in her own palace, linked as it now would seem indissolubly to a husband whom she hates and despises, and whose dislike for her equals hers for him; and watched and controlled by a mother who seems only to be waiting to catch or to create an opportunity to put into her place another and a more favourite child'. He was convinced that the French intended to put pressure on Queen Maria Cristina to encourage Queen Isabel 'in a course of conduct which will lower her in the estimation of her subjects and loosen her hold upon their affections, and thus to prepare the way for the accession of the Montpensiers, or else perhaps to cooperate with Narvaez in driving or persuading Queen Isabel to abdication'.[15]

Within a few weeks everyone knew that Queen Isabel was suffering from acute depression. *Prensa* reported that there had been rumours about her health since the beginning of November, and that 'instead of that cheerful temperament which she heretofore enjoyed, the result of robust health and youth, she has become sad and melancholy'. Every care was taken to prevent the journals sympathetic to the opposition from reaching the palace so she would not be further upset by adverse comment. 'Fits of melancholy and extreme depression of spirits' appeared suddenly, in stark contrast to her 'occasional sallies of the most buoyant gaiety'. Sometimes she remained for hours sitting alone, 'and is often surprised in tears without being able to account for her grief'. She appeared in public much less than formerly, and when she did it was noticed that she had become much thinner, and her face had 'acquired a sad and care-worn expression'.[16]

It was hard to avoid the conclusion that the 'scandal of a divorce' to end this most blatant of political marriages within a year might have meant greater personal happiness in the long run for the sovereign who was still just a child. Unpalatable though it may have seemed to those who regarded the sanctity of marital union as absolute, there were many sympathetic Spaniards who thought that the dissolution of her marriage might be the only chance of ever giving Isabel a 'happy life or creditable reign'.

The fragile match had been patched up but was looking far from strong, and with Francisco's refusal to share his wife's bed, the prospect of a direct heir to the throne looked unlikely. This would strengthen the position of the Montpensiers as rival claimants to the throne, and thus the position of France, whose power in Europe always had to be checked. Almost everyone was anxious to explore an alternative to divorce, though an annulment on the grounds of her husband's impotence might be feasible. Perhaps the less orthodox solution, allowing someone else to father Isabel's heir, might be less troublesome.

Nevertheless there were limits to the licence permitted to the Queen's favourites. On returning to his lodgings from the palace early one morning in November, Mirall found his rooms full of police. They promptly bundled him into a carriage and sent him to Valencia. While they probably had no illusions as to such an action strengthening her marriage, at least they could observe their role in helping to encourage her to behave with greater propriety in future.

THREE

Revolution

During the next few years Queen Isabel had twelve children, though only five lived to adulthood. The paternity of most was open to some doubt, and despite the disapproval if not outright hostility of her husband (who was probably father to no more than two or three of them), her mother and her ministers, the Queen continued to take lovers – and tire of them. Once Francisco threatened to have them all hanged from her balcony.

Serrano and Mirall were not the only ones prepared to take the risk. Another was Don Manuel Lorenzo de Acuñay Devitte, the Marquis de Bedmar, a businessman, diplomat and close friend of Sir Henry Bulwer. He had a room below that of the Queen in the palace, their apartments being connected by a small staircase. The reinstatement of Narvaez almost proved his undoing, for when he learnt that Bedmar was living in the palace, he demanded a meeting with the Queen and lectured her on her shameless behaviour. Furious at his presumption, she ordered him never to enter her presence again. He promptly went to see Queen Maria Cristina, who endorsed the dismissal of Bedmar and the retention of Narvaez in office. Bedmar was transferred to the Spanish legation in Paris, and later became ambassador to Russia.

As Bedmar had been living in the palace when Queen Isabel conceived her first child, he may have been the father. Another candidate was Colonel Gandara, an army officer who also had an affair with her at around that time. When Narvaez announced to the Cortes that Her Majesty was with child, Francisco asked him to let him attend meetings of the Council as the prospective father of the heir to the throne, a request that was greeted with some amusement.

Narvaez refused on the grounds that there was no precedent for a King consort to be present.

At one stage during the pregnancy Francisco wanted to issue a public denial of having fathered the child, but he was told it would be more dignified to refrain from doing so. At first he was angry, but at length he was persuaded to agree. It would be cutting his own throat, he admitted, if he said the child was not his. If the Queen produced an heir to the Spanish throne, then he was at least 'somebody in Spanish eyes'.[1] Queen Victoria remarked that in view of the Queen's 'very peculiar marriage', there was hardly any need to 'cavil as to who was the *real father*'.[2] As the expected date of the confinement drew nearer, Francisco was seen more and more often in public with the Queen, as she drove out almost every day until the time came.

On 6 July the authorities in Madrid announced that the Carlists were contemplating a 'manifestation' on the day of the Queen's delivery, and as a precautionary measure they ordered the removal of all swords and daggers for sale in armourers' shops. Five days later the birth was imminent, but the Queen's chief physician, Juan Francisco Sanchez, decided that the child's position in the womb was unfavourable and an immediate operation was necessary. A baby prince was born, 'apparently strong and robust, but, according to all appearances, devoid of life'.[3] When Isabel saw that the sickly infant had no chance of survival, she cried out 'baptise him!' He was immediately christened Ferdinand, and the doctor tried to find some signs of life in him, but in vain.

Though the baby was probably just too weak to thrive, rumours persisted that he had been strangled or disposed of in some other way, and that the Queen's sister Luisa may somehow have had a hand in hastening his death. Apparently the Queen thereafter took a great dislike to Luisa, and in later years would never allow her or her closest friends to come near the other children. Some members of the public blamed Sanchez for having bungled the *accouchement*, but the Queen did not share their view and continued to place her full confidence in him, refusing to see any other physician. On 15 July the baby's body was removed to the Escorial. Later that week the Carlist journal *Catolico* called the death of the little Prince of Asturias 'a providential event', and was ordered to suspend publication until further notice. One newspaper reported that the Queen had died, though her life was never at risk from the confinement. Though very depressed she made a steady recovery, and was allowed to get out of bed about ten days after the delivery.

Later that year she took another lover, Don Jose Maria Ruiz de Arana, a young army officer who had recently fought on behalf of the crown in an insurrection in Madrid. By the early summer of 1851 the Queen was known to be expecting again, and on 20 December she gave birth to a daughter. No effort was spared to ensure no harm would come to the baby girl, and the Queen would hardly let her out of her sight. At a ceremony two days later she was christened Isabel after her mother, but she was known as 'La Aranuela' by gossips of the day. The godparents were Dowager Queen Maria Cristina and the Infante Don Francisco de Paula, the King's father.

For six years this little girl was the Princess of Asturias and heiress to the throne, in the absence of a male heir. Unlike the ill-fated Ferdinand, she was a strong infant who enjoyed robust health and continued to do so throughout most of her eighty years. As if to dissociate himself from the infant and make it plain that he was not the father, the King retired to his country palace, Riofrio, with his closest friend, Antonio Ramon Meneses. It has been assumed that Meneses was homosexual, though he had been twice married and was also known to have had an affair with a notorious prostitute in Madrid. His friendship with King Francisco was almost certainly platonic.

On 2 February 1852 Queen Isabel went in state to the Church of the Atocha to a service of thanksgiving for the birth of her daughter. As she walked in the procession along a gallery in the palace an elderly priest, Martin Merino, who had just been officiating at Mass at the royal chapel, walked out from the crowd and bent his knee before her. She assumed he was going to present her with a petition, and put out her hand to him in welcome, whereupon he drew out a knife from beneath the folds of his robe, shouted out, 'Take that! You have now got enough!' and stabbed her in the side just above the hip, the weapon entering about an inch under the rib. He withdrew it and tried to stab her again, but was prevented by one of the Queen's attendants, who sustained a minor injury to his hand in so doing. She was saved from serious harm partly by his intervention and partly by the combination of metal embroidery on her bodice and her whalebone corset. As soon as she felt the full force of the attack, she handed her child to the King, then leant against the wall and placed her hand on her side, which was covered in blood, before fainting from shock.

Merino was seized by a halberdier and taken to the quarters of the household guard in the palace, where he was searched and interrogated. When asked why he had attacked the Queen, he said it was 'To efface the opprobrium of humankind, and avenge, as much as in me lay, the criminal ignorance of those who believe loyalty consists in sustaining Kings.'[4]

The Queen was taken to her apartments at once, and remained unconscious for about twenty minutes. When she came round, her first words were to ask for her child. A halberdier had taken the little Infanta in his arms and carried her to the governess. A lady-in-waiting now brought the child to her, and Isabel clasped her to her chest and wept. She then asked that the would-be assassin should not be executed on her account.

Nevertheless he was sentenced to death, and on 7 February he was publicly garrotted, his body burned and his ashes scattered to the winds. Having arrived ten minutes too early at the place of execution, he turned to his executioner and suggested he should chop off the head of the donkey which had brought him in the cart: 'I should like to see the face he makes.'[5] He left behind a letter in which he begged the Queen's forgiveness. Unworthy of being counted as one of her subjects, he wrote, for the purpose of tranquillising his conscience, he 'humbly approaches and prays Your Majesty to condescend, as a Christian, to pardon him the atrocious injury which, in a moment of deplorable madness, he had the misfortune to commit on the person of Your Majesty. The infinite mercy of the King of Kings induces him to hope that he will have obtained his pardon; and to die in peace, he wishes to obtain, and at least, if he is unworthy of obtaining, of imploring that of your Majesty.'[6]

On the following day the Queen was pronounced out of danger. A week later she went back to the Church for a High Mass and *Te Deum* to give thanks again – this time for the preservation of her life. While the crowds were enthusiastic and turned out to greet her in their thousands, she had been thoroughly alarmed by Merino's actions. What upset her was not so much the assassination attempt, but more the fact that the culprit had been a priest, who believed himself the appointed instrument of God. Her escape from death, she believed, was a warning from God that she must live more religiously in future.

Her religion was partly superstition, partly ostentation, and she became ever more devout. She was convinced that the bleeding wounds had been put there by God, and she took to wearing the cast-off shifts of nuns as holy relics to ward off danger. With zeal she took part in such ceremonies as the symbolic washing of the feet of the poor in the Hall of Pillars every Easter, passing along the line of twelve elderly men and kneeling before each one to wash and kiss his feet. When serving one at the supper that followed the ceremony, one of her diamonds fell on to his plate and she told him to keep it, as it was God's will. The Pope sent her the embalmed body of St Felix as a present, and she had it permanently displayed in a glass coffin in the royal chapel.

This new religious fervour had no apparent effect on her private life or any lip-service she might have paid to her marriage vows. The court of Spain might be becoming ever more pious, but it was also increasingly corrupt, and Isabel was still too open to influence from the wrong kind of man, the type of individual who would exploit her for reasons of power or financial gain, if not both. A succession of lovers came in and out of her life, among them the soldier Arana, the singer Obregon, the composer Arrieto and the soldier Puig Molto. One visiting attaché said censoriously that if only a fraction of the stories circulating about her were true, then she was really no better than the prostitutes on the streets of Madrid. It was to be regretted that the fortunes of a once-proud nation were now dependent on the whims and caprices of dancers, ensigns and lieutenants, distinguished only by their loose morals and good looks.

As a result her popularity began to wane. Even the tolerant Spaniards, who had long been used to their Queen's behaviour and easy morals, were starting to resent her scandalous private life, the constant procession of new lovers, and the ensuing corruption at court. When another daughter was born in January 1854 the papers in Madrid took little notice. The sickly baby was christened at once with the names Maria Cristina, but died within three days, a tragedy for the mother who suffered from intense depression. Her woes were exacerbated by news of the growing family of her sister, who had ten children (including one stillborn) during the first twenty years of her marriage. Some heartless individuals saw fit to post rude placards about the Queen and her shortlived infant by night in various parts of Madrid. A report on the state of Madrid later that month painted a picture of general disillusion, corruption and even the threat of revolution. The conduct of persons in high station, it said, was as scandalous as ever, and the very few who dared to speak out against it, or to point out the danger which the throne might incur, were disregarded or condemned. Any generals who dared to warn that the crown's good name was being trampled in the mud risked being posted to some distant garrison.[7] It was rumoured that the Cortes might invite Pedro V, King of Portugal, to accept the crown of Spain as well as his own, or that the Duc de Montpensier would be asked to assume the throne instead.

The unpopularity of the former Queen increased as well. Maria Cristina had been careful to save what she could from her allowance, in case she was to be turned out of Spain again. Her speculations on the Paris Bourse proved profitable, and she was said to be helping herself to funds from the public treasury, as well as part of a government loan levied to meet the needs of those suffering from famine in Galicia, caused by a sharp rise in grain prices due to the blockade of Russia as a result of the Crimean war. She was soon widely known as *la ladrona* – the thief.

On 28 June 1854 O'Donnell issued a *pronunciamento* advocating the overthrow of the ministry and the restoration of a constitutional regime. His movement was joined by Dulce, the general commanding the cavalry in Madrid, and then by most of the big cities across

39

the country. Queen Isabel had been with her latest lover at her summer palace, La Granja, but with Francisco by her side she now drove back to Madrid. Whatever her faults she was no coward, and she intended to show herself to the rebellious troops. Her ministers thought better of it and persuaded her not to appear in public, but to declare a state of siege instead.

The rebellion spread beyond the military. The people of Madrid arose on the night of 17 July, and for twenty-four hours the capital was in uproar with mobs pillaging, burning and killing in the streets. The object of their hatred was not the Queen so much as her mother. They attacked Queen Maria Cristina's house in the Calle de las Rejas, shouting 'Death to the thief!' She had taken refuge in the palace with her daughter, otherwise there was a danger that the mob might have broken into her house and lynched her on the spot. The civil guard put up a half-hearted defence of her property, but the mob forced their way into the rooms, hauling priceless antique furniture on to the balconies and throwing it into the square below, smashing china and glass, burning valuable paintings, and plundering her wardrobes.

Horrified by such destruction, Queen Isabel was prepared to do anything within reason to restore law and order. Diplomats and revolutionaries alike were convinced that she would have to abdicate, an eventuality which must have occurred to her as well. She sent a telegram to Espartero begging him to return, and he sent an emissary, General Allende Salazar, to deliver to her certain conditions, most important among them being that she should dismiss her entire household. When she refused, Salazar was bold enough to try to lecture her on her private life and conduct. She told him she was furious at being spoken to in such a way, to which he retorted that he had no doubt of it, as it was 'not often that truths are told in this palace'.[8] He continued to speak his mind, until Francisco – possibly alerted by a servant – came in to demand how Salazar dared to be so insulting to his sovereign. The emissary replied that he was a plain soldier, and the Queen burst into tears, saying that she was 'much too agitated' to answer him but would retire and consider it.

After the emissary withdrew, the Queen decided she would sooner abdicate than comply with Espartero's conditions to save her throne. She sent for the diplomatic corps. The first to arrive was the French ambassador, who pointed out that if she renounced her throne, the two-year-old Princess of Asturias would be left in the hands of Espartero and O'Donnell. Having experienced life as a child-monarch, and not trusting Espartero, she said she would rather be dragged through the streets than be separated from her child. With this she knew she had no choice but to accept Espartero's terms and remain on the throne. Apart from the considerations for her child's future, there was still fighting and unrest throughout the kingdom and the restoration of peace was a priority. Sending for Salazar again, she asked him to go back to Espartero and tell him that she accepted his conditions.

Foreign observers considered that she had damaged her personal reputation so severely that she had no room for manoeuvre. In London *The Times* thought that she 'had long fallen as a woman before she fell as a Queen', and that it was questionable 'if all the trickery of her ministers, all the violent acts of her military agents, would have succeeded in rousing the country against her throne had she been but true to herself'. Yet though she may have been 'guilty of high treason against the cause of virtue and morality', she was not completely to blame. She had had neither advice nor example from her mother, and neither support nor protection 'from the husband into whose arms she was tricked by an artifice which will remain infamous, even among those of political infamy'.[9] It was as if she was eternally damned by the consequences of her marriage.

On 26 July she published a manifesto in which she threw herself on the protection of her people, and declared that she would faithfully adhere to their ideas. 'A series of deplorable mistakes may have detached me from you, introducing absurd distrust between the people and the throne,' she began. She went on to refer to the sacrifices of the Spanish nation to sustain its liberties and her rights, which 'make it my duty never to forget the principles I have repre-sented – the very principles I can ever represent – the principles of liberty, without which there are no nations worthy of the name'.

A new era, she said, would come to the country, based on the union of the people with the monarch, to dispel the sad events which had just passed; she deplored the misfortunes that had occurred and would strive to forget them, and she entrusted herself 'confidently and unreservedly to the national loyalty'.[10]

At the end of the month Espartero entered Madrid in triumph and drove to the royal palace, where he remained for a short time. Next day O'Donnell, mildly piqued by the fact that the revolution he had initiated had ended in a victory for his rival, entered the city as well. Nevertheless he put personal feelings aside as he went to Espartero's house and both men went out on the balcony to embrace each other in public, resolving to present a united front in keeping their unruly sovereign in her place.

Arrangements were made for the election of a new Cortes. Espartero formed a new cabinet, with O'Donnell accepting the post of Minister of War and the rank of Captain-General, while Salazar was made Minister for the Navy. One of the new administration's first problems was how to send Queen Maria Cristina and Muñoz safely out of Madrid, as the mobs were baying for their blood. Espartero had to promise unruly crowds that she would not leave the city, neither by day, nor by night, nor furtively. Next he privately advised the former Queen that if she wished to stay alive, she would have to stay in the city. Like her daughter, she was nothing if not courageous, and she vowed she would leave the country as a Queen – or not leave at all. She had offered her house for charity, but the mob only wanted to burn it to the ground; they might try to seize her property and put her on trial for treason, but she would not compromise herself nor her husband. Queen Isabel was bitterly upset at the way her mother was being pilloried, and in tears told her ministers that they would 'not compel a daughter to sign the proscription of her mother', as such a 'disgraceful step would dishonour me in the eyes of the world and of history, and it is astonishing that you think I could agree to anything so outrageous'.[11]

Nevertheless it would not augur well for national stability if the Dowager Queen did remain on Spanish soil. Early on 28 August she took her leave of the assembled members of the royal household, embraced her weeping daughter and climbed into a carriage drawn up in the courtyard. The horses picked their way through the deserted streets of a city which had not yet woken, and whose people did not know that their *bête noire* was on her way to Portugal. When the public heard that the Queen's mother and father-in-law had escaped, there were indignant calls for the blood of Espartero and O'Donnell. Most people, however, conceded that their departure from the country was enough.

On 8 November Queen Isabel opened a new session of the Cortes in what was her first public appearance since July. Once again her personal charm had the deputies under her spell; on entering the chamber, she was received 'with deep and respectful silence', and at the conclusion of her speech she was hailed with 'the loudest and most enthusiastic acclamations'.[12] The court had not taken any chances and several people in the galleries had been put there in order to lead the cheering for the Queen. Nevertheless the deputies were clearly content to give their wayward sovereign another chance to redeem herself.

The question of a Spanish republic had not gone away, and one of the first matters the Cortes addressed was a proposition that the throne of Queen Isabel should be declared one of the fundamental bases of the national political structure. On 1 December it was passed by 208 votes to 21. One of the most outspoken republicans, the Marquis of Albaida, said in his speech that since the July revolution Isabel had not been a *de facto* Queen but 'a thing that had remained in the palace without exercising the functions of Queen', and that after the words in her manifesto of July it was no longer possible for her to have 'prestige to reign'. While he was not alone in his views, the republican element was clearly in a small minority, and O'Donnell firmly defended his sovereign: 'Without the throne of Isabel II no liberty can exist in our country.' He qualified his support by adding that it was his desire 'to see her surrounded by the most liberal advisers', and he carried most of the deputies with him in their intention to maintain a constitutional monarchy.

An immediate crisis arose when the Queen protested against the new law providing for the sale of Church property. When she refused to sign the act Espartero threatened to resign, and left-wing *progresistas* in the Cortes threatened to declare the throne vacant. Some of the Queen's supporters suggested to her that she should go to the Basque provinces and issue a manifesto. When the ministers heard about this, more pressure was brought to bear on her, and she signed the bill under protest. About ninety new acts were passed by the Cortes in less than six months, and the deputies were generous to themselves and their adherents with honours, awards and lavish pensions.

The ministry gradually lost momentum, with the *progresistas* becoming *moderados*, at length leaving Espartero as the only genuinely radical leading minister. There were more risings in various provinces, and the Carlists, scenting renewed instability, became active once again. The Queen saw that the only way of achieving what she wanted was to play off O'Donnell against Espartero, and then Narvaez against O'Donnell, when the chance presented itself. O'Donnell, as minister for war, wished to take a firm hand against the rioters, but Escosura, the minister of the interior, was inclined to be more lenient, and an increasingly weary Espartero gave his backing to the latter. The three decided to go to the Queen. Espartero thought that she regarded him as irreplaceable, so she would not dare to lose his services. He was unaware that the Queen and O'Donnell had a secret understanding. Escosura threatened to resign if his policy of clemency against the rioters was not accepted, and the Queen accepted. When Espartero played his trump card by offering his own resignation, to his surprise she accepted that as well.

O'Donnell naturally assured her that he would not desert her. He had drawn up a list of ministers, which she had approved beforehand, and on 14 July 1856 he was sworn in as Prime Minister. The result was a further wave of unrest for two days, at the end of which the *progresistas* and militia were defeated. Queen Isabel bravely encouraged the troops in front of the palace with little regard for her personal safety. O'Donnell became master of Madrid and soon tamed the restive provinces, declaring the whole country to be in a state of siege. Deciding that now she could have her own way on legislation regarding the sale of Church property, the Queen suspended all further sales and lifted the embargo on her mother's property. Having fought for her, saved her from the *progresistas* and championed her in the face of hostility from some of the deputies, O'Donnell felt let down.

Next she summoned Narvaez back in secret, and when he arrived she publicly welcomed him with open arms. On 12 October she dismissed O'Donnell from his post. She had evidently learnt that in politics there was no such thing as mercy. On resuming office, Narvaez produced a new constitution which abolished the national sovereignty, established a nominated life senate and established terms of five years for the Cortes. He rescinded the liberty of the press and made the national militia illegal. Yet for all his loyalty and severity, Narvaez was unusually incorruptible and straitlaced. The Queen had just had an affair with José de Arana, Duke of Baena, only to reject him in favour of Antonio Puig Molto, a lieutenant from Valencia. Narvaez treated him with haughty disdain, and at length the Queen decided that her new prime minister would have to go. Maybe she had just acquired a taste for making and breaking chief ministers. He was replaced by General Armero, who she expected to lead a more progressive ministry.

* * *

Soon after the death of her daughter Cristina, Queen Isabel tired of Arana's influence and company. A new influence appeared at court, Sor Patrocinio, a Franciscan nun with a reputation for performing miracles. An ally of King Francisco, she pretended to have clairvoyant powers and abilities, and she assured the Queen that the King was a true man despite his rather effeminate nature. The Queen trusted her implicitly and enjoyed discussing religion with her. She also succumbed to the nun's political influence, especially in matters connected with the appointment of new bishops in vacant sees. Strongly anti-liberal, Sor Patrocinio had firm religious ideas, and before 1854 she and her faction had tried to counteract the influence of Queen Maria Cristina in order to have control over Isabel's will, increasing her worries, her fears and her idea of being a sinner because of her private life. Between them, Sor Patrocinio and the King tried to manipulate the Queen and make her believe that her right to the crown was not hers but belonged to her cousin 'Carlos VI'. Others suspected the nun was trying to involve the Queen in political conspiracies, but in spite of her suspected Carlist sympathies she acted as a valuable go-between between husband and wife, and without her there might have been no reconciliation.

During the summer of 1855 Queen Isabel became pregnant again, but had a miscarriage in September. Another pregnancy soon followed but ended the same way in June 1856. After this she fell into a deep depression, blaming her husband for her inability to bear healthy children, and for a while she could hardly bear to set eyes on him. In April 1857, soon after she had taken up with Puig Molto, it was announced that she was expecting another child. A chronicler commented on the news with some concern lest the impending birth of another royal infant might once again give rise to scandal, and the only way Isabel could placate her subjects was by another change of ministry.

One evening she was in her private apartments, while Narvaez waited in the ante-room with his aide-de-camp. Suddenly Francisco appeared, accompanied by Urbiztondo, the Minister of War. Francisco demanded to be taken to the Queen's chamber at once, but Narvaez tried to dissuade him on the grounds that she was privately engaged. Francisco was adamant; as her husband he had every right to enter her chamber. Wanting to help the King, Urbiztondo drew his sword, and a scuffle ensued, during which he dealt Narvaez's aide-de-camp a mortal wound. In retaliation Narvaez slew Urbiztondo. The two deaths were officially ascribed to a strange epidemic in the palace, an explanation that convinced nobody.

At around the time this child was conceived, Antonio Puig Molto was still the Queen's favourite, but he was exiled from Madrid shortly before the confinement was expected. Others suggested that an American dental assistant named McKeon may have been the father. On the night of 28 November Isabel gave birth to a son, Alfonso, who was given the title Prince of Asturias as his mother's heir. Although he was not the father, Francisco dutifully picked up the newly born child in his arms and presented him to the grandees assembled in the palace. His duty done, he retired to his palace at Aranjuez. Puig Molto had returned, but the Pope put pressure on the Queen to dismiss her favourite. She did so with some reluctance in February 1858, giving him the title of Visconde de Miranda, signing for him the letters patent of the title of Conde de Torrefiel, and appointing him Captain Inspector of Engineers in Valencia. He spent the rest of his life there, eventually settling down with a wife and family. Many years later, it was said, the Queen acknowledged him as the father by sending him Alfonso's cradle as a souvenir.

*   *   *

When the Cortes met in January 1858 the government was defeated, and Armero resigned. He had been appointed by the Queen who was furious at the loss of the man whom she regarded as her ally. She threatened to dissolve the Cortes but was dissuaded from doing so, and instead appointed a *moderado* government with Isturiz, an old friend of Queen Maria Cristina, as premier. He only stayed in office for a few months before resigning, after which the Queen reappointed O'Donnell. Throughout his five years of power Spain enjoyed some political stability and economic good fortune. It had been the Queen's only hope, for one commentator observed that by this time there was no choice for the country apart from O'Donnell's party and revolution. His party, Liberal Union, trod a careful path between the *moderados* and the *progresistas*. The country prospered, commerce more than trebled, roads and railways were built, and a new agreement was reached with the Holy See regarding the sale of Church property.[13] The Queen had evidently learnt from bitter experience that it was as well not to interfere with the government, and for these few years she allowed her ministers a free hand to act as they saw fit.

Family concerns also distracted her, with the birth of more children. On 26 December 1859 another daughter, Concepción, was born, but she never enjoyed good health and much to her mother's grief she died on 21 October 1861 at the age of 22 months. Not long before the child's birth, in April 1859 the Queen had appointed a private secretary. Don Miguel Tenorio de Castilla, a widower who had given Spain distinguished service in politics and diplomacy, had been civil governor of several provinces and had travelled to the Holy Land. He was a man of many talents, also being a lawyer, scholar and poet. Fourteen years older than the Queen, he became her adviser and right-hand man, though he steered clear of all court intrigues and never used the Queen to further his own financial interests.

The King had now moved out and the royal couple were spending little time with each other. Now the Queen found one of the most satisfying relationships of her life with Tenorio. Her next three daughters were probably the result of their life together. Pilar was born on 4 July 1861, Paz on 23 June 1862, and finally Eulalia on 6 March 1864. Pilar had inherited the common Bourbon disease of tuberculosis and died in her eighteenth year, though the other two would enjoy long and healthy lives, Paz living until 1946 and Eulalia until 1958. When Narvaez was restored to power, he pressed the Queen to dismiss Tenorio and the estranged King's favourite, Meneses. Tenorio retired gracefully to his palace in Almonaster.

As a mother Queen Isabel was inclined to be impulsive and sometimes very affectionate. Preoccupied by her affairs and very much a slave to court etiquette, she did not have much time to devote to her children. Not surprisingly Francisco had very little to do with them, finding them a reminder of her infidelities. Each of the children had eight ladies and eight maids, with each of these groups of sixteen watched over by a lady of higher rank, who herself was responsible to an *aya*, always the wife of a Spanish grandee. These ladies lived with their families in a wing of the palace known as La Porteria de Damas. On feast-days they were dressed in taffeta or brocade dresses, cut low at the neck and loaded with jewels and orders. They would sit on satin-covered chairs in the antechamber to the throne room, then the Gentlemen of the Household and the officers of the palace guard would pass before them, every man kneeling on a velvet cushion to kiss their hands.

The heir, Alfonso, was a small, slight, good-looking boy, who was given a somewhat narrow education. One of his playmates complained that the future sovereign was taught nothing but religion and drill. Though not very academically minded, he was a lively boy who always greatly enjoyed and excelled in sports. In childhood he did not see much of his mother, except when he was allowed to accompany her on her drives in public, stand beside her at receptions or sit beside her at Mass. Oppressed by this regime, he became bored, restless, and sometimes fractious with his tutors.

When he was old enough to do without nurses, an Austrian woman who had served as one of his foster-nurses came to the palace to seek financial assistance. The Queen sent for the steward and asked him to present the woman with 10,000 duras. He protested that this was surely too much, but she overruled him; it was her command. He accordingly collected 10,000 pieces, and spread them out until they covered all the tables in her apartment. When she returned later that day from a drive she asked what all that money was doing there, and the steward told her it was the amount she was giving to the servant. Only then did it dawn on her that she might have been a little too bountiful, and she suggested that ten of the pieces would be a sufficient reward.

*   *   *

During O'Donnell's administration Spain became embroiled in a series of foreign wars. A campaign in Morocco proved successful albeit a drain on the national exchequer, and O'Donnell was made Duke of Tetuan. It was followed by a military expedition to Cochin-China, and in 1861 an expedition to Mexico led by General Juan Prim. England, France and Spain were jointly involved, but the English merely had some debts to collect and withdrew after obtaining them. Queen Isabel briefly entertained hopes of placing one of her Bourbon relatives on the Mexican throne, but common sense soon prevailed. Prim, whose wife was Mexican, soon saw for himself that the nation bitterly resented the presence of the Spanish, whom they saw as greedy imperialists intent on exploiting them; he understood that there was no monarchist feeling there, and knew the people would never accept the rule of a Spanish viceroy or a Bourbon prince. Keen to set up a new monarchy in Mexico, Emperor Napoleon of France and his advisers kept forces to help set up a new regime, disregarding Prim's warning that without the protection of foreign troops in Mexico a European prince or archduke could not hope to rule successfully.

In January 1863 the British ambassador in Madrid, Sir John Crampton, reported to the British government with approval on the appointment of Isturiz as ambassador to Paris, 'because his opinion from the beginning was so decided against intermeddling with the internal affairs of Mexico, that he will not be inclined to enter into any rash engagement with France on that subject. He says "I don't know whether Prim was right or wrong in the *manner* he did it, but I feel grateful to him for having got us out of Mexico at any rate."'[14] This rash French venture, or wanton interference as some would have said, proved the tragic undoing of the man chosen as Emperor. Ferdinand Maximilian, Archduke of Austria and brother of Emperor Francis Joseph, sailed to Mexico in 1864 as Emperor, only to be captured and executed three years later.

At this time Serrano was minister for foreign affairs. It was a precarious position, as Crampton understood; the position of such a minister, 'who is known as an ex-favourite of the Queen's, and who owes his political career to that circumstance, is even in Spain a false one; no matter what his personal qualities may be'.[15] O'Donnell's interest in foreign affairs precipitated his downfall. He wanted to recognise the new kingdom of Italy, but the Queen strongly objected on religious grounds. In the process of unification King Victor Emmanuel had dismembered the Papal State, and endorsement of his policy, thereby accepting 'atheist' Italy, was in effect undermining the Pope and his authority. O'Donnell resigned in February 1863 and early next month Isabel appointed Miraflores instead.

Her political partisanship, Crampton knew, was self-evident. 'The Queen, I need scarcely say, is inclined towards the "Moderado" or reactionary party; not from any deep political convictions (with which I imagine she is not much troubled) but because they talk more of supporting Royalty, and are easygoing people in regard to jobs for her as well as for their own friends.'[16]

Miraflores lasted in power for just over a year. When asked by Crampton some months later as to the political prospects of his administration, he 'did not appear to be very sanguine as to its permanency'. He admitted that he would 'willingly devote all his energies to the great questions foreign or internal which affected the real interests of his country, and that I might observe from the Queen's Speech to the Cortes that he was prepared to enter upon them all in an honest & liberal spirit'.[17]

At the end of December Crampton wrote to Russell that the Cortes had just separated for the Christmas holidays after passing, at long last, the Address in answer to the Queen's Speech 'by a considerable majority, which I am, however, told "means nothing" as regards the stability of the Administration'. There were discussions about the role of General José Concha, Marquess de Douro, who had been engaged in a military conspiracy in 1856 and had written a letter confirming his plans to expel Queen Isabel and proclaim King Pedro V of Portugal as King of Spain as well. Such a matter would not have been important had it not been seen as yet another of those petty attacks and recriminations which discredited those in public life and unsettled the minds of the people at large.[18]

Within a few weeks Miraflores had resigned. Although the end of his period of office was hastened by other causes, Crampton suspected that its fall 'was accelerated by the Court, which seems not to have behaved well towards him, or wisely in its own interest. A favourite plan of his for regulating the interior etiquette of the palace had given offence, and so much importance was attached in high quarters to this trifling matter, that an intrigue was set on foot to get rid of him. Everybody was surprized to observe that the Senator who, quite unexpectedly, originated the question on which the Ministry was outvoted was the husband of the lady most intimate with the Queen, the Marchioness de Novaliches.' Miraflores evidently realised this himself. Queen Isabel had been unwise to sanction his dismissal in this way. Crampton said she had 'acted imprudently to say the least, because for a small consideration she has probably discarded a faithful supporter who would have stood by her throne to the last on principle', while she became involved with the Marquess de Douro, who had been conspiring to dethrone her in favour of the King of Portugal not long before.[19] He was succeeded by Narvaez, but such was the volatility of Spanish politics that in June 1865 O'Donnell took office yet again.

* * *

For the first half of her reign Queen Isabel had been relatively popular. Though plump, she took care to dress regally and look every inch a queen. She was always approachable, and her good nature won many hearts. Although life at the Spanish court was always formal, the atmosphere in the palaces was never stultifying. While her moral life was hardly beyond reproach, she impressed her subjects with her extreme piety. She fasted regularly, though it never seemed to have any significant effect on her ample figure. Politically, she had a less sure touch. The Cortes had long been a byword for corruption, and she had no choice but to rely on whichever military leader came to power each time. Government alternated between liberalism and conservatism, according to the politics of the leaders, with new ministries following in quick succession, and power remained in the hands of cliques.

Despite her occasional intervention, Queen Isabel never pretended to have any political cunning. Amoral (some might have said immoral), lazy and prone to influence by those who surrounded her at court, she gradually lost her popularity. Some have sought to defend her from too harsh a judgement 'because her piety did not always seem to accord with her worldly ideas and practices', on the grounds that such criticism took no account of her Spanish mentality and national customs, or the fact that she was possessed of 'that childlike simplicity of mind which came from an open, generous heart'.[20] In other words, she might have been forgiven her loose morals had she not involved herself in political meddling and laid herself open to charges of surrounding herself with corrupt advisers. Her affairs had counted against her less than the corruption endemic at court. Her *camarilla* had exerted excessive influence in public affairs, and she was trusted neither by her ministers nor by the people. She did not appreciate that the state of opinion in the country required the appointment of a more progressive ministry, and her failure to make more use of the progressives left their leaders without a chance of electoral victory, and with no alternative but to force her hand by taking the country to the brink of revolution. Neither did she understand that the threat of the *progresistas* – if threat it was – that 'revolution' could only be held at bay by a genuinely liberal ministry was not an attempt to erode the power of the crown, more an effort to make the monarchy come to terms with the modern world. If the *progresistas* were allowed or driven to assume revolutionary attitudes, which might culminate in demanding the abdication of the sovereign, the party rank and file would be unlikely to let them desist until their aims were achieved.

After O'Donnell's departure from office in 1865 the *progresistas* boycotted political life, in protest against electoral corruption and against the Queen's refusals to modify the electoral law, which would have led to the succession of a progressive ministry that would have quelled much disquiet in the country. Basically what they sought was a liberal Spain with limited concession to democratic demands, as laid down in the constitution of 1837. A wiser monarch than Queen Isabel would have heeded the words of the British minister who told her that it was apparent 'even to the most superficial observer' that the excluded Progressives were increasingly coming to represent 'the prevalent opinion in the country'.[21]

Economic conditions precipitated discontent throughout the country at large. A slump in the economy caused by several poor harvests, disenchantment with ultra-conservative governments and a growth in democratic agitation among university intellectuals, dissatisfied with the strong influence of the Church over education, all combined to undermine respect for the throne.

Over the years everyone had continually suspected Montpensier's ambition to become King of Spain, while Queen Isabel's hold on her throne was looking increasingly insecure. She could no longer count on the wholehearted support of General Prim, although he still retained his preference for a constitutional monarchy as the form of government best suited to Spain, and Montpensier decided to court him. Prim needed money to accomplish the deposition of Queen Isabel, which he was convinced would be in the national interest, while Montpensier had the money as well as the ambition to take her place.

Prim was an unswerving monarchist and theoretically as loyal a servant of the crown as any other major military or political figure in Queen Isabel's Spain, but he was also a patriot concerned with the good of the country. Denied the chance of power by legitimate means, at length his patience was exhausted and he saw no alternative to revolution. On 3 January 1866 he placed himself at the head of two cavalry regiments in Villarejo de Salvanes and issued a *pronunciamento*. However, he failed to make any headway and was forced to flee the country. He went into exile in France and then in England, but continued to plan the Queen's overthrow, and persuaded Montpensier to send him money. Before long the Duc and Duchesse were exiled from Spain.

Though the Duchesse was Queen Isabel's sister, they had not been close for a long time, and Luisa's efforts to lecture the Queen on her moral shortcomings had widened the gulf between them. When the Montpensiers boarded the ship that was to take them to exile in Portugal, the captain of the ship quietly told Montpensier that if he said the word, he himself would take prisoner their escort, the captain-general, and sail the ship to the Canary Islands to collect Serrano and other banished leaders. Montpensier declined the offer, and they duly sailed to Lisbon, from where he issued a formal protest declaring his opposition to Queen Isabel's regime.

On 22 July 1866 there was an uprising of sergeants in Madrid, in which three hundred men from one regiment and about a thousand armed civilians joined, but they did not succeed in winning over the cavalry, engineers or light infantry. General Serrano put the revolt down. Two hundred mutineers were killed and five hundred taken prisoner; seventy were shot. The liberals blamed Queen Isabel for their deaths. Prim and the other ringleaders had prudently escaped, to continue plotting, but there could be little doubt that their intention was to bring about a Spanish republic, or at least rid themselves of the Queen and her family. Even O'Donnell thought she was being unduly harsh towards the rebels, for on learning that she had given her assent to the death sentences, he reportedly commented that she must realise that if all the mutineers were shot, 'there will be such profusion of blood that it will flow into her alcove, drowning her'.[22]

Narvaez was keen to press the claims of his nephew, Carlos Marfori y Callejas, the son of an Italian cook and a former actor. He began a relationship with the Queen not long before she gave birth to another son, Francisco, who only lived for twenty-two days. Discretion was not Marfori's strong point. Those at court resented the way in which he appeared to flaunt his status as the Queen's favourite, in particular taking his place in the royal carriage with such airs and graces that he could have been the King Consort himself. However, he provided Isabel with company and devoted friendship at a time when years of sadness and disappointment, partly through so many short relationships, unsuccessful pregnancies, deaths of young children and political misjudgement, had depressed and embittered her. She made him a civil governor, then her minister for the colonies, and minister of the royal household. None of her other favourites had ever been given such advancement. This, following on the unnecessarily severe punishments inflicted on the rebels, convinced O'Donnell that he had had enough. He resigned office for the last time, vowing more in sorrow than in anger never to cross the threshold of the royal palace again while Queen Isabel remained on the throne. Leaving Spain, he settled in Biarritz, where he died in November 1867 aged fifty-eight. Once again Narvaez succeeded him as head of government.

At last Queen Isabel's remarkable good fortune was running out. Slowly but surely the popular mood was turning against her, and even a state visit to Portugal, her first (and last) to another kingdom, was dogged by misfortune. She, the King Consort, the Prince of Asturias and Infanta Isabel, left Madrid for Lisbon on 9 December 1866, to be met by King Louis of Portugal two days later. A large crowd awaited them at the station at Daimiel but it was very foggy, and the crowd was all over the line. Tragically the pilot engine killed five people and wounded twenty-six as it entered the station. Superstitious voices said that it was all the fault of the Queen. After a grand levee, a review of the troops and a gala performance at the Theatre of San Carlos, the royal party left Lisbon on 14 December.

In the spring of 1868 Narvaez fell seriously ill. After lingering for a couple of weeks he died on 23 April, five months after the death of his old rival O'Donnell. Prescient commentators noted that one more link in the Spanish chain had snapped, and one more champion was lost to the Bourbon dynasty, 'which always puts its best servants to the worst uses, and, in the end, invariably repays them with perfidy and ingratitude'.[23] In his place Queen Isabel appointed Don Luis González Bravo as president of the council and minister of the interior, though many wondered whether a mere civilian at the head of the Queen's government could protect her after so many previously loyal generals had turned against her. She was unaware that her last two steadfast champions had gone, and without them her days as sovereign were numbered. Surrounded by friends and advisers who flattered her, and who were hated by politicians and military alike, and unswervingly loyal to those she believed to be her friends, she trusted the wrong people.

Meanwhile Prim had assured Emperor Napoleon III that he was not planning to dethrone Isabel in order to promote Montpensier. Napoleon had no intention of allowing Louis Philippe's son to claim the Spanish throne, and Montpensier, believing that Prim was not to be trusted, never forgave him. Next Prim approached Cabrera, a Carlist commander now living in England, to ask him about the possibility of Carlists joining forces with the Liberals in the coming revolution. Cabrera declined to have anything to do with such a move.

On 18 September 1868 Admiral Juan Batiusta Topete, commander of the squadron at Cadiz, issued a *pronunciamento* there denouncing the tyranny of the government and calling for a constituent Cortes. He had already sent a ship to the Canaries to bring back Serrano and his fellow conspirators. An ally of Montpensier, Topete intended to proclaim Luisa Queen of Spain. Had Montpensier been in Spain at the time, he and Luisa would have stood a fair chance of claiming the throne between them. Prim joined the Admiral, and, when told of the plans involving Montpensier, suggested it would be advisable to let the revolution come first and then allow the constitutionally elected Cortes decide who their sovereign should be. The Admiral and all the other leading revolutionaries agreed.

Queen Isabel, King Francisco and the children had been away from Madrid on holiday since the second week of August, and at the time of the revolution she was in her palace at San Sebastian, on the north coast. Her immediate impulse was to return to Madrid, but Marfori and the rest of her entourage would not hear of it. Bravo resigned on 20 September and a military dictatorship under Manuel Concha took over. He sent troops to ward off Serrano, and the Queen again made plans to go back to Madrid. Concha insisted that if she must, it must be without Marfori; she should come alone, or else with her children. The sight of her favourite, he knew, would only provoke the people of Madrid. Infuriated by being dictated to, she tore his telegram into pieces and insisted through her tears that if she was going to be restricted in her choice of companions, she would not return after all.

On 29 September the Queen heard that Serrano had beaten the loyalist forces in a pitched battle, and the people of Madrid had risen in revolt against her. Reluctant to admit defeat, she wanted to return to her capital, where she would abdicate in favour of her son only as a last resort. She telegraphed the Pope to ask if she could renounce her throne, but he advised against it. While she, the King and the Prince of Asturias were on their way home by train, a telegram was handed to them saying that there was an obstruction on the rail line. She said that they would go as far as they could, and then see if they could continue the journey to Madrid by road, but was told this would be impossible. Later, she learned, this was a trick by the republicans to stop her from returning, as they sensed that her presence would probably result in spontaneous demonstrations in her favour which would frustrate their plans to depose her.

Most of her entourage now deserted her, and the few faithful adherents advised an immediate flight across the French frontier. Emperor Napoleon had given orders that her escort should be allowed to accompany the family to the French town of Hendaye in perfect safety, and she arrived there on 30 September. After a late breakfast she went to Biarritz, meeting Napoleon, Eugenie and the Prince Imperial for about quarter of an hour, before leaving for her new residence at Pau.

FOUR

'King Macaroni'

The vacant Spanish throne gave the Carlist Pretender Don Carlos the chance for which he had long been prepared. In the spring of 1866 he had written a formal letter to his father Don Juan, suggesting they should try to agree on the problem of party leadership and telling him that he had no right to renounce his claim to the throne on behalf of his descendants as he, Don Carlos, still retained his own rights. When he received no answer from his father he assumed leadership of the party, and at the Carlist Council of London in the summer of 1868 he was formally accepted as the new Pretender. Seeing this as a *fait accompli*, Don Juan met his son a few months later, agreed to let him assume the title and signed an act of abdication in Paris on 3 October 1868. From that date the Carlists regarded the new Pretender as Carlos VII. When his father's act of abdication was circulated to the other courts of Europe, the sovereigns replied with a formal acknowledgement. Only the Pope answered more fully, saying that whatever regime might be established in Spain, he hoped it would be in harmony with the Catholic Church.

Considering himself the obvious successor to the rejected Queen Isabel, 20-year-old 'Carlos VII' and his wife, born Princess Margaret of Parma, took up residence in Paris, establishing a court and planning a military campaign. From his retirement in England, the Carlist General Ramon Cabrera was invited to come back to Spain and take command of the Carlist forces. Now in indifferent health, he was unenthusiastic about the idea but reluctantly agreed to do so, but at the same time he warned Don Carlos against any hasty action.

However, the Carlists were impatient for Don Carlos to show his hand, and he crossed the Spanish frontier in July 1869, heavily disguised. He had planned to seize control of Pamplona, the capital of Navarre, but was driven back and returned to Paris. Frustrated and annoyed by the Prince's impetuosity, Cabrera returned to England, but was later persuaded to rejoin the cause. He did but strictly on his own terms, recommending that once Don Carlos had regained the throne of Spain, assuming he was successful, the restored monarchy should be a kind of marriage between Divine Right and Democracy. He also reserved the right to choose the King's advisers, but this demand was too much for Don Carlos. Cabrera resigned yet again, and Don Carlos took over command of the Carlist forces himself.

Meanwhile, after Queen Isabel's departure the Cortes was faced with a vacuum. A hastily formed junta decided that the Bourbons had forfeited all rights to the crown. Serrano headed a provisional government, which convened the Cortes with the express aim of drawing up a new constitution. The result was very similar to the Constitution of 1812, declaring Spain a limited monarchy with the real power in the hands of two chambers. Serrano became Regent, with Prim as Prime Minister.

At least one other Queen regnant in Europe had some sympathy for Isabel. From Balmoral, her retreat in the Scottish Highlands, Queen Victoria wrote to her daughter, the Crown Princess of Prussia, saying she had 'always felt for and pitied her – for she was so cruelly used'. Every excuse, she went on, could be made for her private conduct, 'on account of her cruel marriage. But her misgovernment is to me incredible.'[1]

The former Queen had initially gone to live at the Château de Pau as a personal guest of Emperor Napoleon. It was not suitable as a permanent residence, and she was reluctant to take undue advantage of the Emperor's hospitality. Moreover she could not afford to maintain a large establishment. Much as she regretted having to part with the few faithful attendants who wanted to follow her into exile, she had to order some of them to return to Spain. After five weeks at Pau she, Marfori, her family and a reduced suite of ladies- and gentlemen-in-waiting left for a house in the Pavilion de Rohan, near the Louvre and the Tuileries in Paris. Marfori gave up his military and civil careers for her sake, and she created him Marques de Loja.

Ironically, while Isabel had reigned in Spain, the French capital had been the centre of the exiled Spanish revolutionaries; now staunch royalists came to pay their respects and even propose plans for her eventual restoration. Ever a sociable woman who loved to be surrounded by agreeable company, she relished these visits. She had already been a close friend of the Emperor, the Empress and their son, and now that she was living in their country under their protection, they saw much of one another, and the former Queen and the Spanish-born Empress Eugenie would converse happily in their mother tongue. Louis, Prince Imperial, became a companion of the Prince of Asturias, who was only one year younger, and they often played together. The kindly Emperor was devoted to Isabel's daughters and regularly gave them presents, including a doll with a trunkful of costumes based on the newest fashions, and a complete doll's dinner service.

Queen Cristina and her husband lived in a house in the Champs Elysées. Now mother and daughter could dine together most days. Isabel's little girls were astonished to meet a new family of uncles and aunts, the children of the Queen and the Duke, and they were most amused when the ever-respectful Duke, conscious of his wife's status, addressed her in public as 'Your Majesty'.

Having already spent much of their married life apart, Isabel and Francisco now formally separated, and in the ensuing settlement he was granted an allowance equivalent to about £8,000 a year. No longer burdened with the difficult status of a King Consort, he was at last free to live as a grand seigneur without responsibilities, able to devote himself to his love of the arts, literature and travel. He settled in the Château d'Epinay-sur-Seine, in the Bois de Boulogne, where he remained contentedly for his remaining thirty-three years.

In May 1868, just before the revolution, the Queen's eldest daughter Infanta Isabel had married the Count de Girgenti, a prince of the Bourbons of Naples. Shortly after the wedding she discovered to her dismay that her husband was an epileptic, though he was apparently unaware of the condition himself. As a prince of the deposed royal family of Naples he had no real home, and they spent what was to prove their sadly brief married life in hotels, mostly in England and Switzerland. Depressed by a severe attack of epilepsy, he shot himself in a room in their suite at the Hotel du Cygne, Lucerne, in November 1871. She was so traumatised by his death that throughout her long widowhood she would never even consider the idea of remarriage.

Alfonso attended the Stanislas College in the Rue Notre Dame de Champs by day, and the three younger infantas were educated at the Sacre Coeur. Sometimes the children joined their mother for dinner or drove with her in the Bois de Boulogne, and she would play cards with them for a couple of hours. On other days they might be taken to play with the Prince Imperial at the Tuileries.

One of the Queen's former counsellors, the Duc de Sesto, recommended that what the dynasty, and above all Spain, needed was a young untarnished sovereign. For two or three years after her flight, she still hoped that a restoration might be effected either by a sympathetic military rebellion with support from her courtiers, by some form of compromise with the Duc de Montpensier, or by coming to terms with Serrano. Eventually she had to face up to the futility of any such aspirations. Reluctantly she conceded that if she should abdicate in favour of her son she would at least have a chance of saving the dynasty with a view to restoration in the future, and on 25 June 1870 she signed an act of abdication at the Palais de Castille.

In a message to her former subjects, she admitted that her reign had 'seen many sad and troubled periods – sad above all for me, because the glory of certain facts and the progress realised while I ruled the destiny of our dear country cannot make me forget that, loving peace and the increase of the public good, I ever saw my deepest and most cherished feelings, my noblest aspirations, and my most earnest wishes for the prosperity of Spain thwarted by acts independent of my will'. For over thirty years, she went on, she had 'exercised the supreme representative power of the people committed to my charge by God's law, by personal right, and by national right'. She could not accuse herself of 'contributing with deliberate intention either to the evils laid by my charge, or to misfortunes which I was powerless to avert. A Constitutional Queen, I have sincerely respected the laws. A Spanish woman before all, and a loving mother, Spain's sons are all equally dear to me. The misfortunes which I could not prevent were mitigated by me as far as possible.' In conclusion, she declared that she was filled with faith for the future of Spain, and 'solicitous for its greatness, integrity, and independence, grateful for the support of those who were and are attached to me, forgetting the affronts of those who do not know me or insult me, for myself I ask nothing, but I would obey the impulse of my heart and the loyal sentiment of the Spaniards by confiding to their honour and noble feeling the destiny of a traditional dynasty and the heir of a hundred Kings.'[2]

Not long afterwards Serrano commented that if only she had had the wisdom to abdicate in September 1868 in favour of her son, the Prince of Asturias, he himself would have immediately proclaimed the young heir as King Alfonso XII. Such a move, he knew, would have met with little opposition.

Among those present at the abdication ceremony were Maria Cristina, her husband Muñoz, Isabel's daughters and various members of the aristocracy. She read out the statement on the act, then signed it and thus declared her twelve-year-old son Alfonso King of Spain. Legend has it that as she did so, she descended comfortably on a sofa, declaring with relief that she was 'rid of that great weight'.[3]

Isabel's departure from Spain had precipitated the return of Montpensier from Portugal. He came back to Seville bitter and disillusioned, having gone into exile with the promises of Serrano and Prim to sustain him, but returned to find Serrano Regent and Prim scouring Europe with almost indecent haste to appoint a new King. Luisa, who was convinced that if anybody should replace her sister as sovereign it should be her husband, was likewise filled with bitterness against everyone at his being passed over.

Had Montpensier bided his time and behaved prudently, he might have persuaded the Cortes to consider him. Any such chance was destroyed by an act of foolishness which proved his unfitness to wear the crown. In January 1870 King Francisco's brother Enrique, an outspoken liberal, wrote an open letter to Serrano, declaring that if the Duc de Montpensier carried out his threat to become King or Regent by any means whatsoever, he would join the Duc's enemies and gladly shed his last drop of blood against such treason. In an article published widely in the press, he referred to the would-be sovereign as 'a puffed-up French pastry cook'.[4] Montpensier challenged him to a duel on the artillery ground at Carabanchel, near Madrid, on 12 March, and ended up shooting him dead. The victor was so horrified at what he had done that he had to be put to bed to get over the shock. Enrique was buried in the Escorial, while Montpensier was arrested, court-martialled, ordered to pay compensation to the family and banished from Madrid for one month. While he was in Paris he visited Queen Isabel and offered to sponsor young Alfonso, on condition that he was appointed Regent. She wisely refused to consider the idea.

*   *   *

In Spain's quest for a new sovereign, the decision to expel the Bourbons from the throne not only precluded recalling Queen Isabel, but also excluded her son and heir Alfonso, as well as their rivals Don Carlos, Luisa and Montpensier. The crown was even offered to Espartero but he declined it, as did others including King Louis of Portugal; Ferdinand, King Dowager of Portugal, the widower of Maria II; and Prince Leopold of Hohenzollern-Sigmaringen. The last-named seriously considered acceptance before declining what he must have regarded as a poisoned chalice. Had he done so sooner, the Franco-Prussian war which caused the downfall of Napoleon III's empire might have been avoided.*

---

* Relations between France and Prussia had worsened over reports that the Prussians supported the candidature of a Hohenzollern prince for the Spanish throne. In July 1870 the French ambassador sought a personal assurance from King William of Prussia that his kingdom would never support a Hohenzollern for the vacant crown, a request the King refused. He sent a telegram to his Chancellor, Otto von Bismarck, who altered the text so that it appeared as if the King and ambassador had insulted each other and released it to the press. Feelings between both countries reached such a pitch that the French, mistakenly believing themselves militarily superior, declared war on Prussia a few days later. France's defeat led to the downfall of the empire, the abdication of Napoleon III and the establishment of the German Empire under Prussian leadership.

Yet Prim, like most of the other politicians, thought that only when the vacant throne was filled would they stabilise the revolution. When the King comes, he said, everything would be settled; there would be no cry but *Viva el Rey*, and they would 'box up all those madmen who dream up "liberticide" plans and who confuse progress with disorder, liberty with licence'.⁵ He considered himself duty-bound to preserve continuity with the Spanish monarchical tradition, and for him any sudden break with the past was not to be considered. 'I choose to be a monk rather than a Cromwell,' he said. 'There shall be no republic in Spain whilst I live.'⁶ Next he turned to the house of Savoy, and in particular to the Duke of Genoa, the nephew of King Victor Emmanuel II of Italy. The Duke refused, and Prim approached Amedeo, Duke of Aosta, the King's second son. Like King Ferdinand of Portugal, he had been a candidate for the briefly vacant throne of Greece in 1862,* and he telegraphed his acceptance of the throne on 30 October 1870.

On 4 November Prim announced the news to the Cortes. The main opposition to bringing another monarch to Spain came from Emilio Castelar y Ripoll, a prominent republican deputy and Professor of History at Madrid University. Declaring that a federal republic was the logical outcome of the September revolution, he brought forward a motion of censure on the government for trying to find a candidate for the throne without consulting the Cortes, and for presenting a candidate to the army before communicating with the House. He said that in view of the war currently taking place he could not understand the fervour of monarchical partisans, alluded to the sorry fate of Emperor Maximilian of Mexico, and said he doubted the Duke of Aosta would accept the throne. Nevertheless on 16 November his candidature was put to the vote in the Cortes, where he received 191 votes out of 311. Interestingly, 27 voted for the Duc de Montpensier (and one for the Duchesse), 8 for Espartero,

---

* The unpopular and childless King Otho of Greece, born a prince of Bavaria, had been deposed in 1862. Prince William of Denmark, a son of the future King Christian IX, was chosen in his place, and reigned as King George I.

2 for restoring the Prince of Asturias, and 63 for establishing a republic. There were 19 blank papers.

On 4 December the Duke of Aosta delivered a speech at the Pitti Palace, Florence, in which he swore to be true to the traditions of his ancestors. Though he did not ignore the difficulties of his new position 'and the responsibility to be assumed before history', he placed his confidence in God and in the Spanish people, 'which has given proof that it knows how to unite respect for the law with liberty'. He hoped that the Spaniards would be able to say of the King whom they had elected, 'His honesty could rise above the struggles of parties, and he had no other object but the peace and prosperity of the nation.'[7]

Embarking in the Spanish ironclad *Numancia*, Amedeo landed at Cartagena on 27 December. He travelled without his wife, now Queen Maria Victoria, who was recovering from the birth of a son. It was a grim portent of the shape of things to come that his arrival should coincide with the assassination of his leading champion. Late on the following evening Prim left the Cortes in his coach, and while driving home ran straight into an ambush. A cab blocked the way as armed men approached from both sides, one smashing the muzzle of his gun through the closed windows and firing directly at Prim. He was severely wounded in the shoulder and died of his injuries two days later. In the struggle his aide-de-camp was also seriously wounded, and his right hand had to be amputated.

Though some suspects were rounded up and imprisoned, the assassins were never caught and nobody was charged with murder. Montpensier was suspected of complicity, though no evidence was found to implicate him. Others blamed federalist republican extremists who resented having another monarch imposed on them. The assassination was a political disaster for King Amedeo, for Prim had been the most powerful and most capable man in Spain, the one progressive who was respected by and could unite the progressives. Had he lived, Prim would almost certainly have been able to make Amedeo's tenure of the throne a little more secure.

Early in the afternoon of 2 January 1871 King Amedeo arrived by train in a cold and snowy Madrid. He was welcomed by Serrano, who recommended that they leave the station in a carriage as the streets were so slippery, but the new monarch wanted to go on horseback instead, so that the people who had braved the wintry weather would have a chance of seeing him properly. Next he asked to visit the Church of Atocha to pay his last respects to Prim, whose body had been taken to rest there until the funeral. Deeply affected by the tragic death of his champion, he knelt in silent prayer for a while, and then went to pay a visit of condolence to the Marshal's widow and children, who were staying in quarters attached to the offices of the Ministry of War.

When Amedeo went to the Cortes, Serrano surrendered his regency and the new monarch swore the oath to uphold the constitution. An affable and conscientious young man of twenty-six, he took up his royal duties with every good intention, but this would not be enough. He was under no illusions and had foreseen that his life as a king would not be an easy one, and before leaving Italy had remarked that he knew he was going to fulfil an impossible mission. 'Spain, now divided into various parties, will unite against a foreign king, and I shall soon be obliged to return the crown they offered me.'[8]

Indeed the hapless new sovereign had little chance. To most of his new subjects, 'he was the son of an impious usurper who had deprived the Pope of his temporal dominions and had overthrown a number of long-established thrones, two of which had been occupied by members of the Spanish royal family'.[9] Like Joseph Bonaparte, he was looked upon as just another foreign intruder. He was so ill-prepared for his new position that he could barely speak a word of Spanish, and during his brief reign he had little opportunity to improve the matter, though Queen Maria Victoria was fluent in the tongue. By no means wealthy, he was obliged to depend on financial subsidies from his father, King Victor Emmanuel.

Despite his intention to be a democratic sovereign, the King of Italy advised him that if he wanted to keep his throne, he would have to assume dictatorial powers in Madrid, as this would be the only way for him to impose royal authority over such a turbulent people as the Spanish. Any illusions he might have had that they would welcome him were dispelled whenever he attended the theatre in

Madrid, where he was invariably booed or insulted. Even the aristocracy, so often the mainstay of the sovereign, resented his presence, ostentatiously cold-shouldered him and referred to him behind his back as 'King Macaroni'.

The contrast between King Amedeo and his predecessor could not have been greater. Where she had nearly always gone to bed late and risen late, he was up and at work early in the morning. He and Queen Maria Victoria, who joined him in Madrid at the end of March 1871, were relatively thrifty. Yet such was the perversity of the people over whom he reigned that within a few months they were longing for the 'good old days' of the profligacy and easy morals of Queen Isabel's court. When Amedeo's second son was born, little notice was taken, and the Cortes did not send their congratulations. Even the Queen's charitable work, in particular her founding a new orphanage, attracted little attention.

As Republican leader in the Cortes, Castelar kept up a verbal campaign against him. Who were these wretched Dukes of Savoy, he asked, 'that run like dogs in the wake of the coach of our Kings?'[10] Nevertheless the politician was magnanimous enough to respect the King as a person. The latter often went out to a café for his early meal, and on one occasion he met Castelar, who raised his hat to him. 'My salute was not to royalty, sire,' he explained, 'but to the bravest man in Christendom.'[11]

King Amedeo's first political act was to entrust Serrano with the formation of a ministry intended to be a coalition of all those who supported the regime. A cabinet on such lines was thus constituted, but when it appealed to the country the result was the return of an increased number of Carlist and Republican deputies.

When the new King addressed the Cortes, he told the deputies that when his feet first touched Spanish soil,

I determined to merge my ideas, my sentiments and my interests, in those of the nation who elected me as its head, and whose independent character would never submit to foreign and illegitimate intrigues. My sons will have the good fortune to receive their first impressions of life here; their first language will be Spanish; their education will be in accordance with the customs of the nation; they will learn to feel and think as you feel and think and we shall unite with imperishable bonds our own fate with your fate.[12]

Nevertheless the government was defeated in the Cortes on the reply to the King's first address from the throne. There was a split in the ranks of the King's supporters, and two short-lived administrations followed, under Ruiz Zorrilla and Malcampo respectively. The next Prime Minister was Sagasta, whose personal popularity helped him secure a narrow majority at the elections in April 1872. However, on the point of taking office he was obliged to resign after being charged with embezzlement. He was replaced by Ruiz Zorrilla, who dissolved the Cortes, held fresh elections and obtained a new majority.

Having a new 'foreign' King had given the Carlists another opportunity. Don Carlos crossed the frontier into Navarre on 2 May 1872 with an army of supporters, but government forces surprised them in the mountain village of Oroquieta. Many Carlists, including Don Carlos himself, fled without firing a shot, though about forty were killed and seven hundred taken prisoner.

* * *

France's defeat, the abdication of her protector Emperor Napoleon and the overthrow of the empire had left Queen Isabel, her family and remaining entourage very vulnerable in Paris. She was aware that the moderate republican government would soon be eclipsed by the revolutionary Commune. It would be necessary, she knew, to abandon her house to the risk of bombardment, and leave the country for a while. In September 1870, three months after her abdication statement, she took her family down to the south of France and across the frontier to Geneva. They settled in the Hotel de la Paix, waiting until order was re-established in France. By the end of July 1871 stability had come to the republic, and early the next month they returned to Paris. Although the city had suffered much as a result of the war and the hardships of the French people, her house, which had been used as a hospital in her absence, remained relatively unscathed.

King Francisco had not joined them in Geneva, but at the height of the Commune terrors he prudently spent several months in England. He had long been a fluent English speaker and reader, as well as a great admirer of the people. In his new home in Paris, where he returned once revolutionary fervour had subsided, he wore only English clothes and kept English servants, maintaining that all others were stupid and incapable of moving deftly and quietly.[13]

* * *

Amedeo had never ceased to be somewhat bemused at being summoned to wear the crown of Spain. Some years later he told Infanta Eulalia that he had never found out why the throne had been offered to him, nor why his rule had been rejected; it had all been a mystery to him.[14] His unhappy reign lasted for little more than two years. The instability of Spanish politics, perpetual republican conspiracies, Carlist uprisings and internecine party disputes were too much for him. In the Cortes he could only count on the support of the Progressive Party, whose leaders were passing whatever legislation they wanted without any effective challenge, thanks to widespread electoral fraud which had given themn a comfortable parliamentary majority. The Progressives fragmented into Monarchists and Constitutionalists, inter-party conflicts produced virtual paralysis in the Cortes, the Carlists rebelled in the Basque and Catalan regions, and there was a new wave of republican uprisings. The artillery corps of the army went on strike, and the government instructed the King to discipline them. In July 1872 he and Queen Maria Victoria were shot at while on a drive through the streets of Madrid, though they were unharmed. The would-be assassin was never caught, though once again the finger of suspicion pointed at Montpensier, who was considered the arch-villain behind everything.

The final straw came when Ruiz Zorrilla persuaded the King to confer a high command on General Hidalgo, who had taken the side of the rebels at the time of the mutiny in the artillery in 1866; the general was considered responsible for shooting down the artillery officers and was thus hated by those who survived. They refused to serve under him in his new capacity, preferring to resign their commissions instead. The government retaliated by dissolving the artillery corps and promoting non-commissioned officers to fill the vacancies. Though he did not approve of the government's action, King Amedeo wearily signed the necessary decree. To resist would mean that he would have to call on the *moderados* to form a new government, and thus he would lose the support of the radicals and democrats who had at least shown him some loyalty, albeit on a superficial level.

It was his last duty as King of Spain, for by this time he had decided that he had had enough of this unruly kingdom and her politics. Faced with the likelihood that he would never enjoy any popular support no matter how long he reigned, on 10 February 1873 he told Zorrilla that he had decided to abdicate. Taken aback, Zorrilla asked him to reflect on the matter for twenty-four, even forty-eight hours, and then told the other senior ministers in confidence. Inevitably the news leaked out and it was soon the talk of Spain and beyond.

Next day the King confirmed that he was going. In his abdication statement he said that he had been honoured to occupy the throne, had sought inspiration solely in the good of the country and had pledged to place himself above and beyond all political parties. Ready to make sacrifices to give Spain 'the peace it needs, the liberty it deserves, and the grandeur to which its glorious history and the virtue and constancy of its sons entitle it', he thought his lack of experience in the art of ruling would be supplemented by the loyalty of his character, and he believed that all Spaniards who truly loved their country would support him in putting 'an end to the sanguinary and sterile struggles which have for so long been tearing her entrails'. He had been deceived, for Spain still lived in perpetual struggle, and every day it appeared that the era of peace and prosperity he wanted for the country was further away. If the enemies of her well-being had been strangers or foreigners, then he would have been the first to place himself at the head of the army and face them down. Sadly this was not the case. 'All those, however, by their sword, their pen, and their speech aggravate and perpetuate the evils of the nation are Spaniards. All professed to fight and agitate for her good, and between the din of the combat, the confused, noisy, and contradictory clamour of political parties, amid so many and so opposite manifestations of public opinion, it is impossible for me to discover the truth, and even more impossible to find the remedy for such evils.' He was therefore returning the crown to the people and renouncing it for himself, his children and his successors. He did not lay down his love for Spain, 'as noble as she is unfortunate', and he carried no other sorrow than that of having found it impossible to do all the good for her that he desired.[15]

Early the next day, at around 6 a.m., he and some members of his family left Madrid for Lisbon, from where they would return to Florence. There was no parade, no guard of honour, no cheering or booing crowds as he left the kingdom over which he had so briefly reigned but not ruled. Only a couple of generals, a few members of their household and a few members of the Cortes saw the former King on his way to the station. Queen Maria, still recovering from her third confinement, had to stay in the palace and followed a few days later. Her youngest son Luigi, later Duke of the Abruzzi, destined to become a renowned mountaineer and explorer, had been born on 29 January.

With sadness but an overwhelming sense of relief the former King Amedeo and Queen Maria Victoria,* who would henceforth be known as the Duke and Duchess of Aosta, put their lives in Spain behind them. Yet they hoped that the country would be in good hands. 'I still pray God that He will give to Spain, under other rule, that happiness which I and King Amedeo could not succeed in giving,'[16] she wrote to Olozaga later that month.

---

* The Duchess of Aosta's health, which had always been poor, never recovered. She died on 8 November 1876, aged twenty-eight.

FIVE

'A young and unprejudiced monarch'

Faced with a vacant throne for the second time in less than three years, the Cortes responded by declaring itself a National Assembly, and voting for a Spanish republic by 258 votes to 32. The Republican leader Castelar declared triumphantly that the traditional monarchy had died with Ferdinand VII, the parliamentary monarchy had died with the flight of Isabel II, and the democratic monarchy had gone with the abdication of Don Amedeo of Savoy: 'no one has brought it to an end. It died of itself. No one is installing the Republic; it is due to circumstances; to a conspiracy of society, nature, and history.' While he admitted that he had worked towards the moment when Spain became a republic, he wanted to say that he believed with all his heart that the fall of the institution owed nothing to him; 'the monarchy is dead without anyone whatever contributing to its death except the Providence of God'.[1]

Ill-prepared for this turn of events, the republicans were divided, their various factions unable to agree on what form the new Spanish republic should take. Some wanted a federal nation, like the United States of America, while others preferred a military dictatorship, or a more conservative institution. For the Carlists, this was another call to arms and the Basques, the Navarrese and the Catalonians all rose up on behalf of 'Carlos VII'. The Carlists proved unsuccessful, though Carlos did stage a procession with 'Queen' Margaret through Estella. Other parts of the country descended into virtual anarchy, with one area, Valencia, establishing its own fiscal frontiers. Troops mutinied, priests were murdered and by the end of 1873 Spain was in a dire state. In January 1874 Serrano took control. He dissolved the Cortes and announced that no more elections would be held until the country had been completely pacified. He then took the field against the Carlists, who were soon driven out of most of the provinces, back into a few areas in northern Spain.

To more traditionalist strands of opinion, the only way to unite the country was to recall Alfonso, Prince of Asturias, the true heir to the throne. He had been attending the Stanislas College in the Rue Notre Dame de Champs, but the outbreak of the Franco-Prussian war made it advisable to take the boy away from Paris and he was sent instead to the Theresianum College in Vienna.

On completion of his studies there in October 1874 at the age of sixteen, he was sent to the Military College at Sandhurst in England under the incognito of the Marques de Covadonga. When not at the college he spent much of his spare time with the Prince Imperial, then an artillery cadet in his last term at Woolwich, and his widowed mother, the former Empress Eugenie, who lived nearby at Farnborough. It was inevitable that both young men, who had so much in common, especially with regard to their peculiar position as heirs to thrones of neighbouring young republics, should become firm friends.

On his seventeenth birthday in November 1874, Alfonso came of age. The abdication of Amedeo and the declaration of a republic had raised the family's hopes of being recalled, and the tide had turned against the Carlists. In December Alfonso issued what came to be known as the 'Sandhurst Manifesto', in which he proclaimed that only the establishment of a constitutional monarchy could put an end to oppression and uncertainty, 'and to the cruel disorders from which Spain is suffering. All men of good will, whatever their political antecedents, will soon be on my side, knowing that they have nothing to fear from a young and unprejudiced monarch to whom union and peace are the breath of life. I shall ever be a good Spaniard, a good Catholic like my ancestors, and like the men of my own day a Liberal.'[2]

After the end of his first term Alfonso spent a few days in London over the Christmas of 1874. On 23 December he and his equerry Don Juan de Valasco arrived at the Charing Cross Hotel. They had so little luggage with them, only a greatcoat and a small case, that a deposit of £2 was requested by the management from this young and presumably impecunious young cadet and his friend before they could be allotted a room. His plan was to leave for France in the following week, returning to England on 8 January, and to spend the ensuing five weeks before the next term at Sandhurst began in mid-February in touring the more important English industrial centres. He spent Christmas Day sightseeing in London, sailed to France on 29 December and on the following day arrived at the Palais de Castille, Paris, to see in the new year with his mother and sisters. A few hours after his arrival he received a telegram from Spain to say that, contrary to royalist plans, a General Martinez Campos had issued a *pronunciamento* in his favour and that it had been enthusiastically supported.

The military had anticipated the prudent schemes of the Prime Minister Cánovas del Castillo and the Prince, both well aware that a restoration of the monarchy had to come about by constitutional means. Canovas had long since held the view that a restoration would only succeed if opinion was strongly in favour of Alfonso as King, for unlike his discredited mother he could be sure of support from almost all sides of the political spectrum except the relatively small radical and republican element. Most of the politicians and military leaders who had brought about Queen Isabel's downfall had been opposed to her personally, rather than to the monarchy itself. In several regions of Spain monarchist propaganda had been carried on openly, supported by the better-off and undimmed by the unsuccessful reign of King Amedeo. Some of the more active monarchist supporters, particularly among the military, were impatient for a restoration, believing that any postponement would only weaken the chances of Alfonso returning as King. The longer Spain remained without a monarch as head of state, they knew, the easier it would be for ambitious politicians to assume power – maybe absolute power – for themselves.

The man who would soon be King prudently kept the news to himself. With his mother and sisters (who knew nothing about it), he went to the theatre on the evening of 30 December. On their return to the hotel, they found a Spanish statesman, the Marques de Elduayen, waiting for them. Sadly he told Queen Isabel that one of the military leaders had had the folly to place himself at the head of his troops and proclaim the accession of King Alfonso XII. Unless the whole of Spain followed his example, they were lost. Alfonso let him finish, then turned to him with a smile, saying that he had received the news that morning and had decided to leave for Spain immediately – or rather, the next morning, as he was tired and looked forward to going to bed.

The following morning crowds gathered outside the palace and Alfonso knew that the *pronunciamento* had been successful. When his sisters excitedly went to his room they found the door locked. He called to them, asking them to wait until he was dressed, and when he emerged they asked him why he was looking so serious. His answer was simple: 'I want to make a good name in history.'[3] Over the next three days well-wishers came to congratulate him, and Queen Isabel stood beside her son as they greeted a steady procession of guests. When the widowed former Empress Eugenie, now living in exile in England, heard the news, she wrote to a friend to say it had reached them 'like a thunderbolt'. Don Alfonso, she went on, was 'the first of the birds to pass through the bars of the cage; will it be the same for the others?'[4] Later that week he left Paris for Marseilles, where he boarded a Spanish man-of-war and changed into the uniform of a captain-general. On 10 January he landed at Barcelona to a roar of welcome, and on 14 January he entered Madrid, where the crowds went wild.

Spain was now in the unusual position of having two kings, Carlos VII in his capital at Estella and Alfonso XII at Madrid. Though the latter was not as tall and may have looked less impressive, he was athletic and graceful, of a soldierly appearance and figure, and he had the more appealing personality. A smiling, bright young man eager to please, he had his mother's charm, friendliness and ability to win hearts. Disliking protocol and pomposity, he wanted to purge the court of some of its formality. Unlike his mother he rose early, worked hard, took plenty of exercise and dined early – at 7.30 p.m. He was an excellent shot and a daring horseman. He enjoyed skating and had his own rink. As the sun rose early in Spain, even in winter, he had to be up early each morning to take advantage of the ice, and guests at court – ambassadors, ministers of state and generals – all had to come out and join him.

He often claimed that he had learnt much from his period of exile, and had acquired a sound knowledge of men and things. Early in life he had learned to rely on himself and his own judgement. Immune to flattery, he could take criticism in his stride. One evening after dinner he amazed the company by reading aloud a speech made recently in the Cortes by Castelar, attacking the King himself. When he had finished, his horrified listeners told him that it was outrageous. With a twinkle in his eye, he answered, 'But, Señores – it is magnificent.'[5] Later Castelar willingly recognised the monarchy and in time became a fervent admirer of Queen Maria Cristina.

In contrast, as has been observed, Alfonso belonged to that select group of monarchs including Charles II of England, Louis XVIII of France and (some years later) George II of the Hellenes – restored to a throne after several years of foreign exile. From their youth, all were surrounded by sycophants to whom their slightest whim was law; they had then seen themselves ostentatiously avoided by those who had fawned on them, held at arm's length by foreign powers to whose rulers they were closely related; and they had then seen a 'rush to the bandwagon' on the part of those who had sat on the fence. It all seemed calculated to produce a feeling of cynicism.[6]

The early days of Alfonso XII's reign were overshadowed by the continuing Carlist war and the presence of Don Carlos. The restoration of the monarchy had deprived him of the support of many who were prepared to accept him as the only means of overturning the Republic, while papal recognition of King Alfonso XII had weakened his position with the clergy as well as with many of the people. Alfonso took personal command of his troops on the Ebro and was present at the raising of the siege of Pamplona. A subsequent attack on the Carlist stronghold of Estella failed, and

Alfonso started back to Madrid under steady fire from Carlist bullets. It proved only a temporary setback.

Throughout 1875 the Carlists suffered further defeats from Alfonso's troops, and Cabrera, still in Paris, turned his back on their cause. He acknowledged Alfonso as King, and as the end was evidently in sight, the government allowed King Alfonso to take over nominal command of the army again. On 19 February 1876 the town of Estella was captured and the Carlist resistance collapsed. Don Carlos was forced to flee the country and settled in France; after a brief visit to England, where he soon found he was not welcome, he went back to Paris. The Second Carlist War was over.

To restore law and order was King Alfonso's immediate priority. In March 1876 a committee comprising all shades of monarchical opinion under Cánovas drew up a new constitution, by which Spain would be governed until 1923. According to Article 18, 'The legislative power lies in the Cortes with the King.' Both chambers of the Cortes had equal authority. The Senate consisted of eighty senators elected by local bodies, the universities and taxpayers of the highest class; elections for half the body took place once every five years. The Chamber was elected by districts of 50,000 inhabitants, though full adult suffrage did not come until 1890, and even then the vote was limited to men. In the larger towns there was also a form of proportional representation. The King alone had the right to summon, adjourn and even dissolve the Cortes, but a dissolution had to be followed by the assembly of a new Chamber within three months. He did not have absolute power, in that his decrees had to be countersigned by a 'responsible' minister. While the King appointed ministers, they were answerable to the Cortes; he had the power of veto, but never actually used it. In practice the constitution depended for successful working upon the willing cooperation of the Spanish people.

Cánovas did not believe that his fellow countrymen were ready for such a constitution, but the King hoped it would take root with the passage of time. In this he was to be disappointed, as the political life of Spain continued as something of a sham, but at least he could look forward to a period of political stability. The

Conservatives, led by Cánovas, and the Liberals, led by Sagasta, came to an agreement by which they would alternate in office. As elections were shamelessly rigged, this caused no difficulty. Alfonso was well aware of this, and when his sister Eulalia asked him, on one change of government, whether he believed it would be an improvement on its predecessor, he shook his head, saying it would make no difference: 'They are the same dog with different collars.'[7]

Even so, he recognised his duty as a constitutional sovereign better than his mother, in that he was prepared to adopt a more laissez-faire and, less interventionist (or interfering) attitude by allowing the two-party system to function as it saw fit in the interests of national stability. Both political leaders worked together to ensure at least an outward appearance of normal constitutional life in Spain. During the lifetimes of Cánovas and Sagasta this was maintained, but after their deaths the parties fragmented into different groups, with severe consequences for political stability. Cánovas himself was a hard task-master, and it was alleged that he surrounded the Pardo with troops instructed to report back to him on the King's movements, presumably so he would be aware of the company his young and inexperienced sovereign might be keeping. If the King was ever angered or slighted at such surveillance, he kept his thoughts to himself.

Infanta Eulalia was thoroughly scornful at this pretence of democracy. In theory, she believed, the people of Spain were almost as free to vote at elections as those of the United States of America, but in practice they had no voice at all in 'their own government'. Whenever the Spanish rebelled, they succeeded in no more than making a futile anti-clerical revolt that achieved nothing, 'because they got involved in a quarrel about religion and the burning of churches'. Whenever a republic was declared, with the aid of the army, which was republican because the aristocracy did not serve even as officers, the system of government, or misgovernment, continued under a new name.[8]

King Alfonso XII worked faithfully, trying to oversee the departments of the government which were most easily watched, such as the army and navy. He did not trust official reports, but took great trouble to visit and talk to the officers and men to ensure that the reports were accurate. One day while out driving with his sisters, he suddenly announced that they would visit the French hospital without warning, so the authorities would not be able to make any preparations for their visit. On their arrival, so his sister Eulalia recorded, a man who had apparently been paralysed for years was so startled that he immediately got to his feet and walked. Had it happened a few centuries earlier, she remarked with a touch of irony, her brother might have been made a saint, and she might have been granted her own little shrine.[9]

Every afternoon King Alfonso gave audiences to anybody who wished to come and see him, whether to present petitions, pay their respects or for any other reason. His patience with everyone impressed all around him, though it often seemed difficult for him to learn anything from his visitors, as they were usually too overawed by the formalities of etiquette to be at their ease. He worked hard but had few if any interests outside sport to lighten his leisure hours. Literature meant nothing to him, and he had no ear for music; he told his opera-loving sister that he could not tell the Royal March apart from other pieces, and he complained that the sound of singing depressed him like the howling of a dog.

✳   ✳   ✳

In July 1876 the former Queen Isabel and her daughters returned to Spain. According to her daughter Paz, their seven years of exile or banishment had been a grave personal misfortune for them. Nevertheless the girls' education in a foreign country had done them all much good, for instead of living for years surrounded by court pomp and etiquette, they had been brought up in relative simplicity like private citizens. Nevertheless she was overjoyed to return to her own country, and to see her brother and eldest sister again.[10]

Her younger sister Eulalia was less enthusiastic about their return home. Always the most egalitarian of the family, as she would prove with devastating effect in middle age after the publication of her memoirs, she had thought that the Bourbons' displacement from the Spanish throne would have entailed a life of some privacy. After finishing her education at school, she fondly imagined, she would lead a relatively normal life like other girls of her own age. It was bewildering when her mother summoned her to her bedroom one day and told her that her brother had been proclaimed King. While she realised from her mother's manner that it was an event of great joy, she failed to share in any such elation. 'It was as if someone should tell a little girl of a great inheritance that was to make her very wealthy, when she did not understand what money should buy.'[11]

Queen Isabel could hardly be refused the chance to return to her homeland, but the government viewed her arrival with little enthusiasm. While living in Paris she had continued to spend lavishly, and now she was in desperate need of further funds. At an audience with her son, she promised faithfully to keep aloof from politics, saying that her role in public affairs was now at an end. Nevertheless she had not been back long before she began negotiations with the Treasury over items and arrears in her pension. Next she began interfering in religious matters as well; when some of her hard-pressed friends in the Clerical Party appealed to her for help, she wrote to the Pope, telling him she would use her influence with her son to bring about a settlement satisfactory to His Holiness. The Prime Minister's complaints provoked her into publishing her side of the controversy in the French press, and he responded by putting his case in the Spanish papers. Something had to be done about her, though banishment was considered too drastic. She was asked to leave the Escorial, and was offered the Alcazar in Seville. It did not, however, stop her from continuing to scheme on behalf of her clerical friends.

Though the former Queen might be untrustworthy, she had lost none of her legendary charm. Sir Alexander Hardinge, a British diplomatist who first came to Spain during the reign of her son, recalled in his memoirs 'the queenly dignity and charm of manner which distinguished her, notwithstanding her age and a marked inclination to stoutness. Her voice, and in this she recalled our own Queen [Victoria], was musical; and though she can never have been really beautiful, she preserved a most attractive smile.'[12]

Still she sought happiness in the company of a faithful male companion. Shortly after her son's recall to the throne, Cánovas had ordered her to send Marfori back to Spain, where he was arrested in October 1875 but released four months later as the government could not charge him with any crime. He remained in Spain until his death in 1892. Alone again, she took a new lover, José Ramiro de la Puente y Gonzalez de Adin, an army officer. He arrived in Paris in 1877, and soon after returning from Spain Isabel made him her personal secretary and head of her household. Early the following year she bought and settled in a hunting lodge at Fontenay.

Though now aged forty-five, her childbearing days were not quite over. On 28 March she had another child, apparently stillborn. Very few people, apart from her lady-in-waiting and a few confidantes among her household, knew about the birth. Again she suffered from severe depression as a result, and her relationship with Ramiro de la Puente did not survive much longer. At her personal request the title of Marques de Villa Alta was conferred on him by the King of Italy, and he later returned to Madrid.

This unhappy episode was to have a curious sequel. About twenty years later, towards the end of Queen Isabel's life, Pedro de Répide, a young Spanish writer, arrived in Paris saying he had come with instructions to take care of her personal library. When questioned about his family, he said he was the adopted son of a civil servant with whom he shared a name, and to whose care he had been entrusted by the family of Ramiro de la Puente in 1878. He had always been supported and educated with money from the Duke of Sesto. While staying at the Palacio de Castilla he had had access to the Queen's documents, and after studying these he eventually concluded that *he* was the child born at Fontenay. Nobody ever saw fit to prove or disprove his claim.

Queen Isabel was privately rather disgruntled that she had not been recalled to wear the crown. Even if she had once been glad to 'be rid of that great weight' and no longer bear the responsibilities of a reigning sovereign, she must have been a little irked at not being asked to resume the throne. Nevertheless, it was unlikely that she took neither pride nor comfort in seeing Spain become a monarchy again, with her son and heir as the monarch. If she was jealous of him, she had the good sense to keep it to herself.

Not for want of trying, the former Queen failed to get her own way with regard to her elder – or only surviving – son's choice of wife. She had regarded the Carlist wars as little more than a family argument which grew out of all proportion. If a marriage could be arranged between both branches of the family, she thought, maybe it would put an end to years of feuding. Bianca, the eldest daughter of Don Carlos, was barely ten years old, but Isabel thought that if a betrothal could be arranged, in about four or five years she could marry King Alfonso. This would also put an end to the aspirations of the Duc de Montpensier, whom she still could not trust.

Unfortunately for his mother, King Alfonso had other ideas. In the summer of 1877 he announced his betrothal to his cousin Mercedes, Montpensier's daughter. She was sixteen, and had been on very friendly terms with him for about two years, conducting a secret correspondence for several months. Queen Isabel was outraged. That it was to all appearances a genuine love match did not move her in the slightest, notwithstanding the fact that she had been forced into the most cynical of arranged marriages. It looked suspiciously like a plan by which Montpensier would get one of his descendants on the throne of Spain. When she questioned her son on the matter, he was adamant; he would never marry against his will. In vain did his mother try to warn him that his bride would let slip no opportunity to conspire against him in order to place her ambitious father on the throne. She threatened to cause scandal by publicly auctioning some of the jewellery kept in the treasury of the Church of the Atocha, which he wanted to give his bride as a wedding present. Her arguments and threats were to no avail.

At last Isabel realised that her influence no longer counted for anything in Spain, and in August she told her daughters that she would take them to Madrid and leave them there while she returned alone to Paris. They thought it very hard on her, but accepted her excuse that she made 'the sacrifice because she thinks it better for our future that we should remain with Alfonso'.[13] Torn between loyalty to parent and eldest brother, whom they knew to be deeply in love, they were happy to join him in the Palacio Real. In time they found out the real reason for their mother's departure, and felt saddened that she should have tried to throw a shadow across her son's happiness. On 14 September he told his mother firmly that he and Mercedes were to be married. She left the stormy interview red-eyed, her face betraying the signs of tears of anger, but, as Alfonso told his sisters triumphantly that evening, 'it was all arranged'. Thwarted and overruled, she returned to Paris in high dudgeon.

Mercedes was an attractive young woman with great charm and spontaneity of manner. According to King Alfonso's youngest sister Eulalia, it was purely a love match, 'the only one I ever knew in royalty'.[14] The Duc de Sesto was sent to Seville to ask formally for her hand, and once his request was granted, Alfonso arrived in the city. Their betrothal was formally celebrated at a great ball on 26 December 1877. Mercedes was described as looking radiant, while Alfonso, as was only to be expected, seemed particularly animated as well.

The wedding took place on an unusually warm and sunny winter's day at the Church of the Atocha on 23 January 1878. 'It is too sad that the only one to be absent is just Mamma', Infanta Paz wrote in her diary.[15] With the prominent exception of the still smarting Queen Isabel, all the family were there – the elderly and increasingly frail Queen Maria Cristina, her son-in-law King Francisco, making his first journey to Spain since being exiled after the revolution of 1868, the bride's parents Montpensier and Luisa, and the King's sisters. Though they had often been indulgent towards the personal weaknesses of Queen Isabel, the Spaniards were glad to see that a royal family which had long been notorious for its decadent private life was now bringing a touch of genuine respectability and domesticity to the court. Though she was hardly an objective witness, the bride's sister-in-law Paz echoed the thoughts of many when she noted at one of the receptions that Queen Mercedes, in her simple blue dress trimmed with fur inherited from her grandmother Queen Marie Amélie, widow of King Louis Philippe, 'looked lovelier than ever with all the freshness of her seventeen years'.[16]

Queen Isabel softened the blow of her absence a little by writing to Infanta Pilar that she was sorry she could not be present at her brother's wedding, but she would be there in heart: 'I bless them, and wish them long years of happiness.'[17]

As Eulalia would testify, her brother and his wife were idyllically happy in their married life. Queen Mercedes was adored by her sisters-in-law. She helped them with their lessons, painted them flower studies and would gladly do anything to help them. Though her father had been unpopular among the public and the match had been viewed with suspicion at first, her radiant, unaffected personality soon swept opposition away.

Tragically their married life was to be all too short. On 18 June, the Infanta Paz noted sadly in her diary, the Queen had been feeling unwell for over a month, 'but at Court no one ever acknowledges that a member of the Royal family is ill, and when one inquires the answer is always the same, even when it is not true'.[18] When the family came to see her and sit round her bed, a large portrait of her fell from the wall and broke into several pieces. To the superstitious, it was a bad omen.

Six days later, five months after her wedding, it was her eighteenth birthday, but neither she nor anybody else was inclined to celebrate. On the contrary, as the guns outside the palace in Madrid were firing a salute, she was receiving the Last Sacraments. Two days later a deathly silence hung around the rooms of the palace as the Archbishop of Toledo read the prayers for the dying while ministers, ladies-in-waiting, aides-de-camp and generals joined the family as they knelt in the chamber. The King held her hand and his eyes never left her white face, until at midday she died.

Officially the cause was gastric fever and possibly typhoid. According to her sister-in-law Eulalia, the real causes of death were miscarriage and blood poisoning thanks to incompetent doctors, who had treated her for typhoid fever and mismanaged her case until a putrefaction set in which no medical treatment could alleviate.[19]

Afterwards Alfonso's sisters were among the first to kiss her. As they left the room, the King asked for forgiveness for calling them in: 'I still hoped that perhaps the prayers of such innocent hearts might help.'[20] To his mother in Paris who had not looked kindly on the marriage, he sent a telegram: 'Pray to the good God for the soul of my poor Mercedes, who is now in Heaven.'[21]

Later her body was dressed in the black and white habit of a nun, and she was taken to lie in state in the Hall of Columns in the Palace.

A funeral service was held in the Church of San Francisco, after which the body was deposited in the Escorial. As she had not been the mother of a King, she could not be laid in the royal vault, and rather than have her buried among the lesser members of the royal family, King Alfonso had a special tomb constructed above the high altar of the church. He was shattered by her death, and after the funeral he refused at first to leave the Escorial. Each day he would shut himself away for hours in the crypt where her body lay, and when the family tried to coax him away he would not speak to them. He did nothing but grieve, could not sleep and appeared 'sunken in a mood of passionate despair' that seemed to have put him beyond reach of the family. Friends and sisters worked hard to persuade him out for fresh air at dawn and again at sunset, but they did not get him on horseback again for several months. Infanta Eulalia thought he had 'lost interest in life entirely; and as the months passed, we were afraid that his health would be destroyed'.[22]

For the rest of his days he never really recovered from the death of Queen Mercedes. He remained a dutiful monarch and a sympathetic friend and brother, but his former high spirits now gave way to a world-weary cynicism, his boyish enthusiasm to a frenetic search for distraction, an increasing flippancy, restlessness and immorality. One of his aides saw him a few days after her death, and thought that while he seemed outwardly calm and self-contained as ever, he looked as if he had aged ten years in less than a week. Dark rims under his eyes testified to sleepless nights. When the man tried to express his sympathy, he dismissed his words with a gesture of pain, and the faint trace of a friendly smile that seemed to say that he appreciated such thoughts but could not bear to talk about it at present. He then turned to the business they had been discussing a few days earlier, and seemed as enthusiastic and determined as ever. As the man left the audience chamber, he said that they should try to be successful this time: 'I feel that there is nothing else for me to spend my energies upon except the future of Spain now.'[23]

Two months later Spain lost another of her queens. A widow for five years since the death of her devoted Muñoz, Queen Maria Cristina had spent the rest of her retirement near Havre. She had been deeply saddened by the death of her grandson's wife, and by the end of July she was seriously ill. On her deathbed she asked her granddaughters to tell the King, who was not present, that 'he must console himself and make Spain flourish'.[24] She died on 23 August 1878, aged seventy-two. Her body was brought home to the Escorial and laid in the vault beneath the high altar beside that of her first husband, King Ferdinand VII, who had died forty-five years earlier. Still in deepest mourning for his wife, King Alfonso was among those who attended the ceremony, alongside his sisters Isabel, Paz and Eulalia and the Montpensiers. Queen Isabel and King Francisco stayed away, as it was still not thought politically opportune for them to visit Madrid – even for such a solemn family occasion as this. Observers noticed that there was no sign of popular feeling, either favourable or adverse, towards the memory of Queen Maria Cristina, but only an air of indifference. It was as if the heavy pall of gloom that had descended after the death of Queen Mercedes had failed to lift.

Nevertheless there was one positive result for the elder generation of the royal family. Though neither of them attended the obsequies, her daughter and son-in-law exchanged messages after her demise. They consequently began to become friends at last, and in their exile in separate houses around the French capital they drew closer to each other than they had ever been during their twenty-two years of living in Spain, unhappily married and often separated.

In the afternoon of 25 October King Alfonso made his first official appearance in Madrid since the Queen's death. The escort and his horse were waiting at the railway station as he rode through the streets on horseback, going to the Atocha to attend a *Te Deum*. As he was returning to the palace a man pointed a revolver at him and fired twice, but missed. The culprit, a workman named Juan Oliva Moncasi, was put on trial at the end of the month. A diary was found on him, the last words written inside being, 'I have not much longer to live; Alfonso passes by in an hour's time; then I shall be condemned to death.'[25] Despite a general expectation that the King would commute his sentence of death to one of life imprisonment, he was executed in January 1879.

A third family death, as sudden and unexpected as that of the young Queen Mercedes, followed later that year. In the summer of 1879 King Alfonso's sister, the Infanta Pilar, died after a struggle with tuberculosis. The disease had long been hereditary among the Bourbons, but knowledge of their sufferings was kept from the public. Pilar had always been delicate, and while enjoying a holiday with her sister Paz at Escoriaza in the north of Spain which she had been ordered to take by the doctors after developing a skin disease, she attended a fiesta arranged by the people in her honour and thoroughly enjoyed the stalls, donkey rides and a session of open-air dancing.

However, that night she complained of tiredness, and stayed in bed the following day. At lunchtime a servant called Paz to say that she had suddenly become much worse. Her brother and mother were sent telegrams asking them to come at once, but they arrived too late. Early on the following morning Pilar received the Last Sacraments, and died at 7.30. It was rumoured that she had been nursing a broken heart since the death of the Prince Imperial in the Zulu wars in South Africa, though in fact she hardly knew him. Like that of Queen Mercedes, her death was instead laid at the door of poor medical practice in Spain and negligence on the part of the doctors.

For the Queen's eighteenth birthday King Alfonso had bought a very valuable and attractive ring. As she was lying on her deathbed at the time he felt unable to give it to her, so instead he presented it to her sister Cristina. Nine months later she realised that she too was dying, so she gave it to the Infanta Isabel, asking her to return it to him. He then gave it to his sister Pilar in memory of them both. Within four months she too was gone. After her death he put the ring on his own finger, and was wearing it on the way back from her funeral when the carriage overturned and he was thrown on to the road, dislocating his arm. Yet he refused to be superstitious about it and wore the ring for the rest of his life. And though he attained a greater age than his tragic wife, her sister and his own sister, his life was not destined to be long either.

SIX

'He had so longed for a son'

At the age of twenty-one the widowed King Alfonso XII – and his country – badly needed an heir, and court officials did not wait long after the death of Queen Mercedes before they began drawing up lists of prospective brides. The duty of taking a second wife was one which Alfonso viewed with little enthusiasm, but it had to be done.

Fortunately for the kingdom, there was one obvious choice. He had first met Archduchess Maria Cristina of Austria, a second cousin of Emperor Francis Joseph, during his adolescent years in Vienna. Another meeting between them was arranged for August 1879 at the French resort of Arcachon. At this time King Alfonso still had his arm in a sling after the carriage accident. Still in mourning for his sister, as well as his wife and his friend the Prince Imperial, he was not the liveliest of company, and can hardly have given the best possible impression to any would-be consorts. However, the Archduchess knew her obligations; she was sympathetic towards the young widower, and was aware that the object of this rendezvous was to lead to her becoming his wife. She realised that she would be expected to make Spain a good queen, not least by providing the country with a future sovereign. Moreover, it was not every archduchess or princess in Europe who was offered the chance of taking the hand in marriage of the king of one of the few major Catholic powers in Europe – a prize indeed.

After King Alfonso had spent a week with the Archduchess and her mother – the young couple passed much of their time walking around the picturesque gardens of Villa Bellegarde – they were betrothed. As observers pointed out, it would have been remarkable if they had not become engaged as a result, and one if not both of the countries involved would surely have taken offence if a marriage had not been arranged. On 2 September, shortly after his return to Madrid, the King announced his intended nuptials to his ministers, and the wedding was arranged for November. Maria Cristina wrote to their sister Paz, saying 'she hopes we will love her, and says she will do her best to make up for the sister we have lost'.[1]

To his credit, the King was too honest to make any pretence that he was really in love with her. Like that of his mother, this arranged marriage was no more than a dynastic duty. To one of his sisters he remarked cynically that the mother, Archduchess Elizabeth, attracted him greatly, but it was the daughter whom he had to marry.[2] Politicians throughout Europe, particularly in neighbouring Portugal, were quick to speculate as to whether this would be the prelude to a binding political alliance between Spain and the imperial powers of Austria and Germany.

The wedding was celebrated on 29 November 1879 at the Church of Atocha, and this time the guests present included the King's mother. As the bride was a member of one of the most conservative and uncompromisingly Catholic dynasties in Europe, the former Queen Isabel could hardly have wished better for her son than a Habsburg. A month earlier she had written from Paris to her daughter Paz how she was counting the days till she would see all her children again on the occasion, even though she would 'feel it terribly finding a daughter less'.[3] Now, at the end of the ceremony, she knelt at her daughter-in-law's feet and kissed her hand. It must have given some reassurance to the bride, who was said to be looking pale and nervous as she walked down the aisle in her dress of white satin, almost covered with lace, and its silver train embroidered with fleurs-de-lis. Infanta Paz recorded that 'she looked so dignified and at the same time so unassuming, that we could hear a murmur of admiration run through the Church'.[4] After the wedding ceremony a reception was held for over two thousand guests, ministers and diplomats.

'We have a charming sister-in-law who I am sure is going to make Alfonso happy again,'[5] Paz wrote. As a personality, Queen Maria Cristina lacked the spontaneity and charm of her husband's first wife. She was a foreigner, and many of the Spaniards found her too correct, too detached and too controlled. Queen Mercedes, they said, had never let anyone forget that she was a woman, while Queen Maria Cristina never let them forget that she was Queen. Nevertheless she soon gained the respect of her husband's subjects. She might appear reticent and frigid, in severe contrast to her predecessor but she was calm, tactful and had a strong sense of duty.

In contracting an arranged marriage King Alfonso XII may not have expected to find the happiness with his second wife that he had enjoyed with the first, but it was only as everybody had foreseen. Much to Queen Maria Cristina's mortification, he proved himself only too ready to look beyond his wedding ring for distractions and pleasures. Ever since he had returned to Spain from exile, mistresses had been smuggled into the palace, and when necessary he was equally ready to leave the palace quietly in order to visit them. Not long after his accession he had had a brief affair with Adelina Borghi, an opera singer. His relationship with another singer, Elena Sanz, proved more durable, and she bore him two sons, Ferdinand and Alfonso. Elena was about thirteen years older than Alfonso, and he had known her since 1872 as her career had been partly sponsored by Queen Isabel, and she had sung at the former Queen's palace in Paris. His unflattering comparisons between singing and the howling of a dog evidently counted for little when he sought his pleasures of the flesh.

Queen Isabel had been so incensed by her son's marriage to Mercedes, the daughter of her *bête noire* the Duc de Montpensier, that she shamelessly championed her son's affair with Elena, and would refer to her as 'my daughter-in-law in front of God'. It would be pleasing to assume that he was faithful to Queen Mercedes during their sadly short time together as husband and wife, but hardly surprising if he had amused himself elsewhere during his first marriage.

Reserved Queen Maria Cristina might be, but she refused to be regarded as a nonentity. One evening, when she caught a courtier introducing the King to a particularly attractive young singer, she struck the man across the face. Another time, when told that her husband was going to keep a private assignation, she threatened to

leave Spain and return to her native Austria. It took much effort by
the court dignitaries to dissuade her from bringing the scandal out
into the open. Like many another long-suffering royal consort of the
age, she had to learn to accept that there was one rule for princes
and another for princesses.

Nevertheless King Alfonso fulfilled his family duty the best he
could on the right side of the blanket. Their first daughter, named
Mercedes at the long-suffering Queen's insistence, was born in 1880,
and their second, named Maria Teresa, followed in 1882. King
Alfonso did not attempt to conceal his disappointment at the birth
of a girl on either occasion. He had to be persuaded to bow to
Spanish custom and present them to the assembled grandees, while
hoping and praying inwardly that after the next time the Queen
gave birth he would be able to show the assembled company their
future King.

Whatever the King's faults, he never shrank from one of the most
important duties he could perform towards his people – a readiness
to share in their sufferings in the face of natural disaster. In the
autumn of 1879, just before his second wedding, the rich agri-
cultural province of Murcia sustained severe flooding, with villages
and towns destroyed and several thousand people drowned. The
King wasted no time in paying a personal visit to the affected areas.
One day he was wading through the streets of a village, up to his
knees in water, when one victim who had been made homeless and
was sitting on the ruins of his house, recognised his sovereign. He
made his way towards the King and embraced him. Neither said a
word but both were in tears, and when telling others about it
afterwards the King remarked with some emotion that it was the
most beautiful speech he had ever heard in his life.[6] As a result some
of the festivities that were to have taken place at the wedding were
curtailed at the request of the bride and groom, so that extra funds
could be devoted to relieving the plight of the sufferers.

Although King Alfonso was probably already much more popular
in Spain than his mother ever was, there were still some individuals
who were keen to eliminate him. On 30 December 1879, only a
month after their wedding, the King and Queen were returning from

a drive in the streets of Madrid in an open carriage when a man concealed behind the sentry box at one entrance to the palace fired two pistol shots at them. The first ball grazed the head of a groom sitting behind them. On hearing the noise, the Queen bent anxiously forward towards the King, and the second narrowly missed her face. The would-be assassin, Francisco Otero González, was a youth of nineteen. He was arrested, put on trial in the spring of 1880 and sentenced to death; although the King wanted to reprieve him, Cánovas overruled him and the young man was executed on 14 April. Afterwards a confession was found in his papers, saying that he did not wish to compromise anybody, but had been deceived and led astray by others:

> I entered an unknown association, and was subsequently brought to Toledo before a secret meeting of masked men, who decided that I should kill Senor Cánovas del Castillo. Thence I returned to Madrid after receiving 130 francs and a firearm. Shortly after this the original order was revoked, and I was directed to kill the King. The day on which I attempted the life of the King was considered by two of my associates a favourable opportunity, and had I missed it I should have been assassinated. They accompanied me to the gate of the Royal Palace and remained near me. The rest you know.[7]

The King, suggested his youngest sister, was an enlightened monarch in that he believed that the day of the warrior kings was over. He considered it as more important to take a keen interest in attempts to promote the industrial development of the country rather than hanker for the role of figurehead and war leader, particularly in times of peace. Never did he wear military uniform except when attending army manoeuvres or taking part in inspections and other functions on the parade ground, and he did not take seriously his fellow kings who went about dressed as soldiers as if always on parade. While he was aware of the value of the founding and maintenance of arsenals for the manufacture of munitions of war, and devoted some effort to correcting the dishonesty in the expenditure of appropriations for the army and navy, he had little time for the outward showiness of military pomp.[8] Nevertheless he recognised it was his responsibility as a monarch to take due interest in military matters, especially in details of army administration and regulations.

In the late summer of 1883 the King made a personal state tour of European capitals. He believed it was vital for the crowned heads of state to keep in regular contact and to see one another on a regular basis. Vienna was his first stop, because of his close relationship by marriage with Emperor Francis Joseph, after which he went to Berlin, Brussels and Paris. While he was in Vienna he made an impromptu visit to the warden of the Theresianum College, which he had attended as a boy. The warden was not at home, so he decided to leave a note and asked the maid for a pencil. She was unaware of his identity, and she went into the kitchen to look for one. He followed her, and as he had never seen or been inside a kitchen in his life until then, he was fascinated by the sight of the utensils. An egg-poacher interested him so much that he made a sketch of it to show to his attendants.

When he arrived in Germany, the welcome accorded him was particularly enthusiastic. On a personal level Crown Prince Frederick William, who saw him regularly during his visit, later described him as an 'amiable and highly gifted young monarch'.[9] The German Chancellor, Otto von Bismarck, who never missed a political or diplomatic opportunity to strengthen the national interest, was determined to keep Spain from any kind of binding alliance with France, the German Empire's most bitter foe since the Franco-Prussian war some twelve years earlier, and he saw to it that Alfonso was given every attention and every honour. He attended the autumn manoeuvres and was appointed honorary colonel of an Uhlan regiment by Emperor William. At a subsequent banquet given in his honour by the Spanish minister in Berlin, he wore the Uhlan uniform. This was to have unfortunate repercussions, as when he went to Brussels afterwards he was advised by his legation that his acceptance and wearing of German uniform had antagonised the French. It was a particularly sensitive issue as the French resented the Uhlans above all, as most of them were stationed at Strasbourg, which had been French territory until taken from them after the Franco-Prussian war.

The King was warned that there might be hostile demonstrations in Paris. Sitting beside Jules Grévy, the French President, in a carriage as they rode through the streets, he was greeted with angry cries of '*A bas les rois Uhlans!*' While he was at a dinner with the President at the Elysee that evening, the crowds continued to demonstrate on the pavements. Grevy apologised and begged him not to mistake the bad manners of the mob for the true feelings of the French nation, and King Alfonso asked to be given permission to make his apology public, a request which was readily granted.

However, if the gift of a Uhlan colonelcy had been a cunning ruse on Bismarck's part to make a Franco-Spanish alliance less likely, it had been a perfect success. The behaviour of the Parisians had infuriated Alfonso's subjects at home, and on his return to Madrid all the Spaniards loyally gave him one of the most stirring ovations of his reign.

In November Crown Prince Frederick William came to Spain for a visit of three weeks. He was favourably impressed by the court at Madrid and the royal family. Queen Maria Cristina, he noted after their first meeting, was 'uncommonly amiable and natural, and gives the impression of being a talented Princess, who knows what she wants'.[10] He left 'with the most lovely sympathy for the King, his family and his country,'[11] and full of hope that ever-closer relations with Germany would be the result.

* * *

Soon after his return, it was noticed that the King was not looking well. He had always been moderate in his eating habits, teetotal, and taken regular exercise and cold baths. In this respect nobody could accuse him of neglecting his health. But by his mid-20s he appeared pale and listless, and he was losing weight. Officially he was suffering from tuberculosis, but the rumours that he was wearing himself out through his excesses in his private life and that he was venereally affected were more accurate.

According to Lady Cardigan, he was carrying on an affair with the wife of an army officer, who proved too possessive for comfort and was therefore posted for service in Cuba on the King's orders. Though he was given the most dangerous missions, he survived them all. On his return to Spain, the officer was told by one of his colleagues the reason for his being sent to the West Indies. Determined to exact his revenge, he waited at his home, fully armed, until the King paid his next clandestine visit, accompanied by a male member of the nobility. The latter promptly killed the wronged husband with his sword, and the body was secretly buried. When Lady Cardigan questioned the aristocrat about the propriety of such behaviour, he replied that it was the quickest way for an 'interfering husband' to be disposed of.

King Alfonso was impatient at the very idea of being ill, and refused to let himself be treated like an invalid. The racking cough and hectic flush that seemed ever more noticeable made his listeners and associates pity him, but he insisted on carrying out his duties as a King the best he could. In December 1884 and again in the following spring, severe earthquakes occurred in Andalusia, with the provinces of Malaga and Granada particularly affected, and over a thousand people were killed. Almost as soon as the King knew how grave the situation was, he visited the affected region, disregarding the threat of any personal dangers. A letter he wrote to his sister Paz bore witness to his feelings on behalf of the suffering, and his sacrifices of comfort in the name of duty:

I send you these few lines from a portable hut where we have passed nights with the thermometer below zero and our bodies somewhat battered by our fifteen days' journey through these pathless *sierras* on foot and on horseback. . . . You will have seen by the papers that I have kept moving on, that it has snowed nearly all the time, indeed that the weather has been infernal. We have had days of twelve hours on horseback in the middle of the sierra, often without seeing a house for hours, and afterwards, for our night's rest, we perhaps had an earthquake or, if lucky, a hut like this! This country has suffered terribly; throughout the province of Granada the villages are a heap of ruins in the middle of a desert. . . . It is impossible to remove the wounded and amputated because the roads are so bad that no cart can use them. At first the injured had to lie out in the cold, and later were crowded into shelters without air; therefore many of the wounds mortified. My first care was to have ventilated huts erected, and beds, mattresses and linen installed in order to remove the wounded from their beds of straw on the damp ground. . . . The regular supply of food was, however, the most urgent thing to be arranged. I have given orders that roads are to be made immediately; this will provide work and do something to remedy the half-savage state of affairs existing here. The next most urgent thing is the rebuilding of the villages. Using the funds and subscriptions placed at my disposal, I shall occupy myself with this task until it is completed as it is impossible to allow the inhabitants to live any longer like this.[12]

In the summer of 1885 a cholera epidemic swept through Valencia and Murcia in south-east Spain, reaching Madrid by the end of June. At its height people were dying at the rate of about five hundred per day, but the King decided that he and his family would remain in the capital. Queen Isabel had fled the city during a similar epidemic twenty years earlier, a move that had caused some ill-feeling, and he was determined to set a better example. Admittedly Madrid was not the most seriously infested area, but the King was keen to visit those places which were suffering more severely. Aranjuez, the village near his summer palace, was badly affected and he wanted to go there, but Cánovas and his Conservative ministers were very concerned at his state of health and wanted to prevent him from taking unnecessary risks. If he ignored their wishes and set foot in the village, they warned him, they would resign, and they were supported by Sagasta and the Liberal opposition.

One morning in July the King said he was going for a walk in El Retiro, the public park in the centre of Madrid, accompanied only by his aide-de-camp, Colonel Don Felix Ingosoto. Instead he went to the Atocha station nearby, telling his aide that he was going to Aranjuez. The officer refused to leave him, so they bought tickets and together they boarded the train to the stricken town. When they arrived, the King made a tour of the hospitals and arranged for the palace to be turned into a convalescent home. He asked to see the Mother Superior of the Sisters of Charity, who were nursing in the hospital. On being told that this would be impossible as she herself was dying of cholera, he said that the least he could do was thank her. They led him to her bedside and he kissed her hand in gratitude for her efforts.

When he returned home that evening, everyone in Madrid had heard of his unselfish gesture, and gave him a hero's welcome. No more was heard of the government's threats to resign. On the contrary several ministers went to greet him on his return. To those who asked him why he went, he replied that he did it 'following an impulse of my heart, but not ignoring my oath to the Constitution'.[13]

In the following month Germany attempted to take possession of the Caroline Islands in the Pacific. Spain had always claimed them as part of her own empire, but never effectively occupied them herself. The German action roused the Spanish people to fury, and a mob attacked the German embassy, demanding war. Only the restraint of the German government and King Alfonso's prudent manoeuvres solved the problem. His carefully cultivated friendships with other European rulers had helped, and he persuaded the German Emperor William to ask Pope Leo XIII to arbitrate. The latter decided in favour of Spain, while allowing Germany trading rights in the islands.

Towards the autumn the King's health deteriorated sharply, and those around him became increasingly anxious. The doctors wanted him to be sent to a milder climate during the winter, and suggested he take advantage of the fact that Eulalia was about to marry Montpensier's son Antoine, and this would give the King a chance to spend a few weeks amid his uncle's sun-warmed orange groves. Cánovas was anxious lest rumours of the King's illness should prove destabilising to the government. His sudden death, the politician believed, would provoke republican and Carlist agitation, and more disconcertingly for him, such forces would probably be held in check more effectively by the Liberal opposition than by his own party. Even members of the royal family were unaware of how ill the King really was. When rumours of his ill-health reached the other capitals of Europe, they were immediately denied by the Spanish embassies in those cities.

One afternoon that autumn he was standing in the dining room of his palace watching a young workman carrying his small son in his arms. The child was persistently pulling his father's cap off and throwing it on the ground. The King watched them until they were out of sight, and then turned back into the room, and a courtier observed the look of sadness on his master's face. The King told him that he had a feeling he would never know the same joy as that workman, namely being able to kiss his son. Queen Maria Cristina was expecting her third child, and he had a premonition that it would be a son – but he believed he would probably not live long enough to see the child.

At the end of October he was moved to the palace of El Pardo, on the edge of Madrid. Some days he could not even leave his bed. On 22 November his mother, Queen Isabel, his wife and his aunt the Duchesse de Montpensier came to see him, and he suggested they should all go for a drive. Though the doctor recommended a closed carriage, the King insisted that he would ride in an open one. The mountain air proved very cold, and when they returned he stood close to the wood fire, trying to get warm. When the Duchesse de Montpensier reminded him that it would be his birthday in six days' time, he remarked bitterly that it would be 'a nice way' to spend his birthday, meaning that he would probably be in his coffin by then. A reception that had been planned in Madrid for his birthday, it was announced, would be cancelled unless there was a marked improvement in his health, as there was no question of jeopardising his convalescence by any long, tiring ceremonial.

On 24 November the government finally had to admit that the King was gravely ill. He had been suffering from consumption for some time, and now the doctors reported 'a recurrence of dysentery, accompanied by great debility'.[14] Ministers informed correspondents from the press that telegrams on his state of health had been stopped by the censor, as they were merely calculated to create unfounded alarm or even provoke wild talk of imminent revolution. But the

King could not leave his bed, and the Queen was constantly by his side at the Pardo. For some time she had been kept away from her husband by order of Cánovas, in order to dispel rumours of his illness, but now she and the family could see that they were anything but rumours.

'I don't deserve to be cared for as you have cared for me,' he whispered to her. 'I know that when I have gone you will care for Spain as I have myself.'[15] At 8 a.m. the next day he was obviously dying. He asked for his little daughters to be brought to see him for the last time, and the Queen sent word for other members of the family and a select few friends to come and take their leave as well. It was her misfortune to fall in love with a husband who had never been able to reciprocate her feelings, and never made any pretence of trying to do so. However, like many a cuckolded queen before her, she was magnanimous enough to summon Elena Sanz and conduct her personally to his bedside to see him for the last time. The death rattle was already sounding, and shortly before 9 a.m. he passed away.

Throughout Spain the reaction was one of general uncertainty at the unstable situation which might lie ahead in the event of a long regency, and fears that such a situation might be a source of serious weakness and danger to the well-being of the public. In Madrid troops were confined to barracks and the guard at the German embassy was doubled, to forestall any possibility of uprising by republican elements. A few ministers feared that there was a danger of a relapse into political confusion, possibly even civil war, thanks to the machinations of rival factions, particularly the Carlists, and unscrupulous pretenders. However, the danger of an outbreak of Carlism was thought unlikely, as the economy of the northern provinces was much stronger than it had been at the time of the last interregnum. A relatively prosperous nation, it was assumed, did not hanker after unrest or civil war, and the common sense of the people would surely prevent any disturbances.

The shock of the news was felt far beyond the borders of Spain. At Windsor Castle Queen Victoria wrote sadly in her journal of the death of 'the poor young and distinguished King of Spain, only twenty-eight, so clever, and full of promise', and remarked that it was 'such a calamity for Spain'.[16]

There was anger when it was revealed that for the last two months of the King's life, there had been a 'system of elaborate deception', beginning with those who surrounded him and confirmed by daily statements in the official gazette that his health was excellent. Nothing, they soon learned, could have been further from the truth. He had died like a shepherd on the mountains, they asserted, with no help from those around him.

On his death his elder daughter, five-year-old Mercedes, officially became Queen of Spain. Cánovas remembered the political instability which had followed the death of King Ferdinand VII in 1833, and he wanted to avoid any complications that might ensue by declaring the infant Queen. Moreover the Queen Dowager was *enceinte*, and the late King had been convinced that she would give birth to a son. According to the Spanish constitution, the widowed Queen would be Regent until Mercedes came of age. As she was expecting another child, the monarchy in effect remained in abeyance until the infant's birth, as she went to the Cortes and swore fidelity to the constitution in the name of 'the heir of Alfonso XII'. 'My poor brother!' wrote Infanta Paz. 'He had so longed for a son and did not live to see him!'[17]

Initially the Queen refused to consider any political matters, saying she would not receive any resignations as she wanted to be left alone with her grief, at least until the following week when her husband's body would be deposited in the crypt of the Escorial. However, the business of government had to continue. In accordance with regular practice Cánovas tendered his resignation as prime minister, recommending that Her Majesty should govern with the Liberals under Sagasta, while adding that he himself would always be ready to serve her if his advice was required. Castelar, the Republican leader, gallantly declared that he 'could not fight against a woman and a cradle',[18] and Sagasta accepted responsibility for forming a new cabinet.

As Regent, one of the Queen's immediate public duties was to receive the various members of the diplomatic corps who came to deliver their messages of condolence. One onlooker, Xarco del Valle, remarked afterwards that she 'seemed crushed by grief and despondency', her face and eyes swollen by weeping, her hands trembling in her lap. He found the sight so poignant that he hesitated at first to disturb her, before plucking up courage to announce to her 'his Eminence the Apostolic Nuncio'. No sooner had he spoken than she turned and stood upright before him, 'a Queen and a ruler from head to feet, her forehead erect, a fire of resolution burning in her brown eyes'.[19]

The body of King Alfonso XII was embalmed two days after his death and taken to lie in state in the Grand Salon of the Palace at Madrid for three days. Several thousand came to file past their late sovereign who lay on the bed, his hands crossed upon his breast, holding a silver crucifix. By the side of the coffin lay the crown and sceptre, while on the top were several wreaths of flowers. A guard of honour was stationed around the catafalque.

The natural disasters which had dogged Spain during the last months of King Alfonso XII's reign had not yet run their course. In May 1886 Madrid was hit by a hurricane in which thirty-two people were killed and over three hundred wounded. Though her confinement was expected in less than a week, the Queen spent nearly three hours on 13 May visiting the worst affected areas, and talking to the wounded in the hospitals, to several of which she made large donations.

Even three days later she was seen to be leading a normal life, with little cutting back on her court activities and appearances. Not until 2 a.m. on 17 May was it announced that her position was 'critical', with principal officers of state being summoned to the palace in anticipation of a happy event.

SEVEN

'The smallest quantity of King'

Early in the morning of 17 May 1886 crowds gathered outside the palace in Madrid and in the Plaza de Oriente, as ministers waited and ambassadors hurried inside. As the clock struck midday, there were murmurs of impatience from those anxious for the salute of fifteen guns to signify an Infanta, twenty-one guns for a King. A few minutes later the Lord Great Chamberlain, the Marques de Santa Cruz, burst into the Regent's audience chamber to announce that Her Majesty Queen Maria Cristina had given birth to a son, about half an hour after midday. *'Viva el Rey! Viva la Reina!'*

The child was born a king.* Sagasta, the Prime Minister, carried him on a red velvet cushion on a golden tray, saying with a smile that they had 'just about the smallest quantity of King we could possibly have'.[1] The mother wept for her 'poor Alfonso, not to be able to see him, he wanted it so much'.[2] Martos, the President of the Cortes, immediately hailed the birth as a good omen: 'If by the will of Providence, King Alfonso [XII] has been prematurely taken from us, to the profound grief of Spain; if his loss has cast a gloom over the nation, there is now a rift in the dark clouds which had over-shadowed us.'[3]

On his birth he inherited an impressive panoply of titles. He was King of Spain, Castile, Léon, Aragon, the Two Sicilies, Jerusalem, Navarre, Granada, Toledo, Valencia, Galicia, Majorca, Minorca, Seville, Sardinia, Cordova, Corsica, Murcia, Jaen, Algarve,

---

* The last time a child had been born a king in Europe was in 1316, when John I of France was born in succession to his late father Louis X. He only lived for five days.

102

Algeciras, Gibraltar, the Canary Islands, the East and West Indies, India and the Oceanic Continent; Archduke of Austria; Duke of Burgundy, Brabant and Milan; Count of Habsburg, Flanders, the Tyrol and Barcelona; Seigneur of Biscay and Molina; and His Catholic Majesty.[4]

He was baptised five days later in the palace chapel. With the narrow scarlet band bearing the Golden Fleece around his neck, he was carried through the tapestry-hung great gallery to the royal chapel, and in the presence of a brilliantly dressed gathering, and with water sent from the River Jordan, he was christened Alfonso Leon Fernando Maria Santiago Isidro Pascual Anton. His father had wanted him to be known as Fernando, and his sisters initially called him thus as the Queen told him that would be his name. As soon as the news spread, however, the people of Madrid wanted him to be called Alfonso in memory of his father, and some even came to the palace to make their wishes known, insisting that they had nothing to fear from the fact that he would be the thirteenth king to bear the name. They pointed out that Pope Leo XIII would be the baby's god-father, and therefore thirteen must be lucky. Queen Maria Cristina was soon persuaded, and agreed to the change.

By her orders the doors of the gallery were thrown open so that any member of the public who wished to could come and see the procession to and from the chapel, led by the chief usher, followed by chamberlains, majordomos, mace bearers and the grandees whose role it was to bear on golden trays the salt cellar, robe, cap, basin, ewer, damask cloth, veil and marchpane. The sign of the cross was made on the baby's forehead, the sacred salt as the symbol of wisdom was placed upon his tongue, he was anointed with oil, the water of regeneration was poured upon his head, and a small lighted candle was placed in his hand. At the conclusion of the ceremony a *Te Deum* was sung and a salvo of twenty-one guns was fired. When Mercedes, then aged five, asked who had sent them her little brother, Maria Cristina answered simply, 'your father in heaven'.[5]

There were immediate questions as to who should be Regent. Some thought that the baby's paternal aunt, the widowed Infanta Isabel, would be the right person, on the grounds that a Spanish princess who had devoted the best years of her life to the regime of the country had more right than a foreigner who had only been in Spain for six years. Maria Cristina was warned that Infanta Isabel was 'a most ambitious and dangerous woman', and might have connived in the death of Queen Mercedes through poison. Others supported the former Queen Isabel, the baby King's grandmother, saying that as her abdication had never been formally published, she was entitled to resume her rights as Queen of Spain. She was not at all diffident about pressing such claims to the throne that she considered she still had.

Though Maria Cristina had taken the oath of regency, it did not stop Queen Isabel from approaching her former enemy Montpensier and trying to conspire with him. The government suspected that they were trying to oust the rightful Regent, and as a result Queen Isabel was 'officially invited' to quit Spain and return to France. Montpensier, who was in France at the time, was ordered to stay there, but he ignored this order and came home regardless. The Duke of Seville, son of the man who had been killed in a duel by Montpensier, stalked into Maria Cristina's bedchamber one day shortly before the baby was born, and demanded an interview. When told that the Queen was tired and had given orders for nobody to be admitted, he threatened violence unless he was allowed in, and said loudly that Maria Cristina could not possibly be trusted with the regency. He was arrested, discharged from the army, and sentenced to eight years' prison in the Balearic Islands. From his cell he wrote a letter to the press attacking the Regent, and on his escape a few months later he published a democratic manifesto in the Parisian journal *La Republique*.[6]

Another difficulty the Regent had to settle was that of Elena Sanz and her two sons by King Alfonso XII. He had left them generous sums of money in his will, but the Queen did all she could to prevent any payments being made. Elena was banished from Spain and settled in France, and after several months of negotiations it was agreed that she should receive a sum of around 738,000 francs in compensation. The payments were delayed on the order of the Queen and Elena died almost impoverished in Nice in 1898. Her sons, who went to live in Mexico, took out a court case against the Queen in 1907, which was successful in obtaining them a certain amount of extra money.*

For the first few years of his life the Regent ensured that she was not separated from her son for a single day. Often she would get up several times during the night and enter the nursery to check that the temperature was satisfactory and that the infant King had not thrown the bedclothes aside or become overheated. From the moment of his birth all the family watched Alfonso's health with anxiety. His father had never been strong, and every illness the boy suffered made them apprehensive. Throughout early childhood he seemed frail and sickly, and his head seemed too large for his thin, puny-looking body.

In January 1890, at the age of three, he suffered a severe bout of bronchitis. While apparently recovering he had several violent convulsions, as a result of which he remained unconscious for some time, and for a short while his heart ceased to beat altogether. Though the doctors could not agree on the cause of his illness, it was feared that he might have meningitis. As all telegrams on his condition were subject to the strictest censorship, rumours multiplied, and by 9 January a series of carefully worded bulletins was preparing the country for the worst. If he had another similar attack, his mother was warned, he would probably not survive. Some people believed that he had already died and the palace was trying to keep the news secret. Doctors, nurses and members of the family crowded into his room, while churches throughout Spain resounded with prayers for his recovery. Members of the leading political parties agreed to support the government in its maintenance of public order in the event of his death. Not for two or three weeks was he pronounced out of danger. Towards the end of the month ex-Queen Isabel wrote to her daughter Paz that it was 'a perfect miracle that he is alive'.[7]

* The elder boy Ferdinand died in 1922. The younger, Alfonso, who later became director of the French car company Peugeot, died in 1970.

By coincidence, one of Spain's former Kings and another man who had lived his life close to the throne were to die within the first few weeks of the year. The Duke of Aosta, who had worn the crown for two troubled years as King Amedeo, died on Turin on 18 January at the early age of forty-four. Like King Alfonso XII, he had long been suffering from consumption, and in his weakened state he fell an easy prey to the influenza epidemic then sweeping parts of Europe. After remaining a widower for twelve years he had married his niece Princess Letitia, daughter of Prince Napoleon and Princess Clothilde of Savoy, by whom he had a fourth son. At Madrid the court acknowledged its former sovereign and declared a period of mourning for three weeks. Though he had technically been something of a rival to the Bourbons, they did not bear him any ill-will. 'The death of poor Amadeo will have grieved you,' Infanta Paz wrote to her mother; 'he was respected by everyone, and it is sad to think he should die just as he had begun a new and happy life!'[8]

On 4 February, while walking around his estate at Sanlucar de Barrameda, Montpensier collapsed with a stroke and died at the age of sixty-five. In view of his persistent intrigues, he was mourned by very few. His hopes that Queen Isabel and Don Francisco de Asis would be unable to have children, thus leaving the way clear for him and his wife to claim the succession by providing heirs to the throne, were not to be realised, and the early death of his daughter Mercedes had extinguished any final possibility of perpetuating the dynasty.*

* * *

Alfonso had been born a king, and it was only to be expected that he grew up with something of an inflated sense of self-importance. As his cousin Infanta Pilar, co-author of one of his first biographies, was to write, the circumstances in which he was born and brought up had to be taken into account in any assessment of his character.

---

* His widow Luisa outlived him by almost seven years, dying on 1 February 1897.

'Standing high above everyone, the boy inevitably stood alone.'
While other boys of his age might have had fathers, uncles, tutors,
schoolmasters and others of whom they stood in awe from birth,
and had to pay deference, the case of King Alfonso XIII was very
different.[9] His father had spent part of his adolescence in exile, as a
king in name only and with an uncertain future before him, but he
had accepted the insecurity of his position with equanimity. Despite
being surrounded with flatterers, he had probably become a more
well-balanced personality as a result. By contrast, his son had been a
king while still in the womb, and therefore was born into a milieu of
flattery and obsequiousness without having experienced the
insecurity of exile to provide some kind of balance.

Though his mother was generally firm with him, he was intelligent enough to see that she was merely acting on his behalf and that
he was the one to whom everybody would look up once he was of
age. On state occasions she would be seated on the throne, and as he
was too small to sit by himself, he was held in the arms of a nurse
sitting in a chair to the right of the Regent. He was bowed to, and
stood aside for, and when a courtier once carelessly addressed the
three-year-old as 'Bubi', his mother's pet name for him, the exalted
child told him firmly that only the Queen was allowed to use the
name: 'to all others I am *el Rey*'.[10] When a hairdresser came to
attend to the royal locks, he ordered him to cut off a large curl in
the middle of his forehead. The man knew that the Regent was
rather proud of her son's curls, and told him that she would be very
angry. The child insisted that it must be removed; it was his hair, and
he was the King.

The Regent knew that her son could easily become insufferable if
not checked. Until he came of age, she maintained, her will would
prevail, not his. She never hesitated to punish him when he was
naughty, nor to check any tendency to wilfulness and arrogance. She
insisted that his teachers should always pass through the door before
him, and he should wait for them to seat themselves before he did
so. When a new teacher did so one day, he said apologetically that
'the King is always the King'. The boy agreed, 'but here I am only
your pupil'.[11] Another day one teacher gave him a long lecture on

the dangers of sycophancy, and in the afternoon praised him for a piece of good work. 'Have I really done well,' the boy asked with a smile, 'or is it only flattery?'[12]

Sometimes he indulged in the odd display of mischievous temper. One day he was locked up in a room in the palace of Aranjuez for misbehaving. When nobody would answer his shouting or kicking on the door, he opened the window and shouted to everyone in the courtyard below, '*Viva la republica!*' On another occasion he told his mother that he would not be King any more, and would prefer to be the son of the head gardener, as then he would be allowed to climb trees, and a king was only allowed to sit under them.[13] Once when he was six and his second sister Infanta Maria Teresa was ten, they planned to go and explore Madrid on their own, taking a picnic lunch which included a large bar of chocolate and two apples. They had made their way outside the palace gates when they were discovered and sent back indoors. 'I will take both punishments', the Infanta insisted. 'Alfonso was just seeing me off.'[14]

Another commentator thought that the 'courtly flatteries of his childhood (had) so strongly fixed in the King's mind the idea of his authority that no one could be more jealous of it even in the intimacy of his own hearth. The King feels himself King, and is always King.'[15] It was inevitable that much, perhaps too much, attention would be paid to him in his early years by his doting mother and the over-indulgent court, and that such a childhood was unlikely to produce a fully balanced adult monarch.

Until he was seven years old, Alfonso's time was divided between Madrid and the seaside resort of San Sebastian on the Atlantic coast, where he stayed at Maria Cristina's holiday residence, Miramar, a cross between a cottage and a castle. His mother was anxious to maintain the boy's health, as she feared he might have inherited his father's tubercular tendencies. When they were at Miramar she encouraged him to spend as much time in the sea as possible, and he became a good swimmer and sailor. He could row a boat and sail a yacht as well as any fisherman, and he loved racing along the fine sand beaches. This open-air regime clearly benefited him, and on his return from Miramar he always seemed stronger and in better spirits. While he never looked particularly robust, and was always subject to minor ailments, he now appeared less delicate than he had been in early childhood.

Despite the problems with his health, he was always fearless as a boy and would remain so throughout adult life. This might be explained in part by the natural defiance of a boy who feels he is being cosseted and protected by an over-anxious mother, and is determined to prove he is strong enough not to need such solicitous treatment. Those around him soon found that the only way to make him forget some dangerous desire, repress some incorrect or unbecoming habit, or simply become less obstinate about something, was to utter the phrase, 'Sire, Don Alfonso XII would not have done it.' He never ceased to revere and respect the memory of the parent he had never known, and would often ask, 'What would my father have done?'[16]

Even so, this did not always succeed. Once his mother gave him a new thoroughbred, and he was so excited he rode it up the staircase into her salon. To get it down again without breaking its legs, he had to have a carpet laid on the staircase.[17] Whether King Alfonso XII would have done such a thing, one can but wonder. The young Alfonso had been fascinated by horses almost since he could talk. At the age of three he was promised a pony, and when his mother presented him with a rocking-horse, he retorted, 'I want a real live horse!'[18] He adored riding and, said his mother, 'when he was quite little he would make regular scenes when the time arrived to alight from his horse. I used to be quite ashamed of him!'[19]

On one occasion the Regent talked to Helene Vacaresco about her love of San Sebastian, and how much good it was doing the children. Her son, she was sure, would have been a sailor if he was not a king, and he would probably only come ashore for bullfights and other sporting activities. Queen Maria Cristina never completely overcame her repugnance of bullfighting, which she thought was a brutal and sickening exhibition. It was a view widely shared by many Spaniards of the time as well as most foreign visitors to the Spanish court, but it was Spain's national sport and as one commentator remarked at the time, 'an English Prime Minister would have as much chance of putting down cricket and football as a Spanish King has of ending the bull-fight'.[20] Nevertheless, as an adult King Alfonso did make one concession to humane feelings, by issuing a decree forbidding children under fourteen to attend displays of the sport.

When Alfonso reached the age of seven, all the women in his suite were replaced by men, he was given his own establishment and lessons began in earnest. He was taught French, English, German, Italian, physics, chemistry, military and general history, geography and literature, with a special emphasis on languages and history. Portraits of his ancestors fascinated him, and one day he was seen standing for a long time in front of Velasquez's painting of King Felipe IV, saying, 'I will have a chin like that.' For some time afterwards he tried to model the chin on his face with his hands.[21] Twice a day there were periods of physical exercise. He became a skilled and enthusiastic horseman, and looked forward to his sessions of military instruction, at which he was joined by a dozen boys using specially made small rifles to practise their drill.

Later, law, politics, economics and social questions were added to his curriculum. His mother wanted him to attend Madrid University as an ordinary student, but this was unthinkable. The best she could do was choose a tutor whom she respected, and on whom she could rely to tell the young man the truth. The man selected for the task was Don Gualberto Lopez-Valdemoro y Quesada, afterwards Count de las Navas. When he hesitated to discuss too critically some aspects of the reigns of King Ferdinand VII and his grandmother Queen Isabel, the King asked him to speak freely: 'these matters belong to history and I must know the truth'.[22] He knew his education would be incomplete without reading the views of socialists and republicans, and he insisted that he should be given access to journals illustrating all shades of political opinion. When a minister found him reading a newspaper renowned for its strident left-wing and anti-monarchical views, he asked him why he should trouble himself by doing so, as the writer was 'an agitator of the worst and most dangerous class, a hothead, a firebrand'. The King smiled; 'Since I am to rule over fire-brands, it is well that I should have some idea of quenching them.'[23]

Maria Cristina adored spending time with her children, and admitted that she found more pleasure and excitement in their telling her of what they had done each day than in all the affairs of state. They were equally devoted to her; each morning she supervised their baths, their dressing and their breakfasts, then arranged the programme for the day with their tutors and governesses. They lunched together at 1 p.m. and went for a drive about two hours later. Tea was followed by two hours of study, and they met again for dinner. Evenings were spent quietly, with the women knitting and sewing, the men playing cards. The Queen might play the piano, or the children organise a small orchestra, with their mother 'tactfully professing great pleasure in the noise that resulted'.[24] Sometimes amateur theatricals were staged, and only extremely urgent state business was allowed to interrupt these evenings. At 10 p.m. they had family prayers, said goodnight and went to bed. Within an hour all the lights were out.

* * *

Meanwhile trouble was brewing. Cuba and Puerto Rico were the only Spanish dominions still left in the Americas. Both had long been a field for exploitation, but neither was properly governed. The governor in each was a captain-general. Both had been restive for some years, and in 1868 the Cubans had risen against their Spanish masters, demanding closer relations with the United States of America. This robbed Spanish merchants of a ready market; they resisted, and for the profit of a few Spaniards, mainly Catalans, both Cubans and Americans saw their trade declining. The islanders had the sympathy of their large and mighty neighbour, and the government of Madrid, in the interests of Spanish capitalists and the army's pride, had been fighting a guerrilla war since 1895. On 15 February 1898 the *Maine*, an American cruiser, was blown up in the harbour at Havana with the loss of 266 of her crew. This triggered active American intervention. An ultimatum was sent to Spain, and on the Queen's advice the Spaniards returned a conciliatory but not abject answer. Within a few weeks Havana was invaded and Spain had lost Cuba.

111

At the same time Admiral Dewey sailed from Hong Kong to Manila to destroy a Spanish squadron there. The collapse of Spanish naval strength produced an insurrection in the Philippines, and the islands provided a useful base for American ships patrolling the Western Pacific and guarding American enterprise in China. Commissioners met in Paris in October to arrange peace terms, and under the treaty signed there between America and Spain at the end of the year Spain gave up the last of her American possessions, retaining beyond the mainland only the Canaries, the Balearics, and certain rights on the Mediterranean coast of Morocco.

This defeat dealt a heavy blow to Spanish pride. King Alfonso had closely followed the progress of the campaign, and several times said he regretted that he was not old enough to take part. When he was told that his country's navy had been destroyed, King Alfonso promptly ceased to play with his model yachts in the Royal Park.

* * *

In February 1901 the King's eldest sister, Infanta Mercedes, married Infante Charles de Bourbon, son of the Count of Caserta, head of the Neapolitan Bourbons and Pretender to the throne of Naples, which had not had a monarchy since 1861. It was an unpopular match, as the Count had been a general in Don Carlos' army. Although Charles was made a naturalised Spaniard and an Infante of Spain, it had little effect on public opinion. On the day of the wedding many of the streets had to be barricaded against the mob and troops were deployed throughout the capital to keep order. Three years later, after producing a third child, Mercedes died in childbirth.*

Among the elder generation, two more senior members of the house died shortly afterwards. After leaving Spain and separating from Queen Isabel, the former King Francisco had acquired a home at Château d'Epinay sur Seine in Paris and lived there quietly for

---

*   A similar fate befell her sister Infanta Maria Teresa. In January 1906 she married Prince Ferdinand of Bavaria, but died in September 1912, a few days after her fourth child was born.

over thirty years. According to his youngest daughter – or, to be more accurate, the Queen's youngest daughter – he was 'a small, grey man, very silent, very formal, fond of books and solitude, and contented to be out of politics and affairs of Courts'. Infanta Eulalia admitted that there had never been any sentiment in her stepfather's marriage to her mother, and none in his relations with her and her siblings.[25] Almost to the end of his days Francisco's main occupations were walking his poodles in the nearby Bois de Boulogne and holding forth on his ideas on the Divine Right of Kings, which his audiences – usually unsuspecting fellow-walkers in the park who may have wondered as to the identity of this eccentric old gentleman – found very bigoted.

To the last he remained on friendly if not particularly close terms with his wife. Sometimes they passed each other in the Avenue du Bois and they would greet each other, exchanging visits on their birthdays at their respective homes, talking over old times as they smoked and drank coffee. In April 1902 Isabel was told that he was seriously ill with inflammation of the lungs, and immediately came to see him. Knowing that he would probably not recover, she asked when she should visit again. He asked her not to; 'let me, at last, have my desire for solitude. Let me die alone.'[26] Early on the morning of 17 April he breathed his last, one month short of his eightieth birthday. In his will he left everything to his widow.

For Queen Isabel time was running out as well. In her Parisian home, the Palace de Castille, she had become 'une grande dame Parisienne, an Epicurean, whose natural southern extravagance had been much tempered by contact with the more delicate tastes of Paris'.[27] Her health had been failing for some years, and it was said that her country's humiliation in the Spanish-American war had broken her indomitable spirit. Her vast figure started to shrink, and she suffered increasingly from heart trouble and arthritis, being unable to walk without the aid of a stick. In the spring of 1904 Empress Eugenie, passing through Paris on her way back to England, called to see her. Isabel had influenza and a severe cough at the time, but nothing would stop her from getting up and standing in a draught in the bad weather to see her old friend. Aware that she was slipping away, she asked to receive extreme unction from the vicar of St Peter de Chaillot. At around 8.45 a.m. on 9 April 1904, she said to her son-in-law Prince Louis Ferdinand of Bavaria, 'Take my hand and pull my right arm as hard as you can. There is something very strange in my chest, I think I am going to faint.' With that she breathed her last. She was aged seventy-three. As her daughter Infanta Eulalia remarked, it was a peaceful death after 'an agitated existence', and 'she had fought from the age of three in the midst of intrigues and *pronunciamentos*'.[28]

The French President Emile Loubet accorded her military honours as her body in its coffin was conveyed back to her homeland, with cuirassiers accompanying the hearse to the Gare d'Orsay. After returning to Madrid for the last time she was laid to rest between her father and her son in the Escorial.

* * *

At the age of sixteen Alfonso assumed his full rights. The boy born a king had become a lively, energetic young man, convinced that he could do no wrong. He loved physical exercise, particularly riding, gymnastics, fencing, swimming and shooting. Anything to do with the organisation of the army or navy intrigued him. He was fascinated by the idea of speed, and when he heard that the Duke of Alba had brought a car from England, he would not rest until he had driven it himself. First he hit a cow and then a donkey. The Duke suggested that perhaps he should take the wheel, to which the King retorted that if he felt afraid, he should get out. This silenced the Duke – and the enthusiastic but inexperienced royal motorist proceeded to drive them into a ditch.

On 12 May 1902 Queen Maria Cristina held her last council as Regent, and formally took leave of her ministers. She thanked the Spanish people for their affection and support, and hoped they would surround her son with the confidence and strength necessary to enable him to realise all the hopes she had placed in him.

Five days later King Alfonso celebrated his sixteenth birthday, and drove to the Cortes to assume the full office of Sovereign. Two thrones were placed under the crimson and gold canopy, and beside the King's chair stood a table on which rested the crown and sceptre. The Infantas Eulalia and Isabel were the first of the family to enter the crowded chamber. They curtsied to the foreign princes, then to the ambassadors and ministers, and then to the entire assembly. They were followed by the King's eldest sister and her husband, Prince Charles de Bourbon, then his second sister Maria Teresa. Last came Queen Maria Cristina and the King himself, the latter in the uniform of a captain-general. When he had reached his throne, they brought him the Gospels and, having removed his glove, he placed his right hand on the Bible and took the oath: 'I swear by God, on the Holy Gospels, to keep the Constitution and the Laws. If I do so God reward me for it, and if not, He may ask me to give account.'

The ceremonial followed with the King returning to the palace to join his ministers. He received their formal offers of resignation, confirmed them in their posts and accepted their oaths of allegiance. The ministers, tired, hot and uncomfortable in their uniforms, assumed they would then be dismissed. But the King proposed to hold an immediate council meeting. He seated himself at the head of the table, and after listening to Sagasta's formal comments on the enthusiasm of the Spanish people for their new King, turned to the Minister of War and asked him why he had issued an order for the closing of the military academies. Weyler, the minister, explained why, but the King would not accept his reasons until Sagasta tactfully intervened. Then he read out a clause of the constitution backing up his contentions. The constitution, he told them, conferred on him the right to grant honours, titles and grandeeships, and he told them that he reserved for himself the exercise of this right.

The ministers were startled. For thirty years, during the reign of Alfonso XII and then throughout Queen Maria Cristina's period of office as Regent, they had had their own way. Here was a mere boy talking about his rights and intentions, and apparently intent on governing as he pleased. The Minister of Marine, the Duke of Veragua, drew attention to the fact that all the King's commands had to be countersigned by a minister, and Sagasta, keen to avoid any arguments, left it at that.

King Alfonso was an open-minded monarch with a keen interest in the modern world. He undoubtedly had his full share of adolescent high spirits, and with the natural impetuosity of youth he was bored by certain aspects of the time-honoured routine of court ceremonial in which he had been raised. At the same time he was confident enough and keen to play a political role in the future of his country. He had probably observed that ministers had taken advantage of conditions during his mother's regency – not least her role in bringing him and his sisters up and her subsequent distraction – to take back for themselves some of the prerogatives still left to the crown by the constitution, and they had reduced the power of the crown to dismiss and appoint ministers freely.

At the same time he had doubtless perceived that the royal will was the only stable factor in the delicate balance of power, serving as final arbiter in a country governed by competing political groupings in the Cortes. He believed that only an active monarchy which refused to take the role of passive figurehead could hold the threat of republicanism at bay, and he was determined not to be a young modern king surrounded by a bunch of outdated mentors still living in the previous century. Whether he would reconcile such aspirations with maintaining a position of constitutional correctness as his father had done, or whether he would develop a taste for political intrigue with disastrous consequences like his grandmother, remained to be seen.

EIGHT

'An awful danger'

Once King Alfonso had attained his majority, the matter of his marriage could not be delayed for much longer. He knew that his ministers were anxious for him to bring a Queen to Spain, settle down and produce an heir. Sometimes he would ask with a laugh, 'to whom have they betrothed me this morning?'[1] Other European sovereigns were keen to bring the claims of their more eligible princesses to his attention. Germany had several royal spinsters, some of them Catholics, and nothing would please Emperor William II more than to see a new German-Spanish marriage alliance. A visit he paid to Vigo in March 1904, escorted by his fleet, to meet King Alfonso and to review the Spanish fleet, was planned as a first step towards closer relations between their countries and, before long, a German-born Queen of Spain as well. However the Emperor's visit alarmed public opinion in France, where it was feared that such a meeting might imply that Spain was considering joining the Triple Alliance, an extension of the Austro-German Dual Alliance formed in 1879 and expanded three years later to include Italy.

The Emperor's chief rival on the monarchical stage, his uncle King Edward VII of Great Britain, also saw a similar chance, and sent his brother Arthur, Duke of Connaught, to bestow the Order of the Garter on King Alfonso. As Great Britain had been the European power most friendly to Spain in the preceding years, it was hardly surprising that matrimonial links between them should have been promoted. King Alfonso had a friend in the diplomatist Sir Arthur Nicolson, later Lord Carnock, a former minister in Morocco who had been acquainted with Spain's problems in North Africa. He presented his letters to the King on 7 February 1905, and was

117

received with all the pomp and circumstance of the Spanish court. Everything went according to plan until Nicolson bowed backwards on his way out, tripped over a stool and fell over. The King kept a straight face, but once the doors of the throne room were closed, the ambassador heard peals of schoolboyish laughter. As he later admitted to his son Harold, Nicolson's admiration and affection for the sovereign dated from that very moment.

Like his father, and indeed like his contemporary crowned heads, King Alfonso strongly believed in the advantages of personal contact between European sovereigns. Between them, he and his ministers decided that it would be appropriate for him to make his first foreign visit. On 27 May he set out for Paris and arrived in the capital three days later, on a visit at which his host was President Emile Loubet.

One of the events on the itinerary was a visit to the opera, and as the King and the President were driving back to the Elysée, there was an attempt on the King's life. The carriage had reached the corner of the rue de Rohan and the rue de Rivoli when there was a loud explosion. The horses of the escort reared and some bolted, and the carriage pulled up suddenly. With great presence of mind the King stood up and told everyone around him that there was no reason to be alarmed. To the President he remarked nonchalantly 'that is one of the crackers used in Spain to frighten girls with'.[2] Loubet displayed equal calm, although the device exploded on his side of the carriage. A home-made bomb containing fragments of iron and bullets, it damaged the under part of their vehicle without penetrating it. The deed was blamed on anarchist factions, and though a few arrests were made, nobody was ever charged with attempted assassination.

On 5 June the King and his entourage arrived in London for a state visit lasting five days, and were received at Portsmouth by the Prince of Wales. During a week of magnificent ceremonial, Alfonso was preoccupied with the young unmarried princesses in whose ranks a future Queen of Spain might be found. The prospect of an English alliance had already been commented on favourably by Liberal politicians in Spain, and King Edward VII hoped that attention would be drawn to his niece Patricia, the younger daughter of the Duke and Duchess of Connaught. The Spanish press started to publish pictures of Patricia, but King Alfonso would not be rushed into any decision. He insisted he would not marry a photograph; he had every intention of seeing his future wife in person, in order that he could decide for himself. Patricia herself appeared totally uninterested in him. At a luncheon one day, he turned from her on his right to the Duchess of Westminster on his left, asking her self-effacingly if he was very ugly, as he did not please the lady sitting on his right.

However, there were other princesses at the English court ready to catch his eye. Foremost among them was Princess Victoria Eugenia (Ena) of Battenberg, daughter of Princess Beatrice, the prematurely widowed youngest child of Queen Victoria and sister of King Edward VII. Ena was a fair-haired, lively girl of seventeen, and had been something of a tomboy in her adolescence. King Alfonso first met her at a family dinner party at Buckingham Palace on the night of his arrival, and as Patricia's prospects of becoming his future bride diminished, so Ena's chances increased. As she had thought she stood little chance over her Connaught cousin, she was far more at her ease and at first she behaved far more naturally.

At a state banquet at Buckingham Palace King Alfonso was seated next to Princess Christian, the eldest surviving sister of King Edward. Alfonso was naturally full of questions about the other guests at table, and he constantly plied Princess Christian about who was who. When he caught sight of the elegant fair-haired Ena, he asked her who was the young lady with the nearly white hair? Princess Christian told him, and he looked even more pointedly at Ena. When she realised she was the centre of attention, she was seized with embarrassment at his penetrating gaze. On being told about his 'white hair' remark, her instant horrified reaction was that he must have taken her for an albino.[3]

At first Alfonso could not remember her name and called her 'the fair one', but within a few days he came to know her well. During a second reception at Londonderry House he caught sight of her again. Their third meeting was during a ball at Buckingham Palace, where they danced together and talked freely. As he spoke English poorly and as Ena knew no Spanish, they conversed in French. He asked her if she enjoyed collecting postcards, at that time one of the most popular hobbies among upper-class ladies. Rather surprised, she told him that she did. 'I shall send you some on condition that you reply,' he told her. At the end of the ball he said he hoped she would not forget him, and with some embarrassment she answered diplomatically that it was very difficult to forget the visit of a foreign sovereign.[4] Marriage between them had not yet been mentioned.

Ena's godmother Eugenie, former Empress of France, who had lived at Farnborough for most of her exile but remained a welcome guest at the English court, was an inveterate matchmaker. She thought the two young people would be well suited and was very keen to encourage them. Nevertheless, little if any encouragement on her part was needed, as by the time Alfonso left England a betrothal seemed likely.

As soon as the news became known in Spain, there were immediate rumblings of disquiet. When the King returned to Madrid and told his mother, she was strongly opposed to any such idea. She would have preferred him to marry an eligible princess from the ancient Catholic house of Habsburg, as she objected to him marrying a princess born a Protestant and, like so many other European royalty of the day, she regarded the morganatic Battenbergs as parvenus. Her views were shared by the more conservative Spanish elements, who saw their King's choice of an English bride as a triumph for the Liberal faction at court and in the country. Some of his confidants tried to talk him out of marrying a descendant of Queen Victoria whose brother was known to be a haemophiliac. Though he was forewarned that the 'bleeding condition' existed in the family, and that his proposed wife could transmit it to any children they might have, he did not consider it a serious possibility. Deeply in love, perhaps he believed fondly that such a beautiful and obviously healthy-looking young princess could surely not be a carrier of the dreaded condition. If she was, then he would take the risk.

The exchanges of postcards between them continued during the next few months. Most of them contained appropriately friendly

Above, left: Queen Maria Cristina, widow of King Ferdinand VII, with her infant daughters Queen Isabel and Infanta Luisa. *Above right:* Queen Isabel, engraving by J.B. Hunt after a painting by A. Deberia, 1852.

Below, left: Francisco de Asis, husband and consort of Queen Isabel. *Below, right:* King Amedeo, who reigned in Spain for two unhappy years and then took the title Duke of Aosta.

Above, left: King Alfonso XII and his mother, the former Queen Isabel, shortly before his accession to the throne. *Above, right:* King Alfonso XII, *c.* 1881.

Below, left: Queen Mercedes, cousin and first consort of King Alfonso XII, who died five months after their marriage. *Below, right:* King Alfonso XII and Albert Edward, Prince of Wales, later King Edward VII of England, at Homburg, 1883.

The former King Francisco and Queen
Isabel, outside the Palace de Castile,
c. 1900. Though they had been separated
since shortly after her abdication, they
remained friends until his death in 1902.

Queen Maria Cristina, Austrian-born
second wife of King Alfonso XII.

Princess Ena of Battenberg and King Alfonso XIII during their engagement, with their mothers Princess Henry of Battenberg (Princess Beatrice) and Queen Maria Cristina (behind), 1906.

King Alfonso XIII and Princess Ena of Battenberg.

Princess Ena entering the Church of San Jeronimo, Madrid, for her wedding to King Alfonso XIII, 31 May 1906.

Below, left: King Alfonso XIII and Queen Ena with their eldest son Alfonso, Prince of Asturias. *Below, right:* King Alfonso XIII and Alfonso, Prince of Asturias.

King Alfonso XIII and Queen Ena with Prince Leopold (later King Leopold III) of the Belgians, his father King Albert, and his mother Queen Elisabeth.

Former King Alfonso XIII and his grandchildren, April 1939. Children, from left: Don Alfonso, son of Infante Jaime; Infante Juan Carlos, the future king; Doña Sandra Torlonia and Don Marco Torlonia, the children of Infanta Beatrice; Infanta Maria del Pilar and Infanta Margarita, daughters of Infante Juan; and Don Gonzalo, son of Infante Jaime.

Don Juan, Count of
Barcelona, and his wife,
Doña Maria Mercedes.

Don Juan, Count of
Barcelona, Princess Grace of
Monaco, and Prince Juan
Carlos, at a Red Cross gala
dinner, Monaco, August 1959.

General Franco and Prince Juan Carlos, watching a military parade marking the thirty-fifth anniversary of the end of the Civil War, 3 June 1974. *(© Keystone/Getty Images)*

King Juan Carlos, Queen Sofia, Crown Prince Felipe and Princess Letizia attending the National Day Military Parade, Paseo de la Castellana, 12 October 2004. *(© Getty Images)*

messages as one would expect between a young couple obviously besotted with one another, though one of hers revealed a twinge of doubt. She suspected that she was more fond of Alfonso than he was of her, saying that she was convinced their friendship was stronger on her part, but 'I will fight with you if you feel the contrary!'[5] Towards the end of the year she told him she was beginning to learn Spanish, though she was having great difficulties with the grammar.

Throughout the rest of the year 1905 King Alfonso made further state visits around Europe. In the autumn President Loubet visited him in Madrid, where he drove the French statesman around in his car, much to the latter's embarrassment. Next the King visited Berlin and Vienna, where he took some delight in making a joke of matters in cities where everyone else took themselves far too seriously for his liking. Emperor William had given orders that no hired vehicles were allowed within the gates of his palaces in the German capital, so King Alfonso could not resist teasing his august host by going out incognito, hiring the most dilapidated taxicab available, then being driven to the imperial palace – where he was refused admission by the sentry. Doing his best to keep a straight face, he told the man he was going to see the Emperor, 'and he will make an exception in my favour'.[6] The sentry asked rather officiously who he was, only to be told by the man in the battered, weather-stained vehicle that he was the King of Spain.

Emperor William tried to take his revenge in a rather petty manner. At the state banquet it had been agreed that both monarchs should speak in French. Despite this, when William stood up to deliver his address he threw his notes aside and spoke in German instead. King Alfonso gave every appearance of listening politely, though he could barely understand a word. When his turn to reply came, he decided that two could play at that game. He therefore answered in Spanish, and though the Emperor and many others were equally nonplussed with this unfamiliar tongue, he was still received with a generous round of applause, not only out of politeness but, one must imagine, by those who secretly appreciated the joke.

Vienna proved more accommodating, for despite the formality and stiffness of Emperor Francis Joseph's court, as Alfonso was partly

Habsburg himself he felt more at home in the Austrian capital than he had in Berlin. He took the opportunity to pay a visit to the Theresianum College where his father had been a student.

In January 1906 Alfonso and Ena met again at Biarritz, and became unofficially engaged. Accompanied by King Edward VII and mother Beatrice, they drove over the border and Ena set foot on Spanish soil for the first time. At the Miramar Palace in San Sebastian they were welcomed by Queen Maria Cristina in spite of her earlier reservations. On 3 February 1906 Alfonso returned to Madrid, and later that same day Princess Beatrice informed King Edward VII that her daughter had officially accepted the Spanish King's proposal of marriage. When leading Spanish churchmen voiced their disapproval at the thought of an English princess forsaking her faith, King Edward avoided the issue by declaring that Ena was a Battenberg princess, not an English one, and she was therefore free to adopt any religion she wished. It could be said that as her mother Princess Beatrice had married into a 'foreign family', her children did not come within the scope of the Royal Marriages Act of 1772.

Beatrice was ready to welcome the King as a son-in-law. He and her daughter, she wrote to the Countess of Antrim, were 'absolutely devoted to one another, and I have every confidence in the King making her the best of husbands. He has such a charming nature, that to know him is to love him, and though the thought of my child going so far from me is a real trial, I feel I have really gained a son, who does everything to make things easy.'[7] On 3 February Beatrice, who was staying at Biarritz, suggested that the ceremony of her daughter's reception into the Roman Catholic Church could take place at Empress Eugenie's villa at Cap Martin, but King Edward preferred it to be done at Paris instead. He also recommended that his sister and niece should return to England for the time being, and suggested that Monsignor Robert Brindle, the Catholic Bishop of Nottingham, who had been a very popular army chaplain in Egypt, should give the prospective bride a course of religious instruction. This was duly done, and in March 1906, on a visit to the Miramar Palace at San Sebastian, Ena was received into the Catholic Church.

The ceremony was presided over by Brindle and also by the Bishop of Vitoria and Sion. Ena had to be rebaptised and renounce her Protestant faith.

King Edward wrote to Sir Edward Grey, his Foreign Secretary, that he considered it 'absolutely necessary' for the Princess, having become a Roman Catholic, to sign a paper formally renouncing her right of succession to the English throne. Moreover, though no public grant would be asked for on her behalf, she would receive a certain sum from her mother, Princess Beatrice, 'but that, the King presumes, is a private affair'.[8] He also warned his niece bluntly that, if anything was to go wrong, she must not 'come back whining here'.[9]

The controversy over his niece's engagement had irritated King Edward, but he wisely refused to interfere. Writing to the Duke of Connaught, he said that her change of religion would take place 'as quietly as possible. . . . I get endless letters and some petitions begging me to stop the whole thing, but this I cannot do considering as it is her affair, besides if she marries the King of Spain she *must* change her religion before even her engagement is announced to the Cortes!'[10]

On 12 March Señor Moret made a formal announcement of the betrothal to the Cortes. In Berlin Emperor William was thoroughly affronted, regarding it as far more than a snub to the eligible princesses of the Hohenzollern and other royal German houses. On a report from the German embassy in Madrid on the matter, he scribbled, 'The whole of these pathetic and corrupt Latin peoples are becoming instruments in England's hands, in order to hamper German commerce in the Mediterranean.'[11]

*　　*　　*

Accompanied by Princess Beatrice and a large suite, Ena arrived in Spain for her wedding at the end of May 1906. Madrid was filling up with royal guests for the wedding, and the streets were decorated brightly with banners in the national colours of red and yellow. According to Spanish royal etiquette, in order that pride of place could be given to the bridal pair, no other crowned head was invited. Among the heirs and other royalty who attended were the Prince and Princess of Wales, later King George V and Queen Mary; another of Ena's cousins, Princess Alice of Teck and her husband, Prince Alexander, later Earl and Countess of Athlone; Archduke Francis Ferdinand of Austria-Hungary, the heir of his uncle, Emperor Francis Joseph; Emmanuel, Duke of Aosta, eldest son of King Amedeo; the Count of Flanders, later Albert, King of the Belgians; and Prince Henry of Prussia, brother of the German Emperor William II.

The long procession of carriages set out at around 9 a.m. on 31 May from the palace to the Church of San Jeronimo. Princess Ena, Princess Beatrice and Queen Maria Cristina travelled together in the nineteenth-century mahogany state coach. This was followed by the 'carriage of respect', a state coach which was relatively plain except for its gold panels; kept empty, it took its place immediately in front of the King. Last came the crown coach, surmounted by two golden globes supporting the crown, and emblazoned with the arms of Spain and Naples. (Naples was the home of the wife of Ferdinand VII, who had been the first to use the coach.) This vehicle was to take the King to the church, and then bring the newly married couple back for a reception at the palace afterwards.

King Alfonso XIII, the last to leave the royal palace, was accompanied by the infant Prince of Asturias, heir to the throne as son of the King's deceased eldest sister Mercedes, and his widowed father Infante Carlos, Alfonso's brother-in-law. The bride's procession was due to join the main one near the Chamber of Deputies, close to the church, but Ena was delayed as Moret, the Prime Minister, had been half an hour late in arriving at the Marine Ministry, from where he was to escort her to the church. The King had arrived punctually, with no idea what had caused the delay, and as he waited alone at the altar he became increasingly anxious. Before leaving the palace that morning he had received several anonymous letters, some threatening his life, some that of his bride, and others both. One, accompanied by a picture of a character named Mateo Morales, said that an effort would be made either to prevent the marriage or else to kill them both. He had taken care not to tell Ena, but at the same time he had warned the Queen Mother and begged her to protect his future wife. An attempt had been feared at the door of the church, and the number of police on guard had been doubled.

At last, to his relief, he heard the British national anthem being struck up – the signal for the bride's arrival. She was wearing a dress of white satin glittering with silver and carrying a wreath of orange blossom. As she walked up the aisle she was seen to be clasping the Queen Mother's hand very tightly in her own. The couple had only just taken their places on the chairs prepared for them when the King, a great weight lifted from his shoulders after the long and worrying wait, impulsively stood up, passed behind his bride's chair, went over to his mother, bowed very low and kissed her hand. Taking her cue from him, Ena went to embrace her own mother, a gesture that visibly brought tears to Beatrice's eyes.

The ceremony lasted about three hours and shortly after 2 p.m. the procession set off in brilliant sunshine for the Palacio Real. The royal coach in which King Alfonso and Queen Ena sat side by side wound its way slowly through the streets of Madrid. Some of the guests were concerned that a well-publicised prohibition against the throwing of flowers at the procession was being blatantly dis-regarded. About two-thirds of the way the coach stopped. When the Queen asked why, the King said that it was probably connected with those ahead alighting at the palace. In five minutes, he assured her, they would be there. This momentary delay saved their lives.

Even as Alfonso was speaking, a large bouquet of flowers was thrown down from the window of a house overlooking the pro-cession. It landed just in front of the carriage to the right of the horses. There was a flash of flame, a sickening smell, the high-pitched scream of wounded and terrified animals, and a cloud of smoke so black and thick that for a moment bride and groom could not see each other. The horse-drawn carriage plunged and came to a stop. Ena was lying on the seat with her head back and her eyes closed, and for a moment Alfonso feared that she was dead.

Once he had found that she was all right, he leaned out of the window and was told that the procession could not continue as one horse had been killed and the others were wounded. He asked for the 'carriage of respect', the customary empty coach that always preceded the royal carriage, to be made ready to take them, and for the Queen Mother and Princess Beatrice to be informed that they were unharmed. Bride and groom were both severely shaken and splattered with blood and splinters from the bomb, as he helped her out of the coach; he tried to shield her from the sight of the torn and bleeding bodies of men and horses scattered across the road, then led her to the waiting carriage. Then, in a loud voice which everyone could hear, he ordered the coach to proceed very slowly to the palace. By the time they arrived Ena was close to hysterics, though outwardly she managed to retain her composure. She was heard saying over and over again, 'I saw a man without any legs!'[12]

Twelve people had been killed and over a hundred wounded. If the coach had not been held up, the King and Queen would surely have been among the victims. Rumours swept through Madrid immediately after the explosion, some saying that the sovereign and his bride, maybe even the entire royal family, were indeed dead. The Prince of Wales had to propose their healths at the state luncheon; as he recalled, it was not easy 'after the emotions caused by this terrible affair'.[13] That afternoon they drove in the Casa del Campo and the King visited the wounded in the hospitals. A banquet went ahead in the evening, but it was a tense affair and after a seventeen-hour day the young couple were exhausted.

Members of the public were apparently permitted to roam at will around the colonnades of the palace, with no effort made to prevent them from wandering almost into the guests' apartments. The Prince of Wales was very scathing about this lack of security, the apparent absence of normal precautions and the extraordinarily happy-go-lucky atmosphere. 'Of course the bomb was thrown by an anarchist, supposed to be a Spaniard and of course they let him escape,' he wrote in his diary. 'I believe the Spanish police and detectives are about the worst in the world.'[14] Marie, Dowager Duchess of Saxe-Coburg Gotha, had seen it before. In a clumsy effort to reassure the others, she said that she was 'accustomed to this sort of thing', having lost her father, Tsar Alexander II of Russia, and her brother, Grand Duke Serge, to the bombs of terrorists.

The man responsible, Mateo Morales, had tried to gain admission to the church with his bomb concealed in the bouquet. It had been arranged that fourteen-year-old Infanta Pilar was to take her place in the church with other members of the Spanish royal family. After this the question arose of where the Prince of Asturias should be sitting. As he was only aged four, everyone thought he was too young to be in the main body of the church as he would get tired and fidgety; it was suggested he should be given a seat in one of the tribunes or galleries overlooking the nave, and that Pilar should accompany him and keep him quiet. The day before the ceremony this particular area, which had been allotted to the press representatives, was therefore reserved for the young prince, the infanta and their suites.

Morales tried to enter the church as a journalist, claiming he had lost his ticket of admission. By showing forged press credentials he persuaded another journalist to give up the ticket he had received, admitting him to the tribune in the church. But this ticket also proved useless, and Morales gave up trying to enter the church. Instead, he managed to install himself on the third storey of the house overlooking the procession. Here he was seen apparently idling the time away by throwing oranges into the street and observing the spot where each one fell. Far from playing an ostensibly mindless game, he was using the oranges to calculate how long it would take for an object thrown from the third floor to reach the ground. By sheer chance he threw the bouquet a moment too soon. Instead of hitting the carriage, it fell on the backs of the horses, which weakened the force of the explosion but nevertheless killed a coachman, a footman and several bystanders.

Morales was arrested at an outlying village two days later. While being taken into custody he shot a policeman dead from behind and then turned the gun on himself. A disciple of the notorious anarchist Francisco Ferrer, he was widely rumoured to have been behind the attempt to murder the King in Paris the previous year. The man who had arrested him left a widow and several small children, for whom King Alfonso made generous financial provision. Morales's suicide came as no small relief to the King, the Queen and their guests, and the latter were very glad to leave Spain. The whole fortnight, remarked Archduke Francis Ferdinand, heir to the Austro-Hungarian throne, had 'been equivalent to a campaign'.[15] Eight years later he and his wife would fall victims to the hand of an assassin, on a fateful summer day at Sarajevo.

On the day after the wedding the King and Queen drove unattended through the streets of Madrid in an open car, to the delight of everyone who came to see them. Still nervous from the events of the previous day, Ena was very reserved and it was noticed that she visibly 'shrank back' as the crowds came closer to her. People fought to get near her, and her dress was literally torn to shreds by those who were intent on kissing the hem of the garment. It was no wonder she was apprehensive at their enthusiasm, but sadly it was all too indicative of her English steely reserve which, her subjects noted, would prevent her from establishing a proper rapport with them.

Later that week they escaped from Madrid for a six-week honeymoon at the Palace of La Granja at San Idelfonso. At last they could relax. The King's attentiveness helped to ease the shock of their wedding day. Nevertheless, memory would never erase the incident, Ena wrote to Lady Paget, telling her it was 'a perfect nightmare' and she positively shuddered when she looked back on it:

> The bomb was so utterly unexpected that until it was all over I did not realise what had happened, even then I was not frightened. It was only when I got into the other carriage that I saw such fearful horrors & then I knew what an awful danger we had gone through. My poor husband saw his best friend, a young officer, fall down dead beside our coach fearfully mutilated & that upset him very much.[16]

Nobody could have doubted the bravery of King Alfonso and Queen Ena in the aftermath of this tragedy, but it was soon equally clear that the former had severely underestimated the harm the assassination attempt had inflicted upon Spanish prestige abroad. He might dismiss it as an occupational hazard, the inevitable consequence of being a sovereign, but others were less sanguine. He was keen that King Edward should reciprocate after his official visit to England in

June 1905, and a few weeks after the wedding King Edward referred the matter to Sir Charles Hardinge, then Under-Secretary of State for Foreign Affairs. Sir Maurice de Bunsen, the British ambassador at Madrid, reported to King Edward's private secretary Lord Knollys that King Alfonso was very sensitive on the matter, to the point of threatening to give up his unofficial visits to England if the King did not make one to Spain himself. Knollys replied tactfully that King Edward's engagements made a visit to Madrid during the next two or three months impossible, but the real reason was that the British Cabinet considered the state of Spain too unsettled and incapable of maintaining proper security. Even so Sir Edward Grey thought a meeting at some Spanish port, on board a ship where they would be safer, might be feasible.

As King Alfonso knew, Britain had good reasons for wanting to maintain a close relationship with Spain. London and Paris feared the Spanish government might be prepared to give Germany a cable concession in the Canary Islands, and therefore a footing on the coast of Morocco, where both capitals were anxious to see German trade and influence severely curtailed. Hardinge agreed that his government wanted to do all it could to be on friendly terms with Spain, but not to the extent of taking undue risks with the life of the King. Such a visit, he said, 'was quite out of the question, and entirely unnecessary until the Spanish government have introduced a more efficient service of police, which will probably be never.'[17]

King Alfonso continued to insist, adding that if King Edward did not come to Spain soon, Emperor William might seize the chance and pay his own visit first. This, he knew very well, was the only threat he needed to make, and in January 1907 Sir Edward Grey thought that a meeting at one of the Spanish ports could be arranged. Much, he acknowledged, depended on Spain, and it would be politically awkward if she was to turn away from the Anglo-French entente and look to Germany as an ally.[18]

Though he was no coward, King Edward was irritated by King Alfonso's insistence, telling Knollys on 4 January 1907 that the King of Spain was 'certainly very pertinacious', and that he would have to shelter himself 'as a Constitutional Sovereign' under the wing of the government[19] in order to decline a private visit to such a potentially dangerous area. Nevertheless it was agreed that a meeting of both sovereigns in Spanish waters was feasible, and on 8 April the monarchs met at Cartagena. King Alfonso was not accompanied by Queen Ena, whose confinement was expected shortly, but with him were Queen Maria Cristina and Prime Minister Maura. King Edward was accompanied by Queen Alexandra and Hardinge, who had brought with him the draft of a tripartite agreement between France, Spain and Great Britain, maintaining the status quo in the Mediterranean. Throughout most of the capitals of Europe it was believed that King Edward aimed to strengthen Anglo-Spanish ties and weaken German influence in Madrid.

In November 1907 King Alfonso came to England and spent a day shooting with the Duke of Portland at Welbeck. One of his fellow guests asked him whether Morales' attempt on everyone's lives had not affected his nerves. He replied that it had not. 'You see I really do believe in God.'[20]

✳   ✳   ✳

There has been much debate as to how aware King Alfonso was of the fact that Ena might have been – and actually was – a carrier of the dreaded royal scourge of haemophilia. Queen Victoria's youngest son Leopold was a sufferer, and had died at the age of thirty, while two of her daughters, Alice and Beatrice, were carriers. Two of Ena's three brothers were afflicted, and the risk that she might bring the disease into the Spanish Bourbons was considerable. As time would prove, she too was a carrier.

Early in the morning of 10 May 1907 her first confinement was imminent, and she suffered severely, gritting her teeth at the unsympathetic reaction of her mother-in-law who told her that 'we Spaniards do not cry out when we bring a King into the world'.[21] Later that day she gave birth to a son, who was baptised eight days later at the Royal Palace. He was known as Alfonso, or 'Alfonsito' within the family. He appeared perfectly healthy at first, and only when court doctors tried to circumcise him did they make the same grim discovery about their son and heir that Queen Ena's cousin Alexandra, Empress of Russia, and her husband Tsar Nicholas, had made about theirs. He was indeed haemophiliac, and for the rest of his short life his health would prove a source of perpetual worry.

For the time being the King and Queen gave the impression of being a contented couple, still very much in love. If there were difficulties in the relationship at this early stage, they kept them well hidden. At the end of the year the Queen's mother Beatrice wrote to the Revd William Boyd Carpenter, Bishop of Ripon, of her daughter's 'thorough contentment in her married life with her kind excellent husband, & precious little boy'. The Queen, she assured him, was quite unchanged, 'beloved in her new country, & her upright straight character appreciated'. As for the King, she said, 'if he is only spared to do one half of what he wishes for his country he will indeed be a blessing. To me he is a most affectionate thoughtful son, & he fits so well into our little family circle.'[22]

Now in his late 20s, King Alfonso XIII may have been impatient, dogmatic and supremely self-confident but he was also full of high spirits and unfailingly active. As he had seemed so sickly as a small child, his mother and doctors had ensured an outdoor life for him in order to build up his strength. As a result he developed a passion for sporting activities, and there were many who alternately praised or criticised this 'perpetual young man'. He cared nothing for literature or music, and with regard to art took only a passing interest in anything other than paintings of battle scenes or military marches.

Occasionally he had to brook criticism within his own family. His aunt Eulalia was separated from her husband Antoine, and after the death of her mother, the indomitable former Queen Isabel, she settled in Normandy. To the horror of the King, in December 1911 *Le Temps* stated that she had written and was about to publish a book, *Au fil de ma vie*. It advocated divorce, emancipation of and independence for women, and the same education for all classes. To her nephew this was provocative in the extreme, and an angry King Alfonso telegraphed her, forbidding her to consider publication without allowing him to read the manuscript first. That she had agreed to publish under a pseudonym, that of the Condesa de Avila, made no difference. She replied that she was amazed he should judge the book without even seeing it. He sent his ambassador to inform her that he was not disposed to tolerate such an attitude, but she refused to receive him. She had separated herself from the Spanish royal family and the state of Spain, and she was therefore under no obligation to receive their ambassadors either then or at any other time.

In order not to appear too high-handed, the King declared that he did not censor the publications of his family, and that another cousin, Doña Paz, wrote in books and newspapers. But in such a case as this, when publication threatened to cause scandal, he believed that as head of the family it was his duty to ask her to send him a copy before offering it for general sale. The Prime Minister, José Canalejas y Mendez, discussed in the Council of Ministers the question of depriving Eulalia of her rank and annual pension. If she had so defiantly broken with the family, it was no less than she should have expected. *Le Temps* announced that she had received the title of Infanta at birth and therefore could not lose it. At the meeting of the Council they confined themselves to passing a resolution deploring her attitude.

The book was published, but received little attention in Spain. Some of the radical papers praised it at first, but poured scorn on it when they learnt that she had come to an agreement with the King. In some other countries his intervention had the unintentional but inevitable result of giving her book additional publicity as 'the book the King tried to suppress'. In the United States of America it appeared under the title *The Thread of Life*. It evidently gave her a taste for authorship, for a few years later she published a second book, *J'ai voulu vivre ma vie*.

* * *

Between his coming of age and the year of his marriage, King Alfonso XIII had had to contend with a succession of ministerial crises and eight different prime ministers. Each change of government resulted in alterations to the governmental machinery and subsequent political instability, with the King in sole charge until all changes had been effected. As time went on, he seemed to be the one constant factor, and he came to regard politicians with increasing cynicism and impatience. Like his father, he knew how shamelessly elections to the Cortes were rigged, and how democracy was honoured more in the breach than in the observance. His faith in his own abilities accordingly increased; he had never lacked confidence in his own judgement. By nature he was impatient and disinclined to suffer fools gladly.

In addition to political instability, there were other upheavals during the early years of his reign, particularly beyond the borders of his kingdom. Fighting broke out in Morocco between Moorish tribesmen and Spanish garrisons in 1912, and there was a violent revolution, believed to have been instigated by the anarchist Francisco Ferrer, who was put on trial and executed for sedition. He had long been believed to be the mastermind behind Morales' assassination attempt, and the government was looking for any excuse to eliminate him, but his death changed his status from a national danger to that of a martyr.[23]

On 12 November 1912 Canalejas, whom the King had regarded as the most responsible of his prime ministers, was assassinated. The Liberal premier was so confident of the affection of the people that he used to walk around Madrid without any protection. While on his way to the Home Ministry one morning he had stopped to look in a bookcase in front of a shop window when a man suddenly fired a revolver at him. He was taken at once to the ministry office, but he was already unconscious and died a few minutes later. The King was horrified by the violent death of a man whom he had greatly respected. Despite the advice of his police he refused to allow the streets to be closed for security purposes, and to the horror of his entourage he insisted on attending the funeral, walking in the procession behind the coffin. When the ceremony was over he stood unguarded for more than half an hour, shaking hands with the other mourners and paying his condolences to relatives and friends in person.

Four months later, on 27 March 1913, he had a severe accident while playing polo. While riding at full gallop his horse trod in a hole and threw him some considerable distance. He was stunned, and did not recover consciousness for quarter of an hour. Severely bruised all over, particularly around the head and face, he was forced to rest for several days. Within a few days he was well enough to resume his normal way of life, but some thought he had been badly hurt in the head, and doubted he would ever be quite the same again.

About three weeks later, as he was riding back from a military review, there was another attempt on his life. In the previous month King George of Greece had been assassinated while strolling along the streets of Athens, and pamphlets had been scattered around Madrid predicting that King Alfonso XIII would die on 13 April. There was a discernible air of tension and anxiety in the air that day, but the King refused to yield by altering his programme. A military review was due to be held that day, with an open air Mass followed by the swearing-in of recruits; it would be the first such ceremony to be held as the result of a new compulsory military service law. As the King rode on his charger through the enthusiastic crowds that lined the streets, a man ran out and fired two shots at him at close range. The King coolly rode towards him and as the officers of the royal suite closed around the culprit, he tried to seize the reins of the King's horse and fired a third time, the flash singeing his glove and slightly grazing the horse. 'Polo comes in very handy on these occasions,' the monarch remarked nonchalantly. 'I set my horse's head straight at him and rode into him as he fired.'[24]

The would-be assassin was Manuel Sanchez Alegre, a carpenter from Barcelona with anarchist sympathies, who had been under police surveillance for some time. He tried to turn the gun on himself but the police managed to stop him. When he was put on trial and condemned to death the King reprieved him, and the sentence was commuted to imprisonment. The King met this, as he did every attempt on his life, with no little courage. Some years earlier his advisers had tried to dissuade him from visiting Barcelona as it was regarded as a hotbed of revolution, but he dismissed such talk, saying that he was King of the whole of Spain: 'when I am afraid to visit any part of my kingdom then it is time for me to abdicate'.[25]

NINE

'Neutrality was a murderous risk'

While much of Europe was at war between 1914 and 1918, Spain remained prudently neutral. Her navy was inadequate for a sustained conflict, while her army numbered less than 150,000, with many of its units already committed to the fighting in Morocco. The population was divided in its allegiances, and like his ministers the King knew he had little choice but to keep Spain out of the war, though even he could not prevent the war from entering Spain. Only by remaining as impartial as possible would he be able to retain the freedom to urge peace on his fellow rulers at every favourable opportunity. Meanwhile, as long as hostilities continued he believed they had a humanitarian duty to do their utmost to mitigate the horrors of war for others in any way they could.

An official declaration of Spanish neutrality, issued on 30 July 1914, was endorsed by the Cortes when it met in October. In August the Liberal Prime Minister Count Romanones wrote in the *Diario Universal* that 'neutrality was a murderous risk, while the rival powers were preparing to remould Europe as they wanted',[1] but even he appreciated that participation in the conflict was not feasible.

In the palace at Madrid, there were inevitably sympathisers for both Allied and Central Powers. An Austrian by birth, Queen Maria Cristina naturally endorsed the war aims of the latter, especially as her brother, Archduke Frederick, was fighting on behalf of the German empire. King Alfonso, a French Bourbon on his father's side, had always had an affinity with France, while through his mother's side he was an Austrian Habsburg and an Austrian Archduke; he was also closely connected with England not only by marriage but also by many ties of friendship and hospitality with British officers and sportsmen. Nobody expected Queen Ena to be anything but passionately pro-British as well, with her British birth, upbringing and brothers in the British army.

By common consent the war was not discussed in the palace. Relations between the Queen and the Queen Mother had always been cordial if a little distant, and they remained thus from 1914 onwards, though sometimes the course of events made it impossible for them to hide their feelings completely. When the Italians joined the Allies in the spring of 1915 Queen Maria Cristina could not conceal her fury. Ena maintained a regular correspondence with her cousin 'Daisy', Crown Princess Margaret of Sweden, as, she told Queen Mary in England, 'it is curious that we are in exactly the same position, both living in neutral countries & with our mothers-in-law on the German side!'[2]

The worst moment of the war for Queen Ena came when her brother Maurice was killed in action at Mons at the end of October 1914. He was leading his company in an attack on the German forces when he was struck by shrapnel from a bursting shell and died almost immediately. Ironically Spain's principal Carlist leader, Vasquez de Mella, had chosen the moment that the news of the Prince's death reached Spain to address a pro-German meeting. Several ladies from court were present in the audience, and as he shouted his praise of Germany and his burning hatred of all things British, there was loud applause. When he came to the end of his speech his feet were almost buried with the bouquets of flowers thrown at him.

As the war progressed, Queen Maria Cristina would wait for the news each day with interest, expressing her approval at every Austrian or German military success. If the news for the Allies was particularly good, she would unbend to Ena enough to tell her coldly that 'your side had a good day today'.[3] More reserved by nature, Ena found it easier to keep her views to herself, but not so her mother-in-law. When news was brought to them in June 1916 of the death at sea of Earl Kitchener, en route to Archangel in Russia when his ship struck a German mine and sank west of the Orkney

Islands, Maria Cristina could not conceal her delight. Ena had known Kitchener, a favourite at the English court, since childhood, and he had often paid family visits, letting her sit on his knee. Count Romanones, who was having lunch with the royal family at the time, saw Ena digging her fingernails into the upholstered sides of her armchair in repressed fury.

With a wife and mother whose allegiances were so at odds, King Alfonso was wise to maintain his neutral stance. When asked for his opinion, he would merely say with an enigmatic smile that 'there is no one who wants to fight but the *canaille* and myself'.[4] Winston Churchill maintained that the Spanish aristocracy were pro-German and the middle classes anti-French, and as the King said, 'Only I and the mob are for the Allies.'[5] Even a century later the Peninsular War and the reputation of Napoleon Bonaparte still left their mark on Franco-Spanish relations, but of more recent and bitter memory still was national defeat and the loss of remaining colonial territories overseas at the hands of the United States, which entered the war on the side of the Allies in 1917. 'A plague on all your houses' doubtless summed up Spain's general attitude to the belligerent nations.

The King's enemies in Spain nicknamed him 'the Kaiser's understudy', because of his admiration for German military efficiency and because both monarchs, Alfonso and William II, had such a passion for all things theatrical. Each, it was said, wanted the centre of the stage; each was animated by the same love of attention, the same enjoyment of taking a hand in everything, managing and making speeches about everything, 'and having the leading part in the most pompous scenes that ingenuity can devise or their positions render possible'. Moreover both had the same passion for disguising themselves under 'picturesque trappings'. At 2 p.m. King Alfonso might be seen in the uniform of an admiral; one hour later it would be that of a Death's Head Hussar; another hour on it would be the regalia of the Lancers. When military uniforms failed to provide him with enough variety, his friends and courtiers told each other, he would ride out into the middle of the polo field dressed as a clown. Sometimes the costumes he designed for himself were deemed so ludicrous that the illustrated journals of Madrid were warned not to publish any photographs of His Majesty, as there were 'limits to what even a King may do with his dignity'.[6] Although King Alfonso had some admiration for his contemporary in Berlin, they were both impulsive, showy individuals, desperate to be the centre of attention wherever they went, and too similar to like each other much as individuals. At any rate, his inclinations and personal sympathies lay more with England and France.

According to his cousin Princess Pilar of Bavaria, who was admittedly not the most objective source, King Alfonso XIII was 'the greatest diplomatist alive' and his private inclinations were a mystery, but 'they were strictly subordinated to what he believed to be the best interests of Spain'. At the same time he was 'an impulsive, outspoken man of very strong feelings, emotionally sensitive, and swift to react where his feelings are concerned: in fact a typical Spaniard: he had close ties with France, and the most tender and binding ties with England and Austria; yet it is doubtful if even Queen Ena or Queen Maria Cristina really knew where his personal preferences lay.'[7]

In Spain as a nation the Conservative aristocracy inclined towards Catholic Austria, though as with many in Austria itself, this did not translate into unqualified endorsement of Germany's war aims, while the Liberals and Socialists leaned towards the Allies. The British ambassador, Hardinge, was not alone in his conviction that the King disliked Emperor William II, and was also revolted by the brutal behaviour of some of the German troops throughout the countries they were attacking. Yet for the elderly Emperor Francis Joseph in Vienna the half-Austrian King Alfonso always had nothing but the warmest regard.

The activities of German submarines in its waters were a grave embarrassment to neutral Spain. The Allies alleged that hospital ships were being torpedoed, to which the Germans retorted that the vessels in question were being used as men-of-war or for carrying munitions. To limit this wanton destruction, the French found a solution by carrying German officer prisoners on their hospital ships as hostages. Then King Alfonso intervened by persuading the belligerent powers to agree to an arrangement by which all hospital ships should carry a neutral commissioner to be appointed by the Spanish government. The duty of these officers, if challenged by German submarines, was to certify that the ships in question were not men-of-war in disguise, and thus could not legitimately be fired on or captured. During the war, Spain lost an estimated 140,000 tons of shipping as the result of U-boat attacks, and with each Spanish ship that sank, public opinion moved more towards the Allies.

To his credit King Alfonso found a way of involving himself peripherally in the war while receiving nothing but well-deserved praise from all sides. Less than a month after the outbreak of war a French washerwoman asked the King whether he could help to trace her husband, who had been missing since the battle of Charleroi on 21/22 August 1914, and to find out if he was dead or a prisoner. He answered the letter in his own hand, promising to assist to the best of his ability. Thanks partly to his efforts and the enquiries which he personally initiated, the man was located among prisoners of war in Germany, and he endeavoured to get permission for the man to write to his wife himself. After this he did much to initiate work in ameliorating the lot of prisoners, as well as making enquiries into the fate of missing personnel. Being King of a neutral state allowed him to do much of a humanitarian nature which could not be accomplished by aligned crowned heads. Before long many similar requests came into the Palacio Real. His private secretary, the Marques de Torres de Mendoza, tried to deal with the flood of letters by using his normal staff, but soon found this task beyond his powers, so a special bureau was set up in the palace to deal with similar inquiries.

During the four years of conflict the King intervened to save the lives of twenty men and eight women condemned to death. He also helped in other ways, collecting information concerning prisoners military and civil; forwarding correspondence concerning health and similar matters to and from prisoners in the occupied countries (beginning with Belgium); giving material help to prisoners; arranging repatriation of civilians; watching over the welfare of interned persons; securing the mitigation of punishments; obtaining special indulgences for prisoners-of-war; and acting as the medium of communication between individuals and families in occupied territories and their relations and friends throughout the world. Another case in which he did his utmost, though to his chagrin without success, was to help Nurse Edith Cavell, whose execution on espionage charges in October 1915 did much to damage Germany's reputation. The Spanish ambassador in Brussels, the Marques de Villabolar, did everything he could to secure her reprieve. Had he been able to communicate with the King in time, a personal intercession on her behalf by King Alfonso to Emperor William would probably have saved her.

By this stage King Alfonso shared the views of those who had their doubts about the stability of the post-war world. One month before the execution of Nurse Cavell, he gave an interview to an Argentine journalist which was published widely in various journals throughout the world. Speaking of the war, he said it was impossible to predict when conditions would return to normal. In reply to a remark that if the result of the war was to be general disarmament then one could foresee progress for all humanity, he commented that after the conflict was over the nations involved would arm more than ever. 'When it is seen that a country like Belgium, neutralised by the consent of all the nations, finally found no other defence than by the force of arms, it is easy to understand that other countries, large and small, consider that in order to exist it is indispensable to work with the most positive guarantees.' When asked if he believed that the lower classes would apply sufficient pressure on their governments to prevent them from imposing new burdens to maintain an armed peace, he answered that in his view socialism would 'become daily more governmental. The Socialists will attain the satisfaction of their most just aspirations by legal methods and without having recourse to violence. But I also believe that they will evolve and that they will recognise after the war that, so long as humanity does not modify its instincts, there will be no better way to safeguard their rights than by foresight and force. Besides, I believe that after the war there will be no stoppage of labour, but that work for everybody will continue to be what it is today. In

10 or 12 years we shall be surprised and shall ask ourselves what has happened.'[8]

Towards the end of 1916 President Wilson of America tried to persuade the belligerent Powers to negotiate peace, and appealed to the neutral countries, especially Spain, for support. After giving the idea due consideration, King Alfonso and Romanones declined, on the grounds that they thought the time was not right, but said they would gladly cooperate if a suitable moment later arose.

There was never more than a remote possibility that Spain would enter the war, though when David Lloyd George became Prime Minister of Britain in December 1916, he believed there still was a chance. At that time America was still neutral, and the Allies were losing much of their shipping to submarine attacks, and there would be strategic advantages in being able to move Spanish troops overland to the Western Front. Romanones was also keen that Spain should demonstrate some commitment at least to the Allied cause, and he issued instructions for a number of British officers to be trained for liaison work with the Spanish army. They received three months' training in London, after which they were returned to their units and nothing more was done. By that time Romanones had resigned as Prime Minister in Spain, to be replaced by Don Garcia Prieto, Marques Alhucemas. Lloyd George had a memorandum drawn up on the advisability of exchanging Ceuta, a small Spanish territory on the northern coast of Africa, for Gibraltar, almost directly opposite in geographical terms. How seriously the scheme was taken can only be imagined, but there was no record that the scheme was ever communicated to Madrid. The fall of the Romanones administration may have put paid to it, but by then the submarine menace was beginning to be mastered and the scheme thus became less urgent.

King Alfonso had his own solution to the issue of Gibraltar, which he once submitted to King George V. He wanted Britain to recognise Spanish sovereignty, and in return she should be granted a ninety-nine years' lease of the fortress, for the annual payment of £1 sterling, which the King of Spain should come in person to collect. On this occasion, he suggested, the Spanish and British flags should fly together over the Rock. There should also be a British officer attached to the staff of the King of Spain, and a Spanish one to that of the Governor of Gibraltar. As the idea did not appeal to King George, it was taken no further.

In the autumn of 1917 a Red Cross conference of neutral nations was held at Geneva, the Spanish representatives being the Marques de Torres de Mendoza and General Don Eladio Mille. A resolution was unanimously passed, thanking the King for his humanitarian work. Perhaps uncharacteristically, he remained modest about his role. Just before the end of the war, a deputation of nine thousand mayors came to Madrid to ask the King if he would confer on himself the Grand Cross of the Order of Beneficence in recognition of his efforts. He answered that the honour should not be bestowed on him, but on the nation of Spain.

Even the war years did not bring to an end the attempts on the King's life. In January 1917 an attempt was made near Granada to wreck the royal train, when a large bar of lead was placed across the rails. It was discovered and removed about an hour before the time fixed for the passage of the royal train by a slow passenger train ahead, which was stopped just in time to prevent an accident. Two men were arrested in connection with the incident but later released.

* * *

By November 1918 the war in Europe was over. With joy in her heart Queen Ena wrote to Queen Mary: 'How truly I rejoice with you in this supreme hour & what great pride I feel at having been born an Englishwoman with English traditions. The excitement here has been intense & the Allied Flags are displayed in most of the streets.'[9] King Alfonso's humanitarian efforts during the preceding years were recognised by other sovereigns and heads of state. King Albert sent him a telegram thanking him for his protection of Belgians during the war, while Alexander, Prince Regent of Serbia, did likewise for his care of Serbian children who had sought refuge in Spain; President Poincaré awarded him the French Gratitude Medal to acknowledge his services to prisoners and missing. In a telegram to the President the King said he wished he 'could have done more to assuage the suffering so heroically borne by your nation'.[10]

After the end of the war King Alfonso's thoughts turned to the conflict between the Spaniards and the Moors in the protectorate of Morocco. Not long after he had come of age, it was noticed with concern by his ministers that he seemed to show an alarming sensitivity to army opinion, and they suspected that should he ever need to side with them or with the generals, he would choose the latter. This preference led him to share the army's concern with Morocco, coupled with a desire to see the last of politicians in general. By the terms of the Franco-Spanish agreement of 1912 the dominions of the Sultan of Morocco, with the exception of Tangier, had been divided into two zones, and the attempts of the Protecting Powers to establish order in their respective zones had brought about war. Spanish forces had been involved in fighting in North Africa for over a decade in an inefficient campaign, costing the nation dearly in men and money, and causing mounting dissatisfaction at home. A spectacular victory by his armies, the King was convinced, was essential in order to put an end to this drain on his country's resources, and to enhance the tarnished reputation of his forces.

At the same time he was becoming increasingly disenchanted with Spain's parliamentary system. For nearly thirty years he had tacitly accepted the thin veneer of national democracy as his father had before him, but now he was becoming impatient with the constant political in-fighting, and wanted to see Spain become a great military and Catholic state. A victory in Morocco would considerably strengthen his standing in proportion to that of his nondescript politicians. In May 1921 he made a speech at Cordoba denouncing Spain's parliamentary system. It was followed by a fervent address in Burgos Cathedral at the tomb of El Cid, a legendary warrior who had fought against the Moors, in which he spoke of the greatness of Spain. 'Do not think that in recalling the empire of my ancestors I am moved by any impulse of ambition,' he declared, after speaking of his ancestors who had found glory on the battlefield in earlier times. Spain, he said, was 'great enough still to realise her destiny;

and apart from that, with what Spain is in the Peninsula, and with what belongs to us on the other side of the Strait, we have enough to figure among the first nations of Europe'.[11]

On the same day Spain suffered a crushing defeat in Morocco. Two veteran generals had been responsible for the conduct of the war. Damaso Berenguer was a cautious leader, while Silvestre was inclined to be impetuous, and just as impatient as his King for a spectacular campaign. In defiance of Berenguer's instructions to await reinforcements, Silvestre returned to Morocco after an interview with the King, moved forward to do battle with the tribesmen, and led a 10,000-strong force to Anual. They were surrounded by the Moors, and when they tried to fight their way out through a narrow ravine, the tribesmen shot them down and most of the force was annihilated. Silvestre was so horrified by the disgrace that he shot himself. Berenguer arrived at the scene of defeat to find that his colleague's insubordination had cost Spain dearly in terms of her Moroccan army, guns and equipment.

At home the news was greeted with fury. The government resigned, but there was a widespread feeling that Silvestre had been encouraged, if not actually ordered, by the impetuous King. Among the dead general's papers were found two telegrams from the sovereign, the first reading, 'On the 15th I expect good news', and the second, 'Ho, you fellows, I'm waiting.'[12] While they could hardly be held to place full responsibility on the King for having ordered Silvestre to advance without caution, they merely reinforced any suspicions that he had as good as sacrificed the lives of ten thousand Spaniards in a vain quest for military glory.

Not only had the disaster robbed the King of his anticipated laurels, but it had also thrown the country into greater unrest and turmoil. Since the Moroccan disaster he had been even more impatient with the politicians and with the Cortes in general. On two or three occasions he had threatened to abdicate, complaining that his ministers were 'deserting' him and exposing the monarchy to the slanders of the left and the republicans. At an impromptu speech he issued a rousing royal appeal for reform with or without the constitution, and they looked askance at this threat of a royal dictatorship.

In August 1923 he consulted his Prime Minister Antonio Maura on the matter. Maura warned him that the crown should not sanction dictatorship, as there could be no return to normality afterwards.[13] Had the King heeded his words, he would have saved himself much trouble later on. However, he had been impressed by the situation in Italy whereby Benito Mussolini had overthrown parliamentary government and set himself up as dictator with the approval of King Victor Emmanuel III. There was a similar strong man in Spain – General Miguel Primo de Rivera y Orbaneja, Captain-General of Barcelona. As a young soldier he had fought in his country's colonial wars in Morocco, Cuba and the Philippines, and after the First World War he had successively been Captain-General of Valencia, Madrid and Barcelona. In a speech the King had hinted that he was powerless to dislodge his parliament, but there was no reason why the army could not force his hand. Primo de Rivera was willing to fulfil such a role, and in planning a coup d'etat for 14 September 1923 he was aware that he would meet with little if any resistance from the King.

On 11 September a riot in Barcelona provoked the General into declaring a state of martial law. When the government tried to dismiss him for this act of rebellion, he answered by issuing a manifesto calling on the King to dismiss the government and rule the country with the help of the army. King Alfonso was at San Sebastian when he heard news of the coup. He returned to Madrid and was met at the station by the ministers. The choice was between civil war and the acceptance of Primo's military dictatorship. When the Prime Minister offered his resignation the King accepted it, and later that day he asked Primo to form a government.

The King always insisted that he had known nothing of Primo's plans, but he certainly welcomed the advent of the dictatorship. After three months two leaders of the Congress, Romanones, the President of the Senate, and Melquíades Alvarez, President of the Congress of Deputies, called on him to remind him that, in accordance with the constitution, he was obliged to reconvene the Cortes within three months of its dissolution. Only one month remained if the law was to be observed, and this article had been scrupulously observed since 1876. He received them in a brief audience, but took no further action. In effect, he had now broken the oath which he had taken on coming of age. He thus made clear his personal responsibility in the collapse of the Spanish parliamentary system, and so made it probable, if not inevitable, that the eventual fall of the dictatorship would imperil the survival of the throne itself. In November King Alfonso and Queen Ena paid a state visit to Italy, and he introduced Primo as 'my Mussolini', expressing admiration of the Fascist system at the same time.

*　*　*

By this stage of her husband's reign, Queen Ena's situation had become increasingly uncomfortable. She had long since realised that her mercurial, restless husband soon tired of everything. Marital relations had virtually ceased for several years, and apart from their love of sporting activities and the outdoor life they had very little in common. Had it not been for her reserved demeanour, the poor health of most of their sons, her persistent Englishness and her wariness of Spain, maybe she could have held his affections. But they were like chalk and cheese. She was very quiet and gave off an aura of sadness, which contrasted markedly with his buoyant, lively personality. That he was carrying on unashamedly with other women, thus giving rise to unsavoury gossip, gave her further cause for unhappiness.

Her situation was made more complicated by the presence in Spain of her cousin Princess Beatrice (Bee) of Saxe-Coburg, another granddaughter of Queen Victoria through the latter's second son Alfred. Beatrice had been one of the eligible young princesses who were possible candidates for King Alfonso's hand on his visit to London in 1905. In July 1909, with the tacit verbal approval of the King and the agreement of his wife and mother, but without legal permission from the Spanish government, the King's cousin Infante Alfonso (Ali), Duke of Galliera, married her secretly in Coburg. Beatrice had refused to enter the Catholic Church, and theoretically there was no need for her to do so as, unlike the marriage of King

Alfonso and Ena, hers would not be a marriage of state. Nevertheless Maura had informed the King that the government would not let an Infante of Spain marry a Protestant princess; if she did not change her religion, it would be tantamount to letting a heretic become part of the royal family. When news of the marriage reached Spain, the Cortes stripped Ali of his royal titles, decorations and army commission. Under pressure, King Alfonso took shelter behind his government, weakly going back on his word and declaring that his cousin had married against his (or in effect his government's) will, and therefore insisting that he would have to go into exile. As Ali had always been his most loyal supporter in the family, it was an unwise move by a cowardly man.

After their honeymoon in Munich the Infante and his wife had to settle in Lucerne for a couple of years, until his honours were restored and they were allowed back to Madrid. On their arrival, Beatrice found the Queen was becoming isolated by the more conservative elements of the aristocracy, led by the Duchess of San Carlos and the Marques de Viana. They thought Ena was far too modern in her tastes and outlook and suspected that her cousin, who was also English-born and of a similar age (three years older), would be a bad influence on her. As she still refused to enter the Catholic Church, Beatrice herself was never popular in a court and country where religious bigotry was a positive virtue.

For a long time it was suggested that Beatrice was an inveterate mischief-maker and nursed a grudge against Ena who had denied her the prize – if it could be regarded as such – of becoming Queen of Spain.[14] This seems to be based on hearsay rather than firm evidence. It was all too easy for Catholic ladies at court to blacken the good name of the English Protestant Infanta. Moreover it was said, perhaps with some justification, that Beatrice, her husband and Infanta Eulalia were rumoured to be making comments in favour of the Central powers during the war, in contravention of the consensus that any such talk should be avoided in royal circles. This was compounded by the fact that the King found the lively, pretty, quick-witted and pleasure-loving Beatrice rather a temptation, particularly when compared to the wife who had offended him by giving him so many unhealthy sons. It was as if he now felt he had chosen the wrong wife. He made advances to her which she angrily rebutted, but he was reluctant to take no for an answer, and at length Ali had to write to his cousin, requesting him firmly to leave his wife alone.

It has been alleged that Beatrice became one of the King's confidantes, giving every outward appearance of being Ena's sympathetic friend while doing much in helping to stir up ladies at court against the Queen and, more insidiously still, acting with the King's cronies in helping him to find suitable mistresses, once it was clear that his marriage to the Queen was gradually becoming a marriage in name only. Furthermore, it has been said – though probably without foundation – that she overreached herself, that her activities as a procuress were bringing the court into disrepute, and that Queen Maria Cristina would not stand idly by and condone such behaviour. On one occasion in 1916 when Beatrice and her husband were staying with the family at San Sebastian, the Queen Mother apparently ordered them to leave the country. When Beatrice refused, orders were given nominally by the reluctant King – to whom his mother's word was law – that she should go.

What really happened was that family relations had become so fraught that the King realised he would have to ask his cousin and wife to leave Spain. For a while they settled in Zurich so they could be near Beatrice's ailing mother, the widowed Duchess of Saxe-Coburg. Later they returned to England, taking a house in Esher, but after a few years' penance she was forgiven and in 1924 they were allowed to return to Spain. Reluctant to believe the worst of her unfaithful manipulative husband, Queen Ena had mistakenly believed that Beatrice's flirtatious behaviour was responsible for the difficult situation, but at length she saw the truth. When Ali and Bee came back to Madrid they were all friends once again, though by that time the King and Queen were no longer close. This friendship between the Queen and her cousins lasted throughout their lives and the long years of exile.

The Queen's greatest *bête noire* at court, the Marques de Viana, had been a close friend of the King since his early adult life. The

Marques had been one of the privileged guests invited to witness Ena, before her marriage, officially embracing the Roman Catholic faith at Miramar. Notoriously prejudiced against foreigners, he always resented the fact that his King had married an Englishwoman. In order to help satisfy his master's appetites, he undertook to ensure that Alfonso had enough young women to provide him with the amusements that he considered the Queen could not offer. Within a few years of her marriage, the Queen was convinced that the Marques was her greatest enemy at court.

The Queen's last pregnancy, in 1918, ended in a miscarriage. By then the King had already been indulging himself elsewhere, not only with ladies brought to court by Viana, but also with those he sought out in Madrid's high-class brothels, or in Paris under the incognito of Monsieur Lamy. Queen Maria Cristina, who had been well aware of her husband's promiscuity, was not surprised to find that her son had gone the same way. She once told her sister that if she had to pick out all the grandchildren credited to her, she would not live long enough to be able to do so.

It seemed as if every Spanish monarch had been a parent to at least one child outside marriage. There was not only the dubious paternity of several of Queen Isabel's children, but the illegitimate children of Kings Alfonso XII and XIII had been openly acknowledged. According to the latter, one of the men who worked in the royal stables was a son of the late King Amedeo and the Marchioness of Villalobar. Yet many Spaniards accepted their monarchs' promiscuity as a matter of course, saying with a shrug of the shoulders that 'thus have always been the Bourbons'.[15]

The King was reputed to have had his first extra-marital affair around 1908 (or earlier), with an Irish nurse who was sent away from Spain once it was realised she was pregnant. Rumour has it that the daughter born of this affair committed suicide at a young age. Then there were various ladies from Paris, notably Madame Melanie de Vilmorin, wife of a French wheat dealer, who bore the King a son, Roger, in 1915. She was soon followed by a Scottish lady, Beatrice Noon, piano teacher to the young princesses, who was also sent to France once *enceinte* and gave birth to a daughter in 1916. Of all his mistresses, his affair with the actress Carmen Ruiz Moragas was the most serious. He first met her in 1916, but his relationship with her only started about seven years later, after she had separated from her husband, Rodolfo Gaona, a Mexican bullfighter. She bore him two children, Maria Teresa, born in 1925, and Leandro Alfonso four years later.

Though the Queen was thoroughly hurt by these betrayals, like many a consort before her she preserved her dignity. At least she could find some consolation, no matter how slight, in the fact that her beloved uncle 'Bertie', King Edward VII, had never been a model of marital fidelity either. At the same time she managed to win a victory of sorts over the Marques de Viana. She had been left in no doubt that he was foremost among those who had schemed and done his best to poison King Alfonso's mind against her. One evening in 1927 she summoned him to an audience at the palace, and on his arrival she confronted him, saying how disgusted she was with his abominable behaviour towards her. He tried to turn on the charm and talk his way out of the situation, but she had had enough and made her attitude plain. 'It is not in my power to punish you as you deserve,' she said at the end of the interview. 'Only God can do that. Your punishment will have to wait for the next world.'[16] For the Marques, the next world was nearer than either of them supposed. He left the palace in a state of shock, went home, collapsed with a heart attack and died that night. When she told several friends about it, much later in life, they asked her whether she felt any responsibility for his death. Her reaction was a non-committal shrug of the shoulders. If she believed he had got his just deserts, she could hardly be blamed.

Alfonso's increasingly notorious infidelity won him no plaudits in the other courts of Europe. In the spring of 1929 Infanta Beatrice's elder sister Marie, Dowager Queen of Roumania, took her younger daughter Ileana to visit her in Spain. While she was there the Prince of Asturias became very attached to Ileana and announced that he wanted to marry her. At first Queen Marie was delighted, but after recalling the experiences in Spain which had led her sister into temporary disgrace, and the plight of several other young women, she thought better of it. The greatest argument against such a marriage, she said, would be King Alfonso, much more than the poor haemophiliac husband who would be her son-in-law. King Alfonso, she went on, 'makes up to every woman & then has a way of declaring that they threw themselves at his head. A pretty daughter-in-law, wife of his invalid son, would in no wise be safe from him.' The opposite sex had to be exceedingly careful where he was involved, and 'it would be quite impossible for a young woman to have anything to do with him'.[17]

If King Alfonso was no longer as popular as he once believed he was, Queen Ena was still much loved except, perhaps, by those Spaniards who could not forgive her for producing such sickly sons, and for her reserved English manner. The less prejudiced of her husband's subjects gladly praised her for her charm, her sense of fashion and her ability to retain a slender figure well into middle age and beyond. Her clothes sense was widely admired, even if she had to take care not to appear in anything too stylish or daring if there was a risk of causing offence. She was one of the first women to be seen in public in Spain wearing a modern, tight-fitting bathing costume. Some were scandalised; queens, they asserted, simply did not behave in such an undignified manner. Even when she went into the water, it was considered necessary for two fully uniformed and armed soldiers to accompany her, no matter how deeply she immersed herself. It was not unknown for her to be seen swimming near a beach with two escorts standing either side of her, in full uniform, with the water lapping at their necks as they stared impassively ahead.

At formal state occasions she always performed well, wearing her clothes with ease – her diamond carat, white lace mantilla, gold and silver dresses – and looking as dignified as the role required. Yet it was away from court that she was at her happiest, staying at El Pardo, at La Granja, Aranjua, and at the Seaside Palace, San Sebastian. As a child she had been something of a tomboy, loving the outdoor life with her brothers and cousins at Osborne House on the Isle of Wight, or at Balmoral. As an adult she still enjoyed being out in the open air, and played golf and tennis as well as swimming. There was one exception to her love of sport, something she shared with the staff at the British Embassy in Spain, and that was a profound loathing of bullfighting. It took her no little effort to steel herself to attend such occasions, from which as Queen she could hardly absent herself.

Unlike her husband, she never aspired to a political role in the country. Once she was asked whether she discussed politics with her husband and she strongly denied it, but throughout their married life they did talk about the nation's affairs. Even though their marriage was an unhappy one in the last few years of his reign, he appreciated her advice and feminine intuition, especially when he asked for her opinions on certain individuals, and whom she might or might not trust. However, she was discreet enough not to do so with anyone else, and on the whole she restricted herself to non-partisan activities such as nursing services, and her work on behalf of Spain's hospitals was widely recognised. Her Red Cross Hospital in Madrid, to which she devoted considerable efforts, was in many ways a model institution.

The nearest she came to speaking politics with anyone else was with Sir Horace Rumbold, the British ambassador to Spain. In 1924 she told him confidentially and at great length about the designs of certain ex-ministers. They were trying to involve her in intrigue against the King, she said, and one even went so far as to hint to her that the King would have to abdicate, but she might remain as Regent. Not for one moment did she ever envisage lending herself to any such schemes, and she supposed that they were trying to play on the constitutional traditions which they assumed she had inherited as an English princess.[18] If they saw her as a possible weapon who could be used against her husband, they were mistaken, for she never had the inclination to involve herself in anything of the kind.

The greatest cause of her sadness was her grief at knowing she had failed, having provided her husband with so many ailing sons. Alfonso, Prince of Asturias, born in May 1907, was haemophiliac; Jaime, born in June 1908, was healthy at first; two daughters, Beatrice, born in June 1909, Maria Cristina, born in December 1911, and another son, Don Juan, were perfectly fit; but a third son, Ferdinand, was stillborn in May 1910, and a fifth, Gonzalo, was also haemophiliac. The tragedy of her cousin Alexandra, Empress of Russia, was that she had borne four daughters and then a delicate haemophiliac son. Ena's tragedy was that only one of her four sons, Don Juan, as well as both her daughters, enjoyed perfect health. The eldest son Alfonso, Prince of Asturias, was often too weak to move, and was obliged to spend long periods in bed. For a father who had been taught to lead a healthy outdoor life, and wanted all his sons to do likewise, it was a crushing blow. In this case it was compounded by the totally untrue yet much-believed rumour that a young Spanish soldier had to be sacrificed every day in order that his warm blood might keep the ailing heir apparent alive. Alfonsito, as he was known, spent much of his time at La Quinta, a small house on the royal estate outside Madrid, where he bred chickens and pigs, and grew olives and vines. These activities were a constant source of pleasure, and some compensation for his unfortunate condition and subsequent enforced lack of physical activity.

The second son, Don Jaime, was 6 feet tall as an adult, and looked a strikingly handsome young man. For the first three or four years he was fine, until he had to have an operation for a double mastoiditis. It was mishandled, the auditory bones were broken, and for most of his life he was a deaf-mute, although he learnt to lip-read successfully. Despite this he had a sunny nature, was kindness personified and warm-hearted if somewhat immature. It was on the tall, good-looking Don Juan, who entered the Naval College at Cadiz, that the hopes of the dynasty were centred.

Whereas Empress Alexandra's behaviour and approach towards her haemophiliac son bordered on hysteria, Ena's calm exterior was exactly the opposite. In her case, she did at least have one healthy son, so her situation was perhaps less desperate than that of her cousin. Nevertheless, she was as worried as any mother would be at having several sons whose condition gave such cause for concern. Yet her phlegmatic demeanour towards them gave the false impression that she was unemotional and uncaring, and only made her more unpopular. Some found this English *sang-froid* rather unnatural. A visiting American remarked that 'she was as English as a cup of tea'.[19]

Queen Ena had a resilient streak. Unlike her late cousin Alexandra, and to a certain extent their maternal grandmother Queen Victoria, 'the widow of Windsor', whose years of seclusion in middle age had lost the British crown a considerable degree of public support, she recognised how important it was for the King and Queen to be seen regularly by their subjects. She had never been one to hide herself away from society, and she enjoyed attending concerts, ballets, plays, musicals and other performances in public. Always enthusiastic about Spanish music, singers and dancers of the day, she easily made friends who shared such interests, and became an active patron of the performing arts in Madrid.

The Queen adored music, and as the state of her marriage deteriorated, she found more and more solace in her piano. Among her friends was the pianist Artur Rubinstein. He had first visited the Spanish capital during the war to play in several concerts, and they soon became friends. She attended many of his concerts and later invited him to play in her private apartments for herself, her daughters and a lady-in-waiting. When the piano provided for his public performances began to deteriorate in quality, she offered to have her own Steinway sent to his concerts, as long as it was kept a secret. The King, who disliked music, must not know about it. The arrangement worked well on every occasion but one, when the piano had still not arrived and the concert was an hour late in starting, much to the audience's irritation. Just as Rubinstein was beginning to despair, the piano arrived and the Queen appeared at the royal box. During the intermission she met the pianist and told him apologetically that at luncheon that day the King and the Queen Dowager had been having a lively political discussion which turned into a quarrel – in the apartment where her piano stood. Not until mother and son had gone could the workmen move it.

She also engaged the pianist and cabaret performer Leslie 'Hutch' Hutchinson to teach her children the piano. Afterwards he claimed that he had lived in the royal palace for about a year while giving lessons, though the Queen's daughter Beatrice said the lessons were infrequent and he probably stayed no longer than about six months. He also said that the Queen was devoted to him, and at a London party a few years later, when the Queen and Hutchinson were introduced by a mutual friend who was unaware that their paths had already crossed, she smiled at him and said they were 'old friends'.[20]

Like many of her mother's family she was an indefatigable reader, enjoying serious literature, mainly English authors. She also read contemporary Spanish writers, including Padre Luis Coloma, a Spanish Jesuit whose works appealed to those Spaniards who espoused orthodox views of Catholicism, and surprisingly the tireless republican novelist and travel writer Vicente Blasco Ibañez, whose most famous title was a diatribe against the King. Sometimes during evenings at home together the King would read aloud to the Queen in English, in order to practise the language. She would search out English books for him on army matters and on life in India, in both of which he had some interest. However, he never became more than a reluctant student of the printed word.

Much as she grew to love Spain, like most if not all of Queen Victoria's daughters and granddaughters who married European princes, she always thoroughly enjoyed the visits she and the King made to England. 'Now that I am settled down again in Spain, I want to send you a few lines of heartfelt thanks from us both, for all yours and George's kindness to us in London,' she wrote to Queen Mary after returning in July 1926. 'We so enjoyed our afternoon with you at Sandown & also the dinner-party at Buckingham Palace & it was so dear of you to see us off at the station when we left. The journey back was very trying for me, as besides the heat being fearful I sneezed the whole way & then as if by magic, the same afternoon we arrived here, every trace of hay fever vanished!'[21]

TEN

'He tires of everything'

Throughout his period of rule General Primo de Rivera and his regime brought considerable economic benefits to Spain. Once he had assumed leadership of the government, he gave priority to improving old roads and building new ones, railways, hotels, hospitals and schools; communications were improved, especially with the construction of a tunnel through the Pyrenees which reduced the journey time between Barcelona and Paris by four hours; and large irrigation schemes were put into operation. With French cooperation, Spanish prestige in Morocco was restored and the disaster of Anual avenged by the end of 1925, something the army had conspicuously failed to do before, and the King made a triumphal visit to the country. Law and order were reinforced throughout Spain. Since the treaty of Vienna she had been somewhat isolated in Europe; now she began to emerge, with friendly relations established with Latin America, and a semi-permanent seat on the Council of the League of Nations.

In the second week of September 1925, on the third anniversary of the coup, a plebiscite on the question of adherence to the Spanish government – or in effect approval of the dictatorship – was put to the people. Six million voted in its favour, and in the autumn it was re-established as a civil institution.

Any doubts King Alfonso might have had on the wisdom of the regime had been quickly dispelled, as an interview he gave to a French journalist M. Tharaud in April made clear. If he was by no means as free as before, and had less opportunity for initiative than under the parliamentary system, he felt it was worth the sacrifice to be rid of parliamentary rule. When Tharaud asked him for his thoughts on the matter, the King was very much on the defensive. Did he notice as he travelled through Spain, he asked the Frenchman, any signs that they were living in a state of siege, under military oppression? As a sovereign he read allegations in foreign newspapers that the Directory shot down civilians in cold blood, or arrested them and threw them into prison without trial, and that they were presiding over a reign of terror. In fact they had changed nothing of the tenor of their ordinary lives in Spain, and he would suggest that as far as he was aware there was no other country where the police were less of a nuisance:

> You can stop in the middle of the street for a talk with a friend without a policeman insisting that you should move on. You can after midnight drink any liqueur you like, which I defy you to do in New York or London, those homes of liberty. At Madrid you can cry, howl, or sing, if that pleases you, till five in the morning. The only things changed since the Directory are that one can go about with money in one's pocket and yet not risk being knocked out, that there are no more strikes, that our works are running, and the masters do not every morning have to face workmen who appear with revolvers in their hands to give orders to their masters or assassinate them. You must admit that's something. But, damn it all, you've got to pay for it. Primo has made us break the Constitution, and that, obviously, is serious.

When questioned further, the King said that they had had no alternative but to introduce a dictatorship. In Spain they had fewer Communists than in France, but the climate made them more virulent. While in Barcelona 'they assassinated you in broad daylight and all our economic and social life was breaking up, our Parliament was busy only with miserable finicky questions, or in gratifying personal spite'. It was an untenable situation which General Primo had addressed, saying he could resolve the matter within three months, and then return to legality within the time allowed by the Constitution. That, the King admitted, was not his opinion. He realised that three months would be insufficient, and that they had already gone for almost two years without ministerial or parliamentary rule proved his point. When asked how long it would take Spain to reach beyond it, he would not be drawn. He saw no sign that the party leaders were giving up their old ways, and believed that a premature return to parliamentary rule would only lead the country back to 'its old undoing', thus destroying the work of some twenty months. The Communist leaders would go back to their old ways of fomenting crime and calling strikes, and they would fall back into the anarchy which for almost two years they had been doing their utmost to extricate themselves.[1]

Yet Primo's greatest mistake was a failure to get the coup d'état ratified by the Cortes. In the early years public and business opinion were overwhelmingly on his side, much as politicians and more left-leaning intellectuals resented his presence, and he would probably have secured a large majority had he demanded full powers. As a result he would have been able to transform Spain at will without laying the King or himself open to charges of illegality. In June 1926 Sánchez Guerra, leader of the conservative opposition in the Cortes, told the King that he must dismiss Primo on the grounds that his proposal for a National Assembly to draft a new constitution was illegal, and it would be 'the official death sentence of parliamentary and constitutional government'.[2] The King refused, saying that he did not want to return to the old system, and it was impossible to defend a 'discredited' constitution. Even though the proposed National Assembly might be faulty in composition, it would allow some hope for an agreed return to normality after the dictatorship was over.

The King's political ventures may have been unwelcome, but in other fields his initiative was to be applauded. It was his own idea in 1927, to celebrate the 25th anniversary of his accession, to build a new university, La Ciudad Universitaria de Madrid. It was to be a centre for all students in the Spanish-speaking world, and despite his lack of enthusiasm for scholarship and bettering himself intellectually, he took a particular interest in its construction. This, he was sure, would not only be a worthy investment in the future, but would also help to conciliate the youth of Spain. It irritated him particularly when students rebelled against the dictatorship, circulating anti-

Primo leaflets, writing seditious graffiti on the buildings and even destroying a large bust of the King himself as a protest.

Such unrest was not confined to the students. Years of strict censorship and the banishment of critical intellectuals from Spain had deprived people of legitimate outlets for debate, while a deteriorating economic position as prices and taxes increased and the peseta rose and fell in value resulted in a worsening of the country's export trade. The King gradually became disenchanted with Primo, especially because of his onslaught on the artillery corps. Like his father before him, King Alfonso took tremendous pride in 'his army', and once said that had he not become King he would have been content to become an infantry major.

Primo's military reforms included moves to deal with the closed scale of promotion by which artillery officers refused promotion that went against strict seniority. Like most of the cavalry and infantry soldiers, he looked with distaste on what he saw as the expectations of the generally aristocratic 'privileged corps', who felt they had an automatic right to promotion regardless of ability, and in June 1926 he took away the rewards which compensated artillery officers' self-denial. When the officers went on strike, the government suspended the whole officer corps. The latter soon capitulated, but Primo's authority in the country had been seriously weakened by provoking such a confrontation. The officers were angry with him, and their confidence in a King who did not defend their interests was shaken. The King was displeased that Primo had dissolved the proudest corps in the army without consulting him. One day a group of artillery officers on the road from San Sebastian to Madrid stopped the King's car and asked him to promise that he would revoke Primo's orders. When the King respectfully refused to commit himself, some sections of the army began to reconsider their loyalty to the throne. A few years later this would cost him dearly.

* * *

By now King Alfonso was gradually becoming more isolated, especially after the death of his mother. To the end Queen Maria

Cristina had remained a source of unfailing support. She had suffered from angina for some time, though her death was relatively sudden. On the afternoon of 5 February 1929 she joined several other members of the family at a charity theatre performance on behalf of the Red Cross. She was in her usual high spirits at dinner that evening, and afterwards they went to the cinema in the Palace. On retiring to bed she appeared to be her normal self. At 2 the next morning she collapsed. The doctor was summoned but she had suffered a major heart attack and died about two hours later, aged 72. The King was desolate at her death, and when they had laid her body in the royal chapel he asked to be left alone with her for a while. He remained in prayer beside the body, and when he emerged it was noticed that he had covered her coffin with the national flag of Spain.

Though relations between the two women had rarely been close, Ena was deeply affected by her mother-in-law's death. A letter sent to Queen Mary in England some nineteen months after Queen Maria Cristina's death, and written as Ena and Alfonso were about to return to Madrid from a five-week stay at San Sebastian, gives a glimpse of her feelings, though at the same time it shows that her sense of humour was never far below the surface. 'It was rather painful being in this house at first, having always been here as my mother-in-law's guests. You would have laughed if you had seen me gradually getting rid of endless little Austrian atrocities with which the rooms abound & hoping that Alfonso would not remark it, as he is very touchy about his mother's things!'[3]

Outwardly the King had changed little over the years. He was still devoted to his sporting activities, and despite his clumsy first efforts behind the wheel, he continued to enjoy driving. His fascination with speed soon became legendary throughout Spain. At one stage he used to go out for a regular evening drive in his car, and the police on duty on his usual route had to ensure that the way was kept clear for him.

One day a new policeman was put on duty in a neighbouring village, and informed that His Majesty would be driving through at some considerable speed that evening. The man had never seen King Alfonso before, but was sure he would be able to recognise him from having seen his picture in the newspapers. When the King appeared in his car, he was startled to see the policeman step into the middle of the road and ask him to stop. The royal car did so, and King Alfonso asked whether there had been an accident. The man warned him that there had not been one yet, but there would be if he continued to drive at that speed and the King was ahead. 'I *am* the King,' Alfonso told him. The policeman told him that the King had gone past an hour previously, and since then there had been seven other motorists all travelling at 70 miles an hour. The driver of each one assured him that he was the King of Spain, but all had been arrested and locked up. Only when the real King Alfonso had seen the police superintendent in order to establish his identity were the other 'kings' released.

His health had been a source of anxiety for some time. Though he had a stronger constitution than his frail father, he was increasingly worried about his condition, and by the time of his 40th birthday he was beginning to feel his age. The image he strove to present to the world, that of an ageless and indefatigable sportsman, was misleading. Much of the world at large may have been taken in by the regular pictures of him shooting or playing polo, but those around him were not deceived. He would only play one chukka of polo, ensuring where possible that a photographer was on hand to produce suitable images for publication, and then he would be too tired to continue. His excuse for retiring from the field would be that some urgent affair of state had just called him away. Likewise with shooting – he would arrange to be there for the finish, so he could be photographed as he stood proudly beside the day's 'bag'. Naturally his friends and cronies were ready to play their part in all this subterfuge.

His reluctance to overdo such activities was justified, particularly after he was taken ill with a mild heart attack during a game of polo during the latter years of his reign. He and the Queen suspected that the legacy of tuberculosis was taking its toll on his strength, and his increasing concern about his health undoubtedly impaired his political judgement at a time when the situation was becoming more critical than ever before.

*　　*　　*

After six years in office Primo's health was also beginning to fail. He had long suffered from diabetes, and the strain of overwork was telling on him. The politicians became ever more restive, and with the press which had languished under strict censorship for several years becoming increasingly hostile, it was clear that such a situation could not continue indefinitely. By the autumn of 1929 the global economic boom had passed, and Spain was deeply affected by the repercussions of the slump.

Suspecting that he no longer had the army and navy whole-heartedly on his side, in January 1930 Primo proposed to consult them as to whether he should remain in office as dictator, by means of a referendum of the captains-general. If their verdict went against him, he promised, he would go 'within five minutes'. Some of them refused to reply at all, and none answered him favourably. The King only heard about this consultation exercise from the newspapers, and was furious with the General for acting in a way which clearly violated the royal prerogative. The dictator defended himself by saying that his approach to the captains-general was not intended for political guidance, but merely for precaution in the possible event of widespread rebellion. Nevertheless he was weary of the burdens of office, and no longer had the heart to continue.

Knowing that his term of office was about to come to an end, he left behind a testament outlining his ideals and thoughts. He had no regrets with regard to the way he had governed, he wrote, but had always sought to serve his country with no other intention than to make it great once again. In the short term, he was convinced, there was no other way in which the nation could be successfully governed. 'With my thoughts fixed on God and on Spain, I believe that for ten years we will have to go on with Dictatorship or something very like it, exercised in the form of a Council of Ministers, but with the dictator alone responsible to his country and to the King.'[4]

On 18 January he was summoned to the Palace, and in the presence of the King and General Berenguer he was handed a draft of his resignation statement and ordered to sign it. Having added his signature, he was dismissed from the royal presence without a word of gratitude. He then left Spain and booked into a hotel in Paris. On 16 March, barely six weeks later, he collapsed and died after a heart attack, though it was rumoured that he had been poisoned. His body was brought back to Madrid, where he was given a hero's funeral as silent crowds stood in respect for the man who had done so much to better conditions for many of them.

There was one conspicuous absentee. King Alfonso seemed all too keen to dissociate himself and the monarchy from the dictatorship and from the man who had temporarily saved his throne though ultimately weakened his hold on it. Ironically some people were beginning to look upon Primo de Rivera's period of rule with some nostalgia and to regard the King as incompetent. His failure to attend the funeral provoked much adverse comment, and was regarded as a sign of cowardice and betrayal. It was remembered that he had courted some disapproval, yet for very different reasons, by his decision to walk behind the coffin of the assassinated Canalejas some seventeen years earlier.

Later King Alfonso would declare that the major mistake of the last years of his reign was that he should have asked Primo for his resignation earlier, and appealed to the country with a constitutional government of his own choice for a mandate to carry on the work of the dictatorship through the machinery of the constitution. After the fall of the Directory, the choices were open to him of either establishing a royal dictatorship, as had King Alexander of Yugoslavia, or attempting to return to normal conditions as soon as possible, observing constitutional limits and governing alongside the Cortes. With Primo gone, the King chose General Berenguer, the former High Commissioner of Morocco, as a temporary ruler, to prepare the country for immediate elections. Censorship of the press had been relaxed, and the republicans devoted themselves to preparing propaganda against the monarchy.

Isolated from general opinion, King Alfonso had no idea how much prestige he had lost as a monarch over the last few years. With the end of censorship the old accusations, that he had broken his oath to the constitution and that he was to blame for the terrible loss of life at the ill-fated Anual venture, began to be heard again. Unsavoury rumours about his private life were used against him, and while his grandmother Queen Isabel might have been forgiven many of her peccadilloes, at least for a while, the population of the 1920s was less forbearing. Intellectuals resented him, as he could never pretend that serious people did not bore him. Had he made some effort to court the great writers, painters, scholars and phil-osophers of his time, and paid a little less attention to his sporting interests and military matters, he might have been better placed to weather the coming storm.

Not everybody saw his devotion to sport as a harmful quality, as long as he realised the limitations to his prerogative where the government of the country was concerned. According to the former American ambassador at the court of Berlin, James W. Gerard, it was vital that he remembered at all times he was a constitutional king, and that 'in a country like Spain leadership is dangerous, that he should always stand aside, let the representatives of the nation decide, thus taking no definite position himself. A king who abandons the council table to shoot pigeons or play polo is often acting with far more wisdom than a constitutional ruler who attempts by the use of his strong personality and lofty position to force upon his councillors a course which the majority of them do not recommend.'[5]

Yet too many people around him were losing faith in their mercurial, undependable monarch. As Queen Ena had commented a few years earlier, 'he tires of everything, and some day he will tire even of me'.[6] That day would come, though not before the nation had tired of him. Business had been healthy up to the fall of Primo, but had declined sharply ever since. The cost of living and taxation had risen sharply, and with the worsening economic situation, discontent was growing. Disillusion with the politicians and, by implication, the monarchy as well, became ever greater. Spain was impatient for change, and it only needed a catalyst to bring the edifice tumbling down.

On 12 November 1930 a building under construction in the Calle Alonso Cano, Madrid, collapsed, leaving several workmen dead or injured. The municipal authorities arrested the architect and the contractor, but the casualties' comrades were not appeased. All the workers downed tools to attend the funeral two days later. The procession proposed to pass through the Puerta del Sol in the city centre, but the local authorities refused to grant permission without consulting the police commissioner, who was unavailable. In no mood to take no for an answer, the procession bound for Puerta del Sol made its way into Calle San Jeronimo, where the Cortes stood. A double line of the civil guard, with mounted men in reserve, tried to bar its way. Part of the procession, with members linking arms, charged head down into the police cordon. A shower of stones rained on the guards, who charged with drawn sabres. A lorry and several taxis were overturned, and a mounted charge swept the procession back. Soon the street was empty, but as the horse-drawn hearses galloped away, five more men were dead, and about a hundred wounded. From that fateful moment, some believed with hindsight, 'Don Alfonso's cause was lost'.[7]

In December the garrison at Jaca in northern Spain rebelled. The rebels cut all the telephone and telegraph lines, isolating the town, and killed several men in senior positions, including a military governor of one of the provinces, and three civil guards. Within twenty-four hours the government had suppressed the movement, arrested several people thought to be implicated in it, and court-martialled two of the officers responsible, Captain Fermin Galán Rodriguez and Captain Angel Garcia Hernandez. Both men were sentenced to death, and the government was divided as to whether they should suffer the full penalty of the law. When consulted, the King said that if officers in his army mutinied, they must be taught a severe lesson, and they should be shot that same day, Sunday 14 December. Though he had probably intended their deaths to serve as a warning to others, when the news of the executions broke it had the effect of turning public opinion against him. In fact five other leading rebels had also been sentenced to death, but were later reprieved. Nevertheless, the cause could now claim two martyrs. During his regime Primo de Rivera did not sentence a single man to death. King Alfonso was evidently less inclined to show mercy.

165

Later that week in Madrid a group of rebels seized an aeroplane and scattered Republican pamphlets all over the capital. It seemed that republicanism was on the rise, and when the authors of a manifesto on the subject were arrested and imprisoned, three leading Spanish intellectuals immediately issued another. The monarchy, they wrote, had become 'an association of groups living like parasites on the substance of the nation, making use of public power to defend private interests. In consequence the monarchy has become every year more isolated. It is unequal to the task of regenerating the country, which must be undertaken by a republic. It would be childish to expect the monarch gracefully to bow to the new regime, and the people must be prepared to use their full influence.'[8]

Meanwhile in January 1931 Queen Ena's mother, Princess Beatrice, broke her arm after slipping on the floor in her home at Kensington Palace. Bronchitis set in, and for a while her condition was critical. The Queen hurried to London to be by her side, and while she was away from Spain the standing of the monarchy diminished further. Berenguer realised he could do nothing, and offered his resignation. The King asked Alcalá Zamora, a leading liberal who had just been released from prison for seditious activities, to take his place, but the man declined. The King thought he was the only person who could unite Spain, a conviction reinforced by the enthusiastic reception the Queen received on her return to Spain on 18 February. Stepping off the train at Madrid, she was amazed by the deafening shouts of '*Viva la Reina!*' and the evident enthusiasm of the crowds. At the Palacio Real they were obliged to appear on the balcony to show themselves time and time again to the throng.

The King thought that any fall in popularity the monarchy may have suffered was no more than a temporary aberration. He failed to realise how much his throne was in danger. In fact, his situation was akin to that of Tsar Nicholas II, who had asked an ambassador shortly before his abdication whether it was true that for over twenty years he had tried to act for the best, but for all that time 'it was a mistake'. Convinced that the crisis would soon pass, he asked

Admiral Aznar to form a government, the first duty of which would be to prepare for a new set of elections, municipal ones in April and those for the Cortes in June. Believing that the country was in safe hands, he went to England for a short holiday, announcing that he would return late in March.

When the Spanish electorate went to the polls on Sunday 12 April, many were evidently determined to strike a blow against the existing order. The first returns showed a large swing towards the Republicans. All the large towns except Cadiz, Palma de Mallorca and Pamplona had voted for a majority of Republicans and Socialists, and in Madrid and Barcelona the anti-royalist majority was overwhelming. The rural districts' results were declared later, and these were predominantly royalist. Of the councillors returned across the country as a whole, 22,150 were monarchist and 5,875 republican. The case against King Alfonso XIII was far from negligible, but certainly not conclusive.

Yet the rural votes were still mainly under the control of the *caciques*, and even King Alfonso knew that if the towns and cities were against him, his position was untenable. He remarked dejectedly that he felt as though he had gone to make a visit to a friend, and on arrival at the house learnt that he was dead. If he had had the support of the military, he might have felt able to stay, but the army and the civil guard, under the command of General Sanjurjo, withdrew their support. Even the aristocratic circles, remembering what had happened in other countries well within living memory, not least at St Petersburg in 1917, could not avoid the suspicion that the monarchy had had its day and that it would be better for them to lie low rather than provoke a 'red revolution'. A premature rumour that he had abdicated caused pandemonium in the streets of Madrid, with crowds between four and five thousand strong celebrating as they cried out *Viva la Republica!* and 'Death to the King!'

The ministry could have taken a chance and proclaimed martial law in the towns where there was any likelihood of unrest, and after the restoration of order placed its resignation in the King's hands. Instead the ministers feared for their own positions, and Admiral

Aznar declared to the press with some exaggeration, not to say a degree of panic, that the country had gone republican overnight. The country might be bitterly divided, but it was far from anti-republican as a whole. Nevertheless, without consulting his colleagues in the cabinet Berenguer circulated a message to the captains-general that because of the rout of royalist candidates in the cities, the elections 'were lost'.

Although he could have appealed to the monarchists or the army to rally round the throne, the King vowed that he would do anything to avoid civil strife. Despite his personal misgivings, out of loyalty to the throne Berenguer told the King that the army was prepared to overturn the result of the elections, but the King would not hear of it. To rely on such a measure would have drastic repercussions, and he knew that the chances of any popular uprising in his favour were almost non-existent.

Believing that republican fervour would soon subside, he decided that he would therefore leave Spain for a while, and consent to a suspension of his powers – but he would not abdicate. In the previous fifteen years three European monarchs had renounced their thrones at times of war or grave national crisis, namely Tsar Nicholas II of Russia in 1917, King Constantine of the Hellenes in 1917 and again in 1922, and his son King George in 1924. King Alfonso XIII did not consider that the result of the elections had resulted in such a desperate situation as those faced by his brother sovereigns in Russia and Greece, but he believed it was prudent to act accordingly.

Before leaving his country he entrusted Aznar with a final manifesto to his people. Fearing fierce anti-monarchical repercussions, the provisional government suppressed the document and it only reached Spain after being published in the foreign press. In it the outgoing King admitted that the elections 'revealed to me that I no longer hold the love of my people, but my conscience tells me that this attitude will not be permanent, because I have always striven to serve Spain with all my devotion, to the public interest, even in the most critical moments'. A King may make mistakes, he admitted, and he himself had done so on occasion, but he knew that their country had always shown herself generous towards the faults of others committed without malice. He would prefer to stand aside rather than provoke a conflict which could lead to bloodshed, but he would not renounce any of his rights 'which, rather than being mine, are an accumulated legacy of history for the guardianship of which I shall one day have to render strict account'. Until the nation spoke again, he would be deliberately suspending his exercise of the royal power and leaving Spain, thus acknowledging that the nation was the sole mistress of her destiny. In doing so he believed that he was 'fulfilling the duty which the love of my country dictates. I pray God that all other Spaniards may feel and fulfil this duty as sincerely as I do mine.'[9]

It was arranged that he would leave Spain on 14 April, with all possible speed and without his wife and children. Such a move could easily have been misinterpreted as cowardice, but it was done for a practical reason. In the event of any attempts on his life, it would be better for the Queen and the children if they were not with him. Republican and revolutionary elements might not hesitate to try to attack him, but would surely think twice if there was any danger of a blameless woman and children being injured or even killed as well. That afternoon the King, pale and trembling, walked into the Queen's private boudoir to tell her that he was going that evening. She asked if they could share a meal in that room on their own. Eaten in almost complete silence, it was the only meal they ever ate unaccompanied by anybody else throughout their married life. After they had finished, he told her that the provisional government had guaranteed their safe passage to France the following day. He was leaving them in Spanish hands, and was sure she could trust them.

The King appeared outwardly unmoved as he prepared to leave for France. The only time he showed any hint of emotion before leaving the palace was when he paused before a portrait of his mother, stood there in contemplation for a few moments, raised his hand as if to salute her memory, and then moved on. The Prince of Asturias was unable to leave his bed, so the King went to his room to say goodbye. Don Juan was at the naval college at Cadiz, so next he took his leave of the Queen and their other children. Two cars were waiting outside, and he got into the first; in the second were a valet and some hastily packed luggage. There followed a drive of eight hours from Madrid to Cartagena, during which, he later recalled to Grand Duke Alexander of Russia, he heard the sounds of celebrating crowds. The night was pitch dark, and perhaps he was grateful that he could not make out clearly the fields and groves of the country he had known all his life. Though worried about his wife and children, and concerned lest the Republicans might not honour their word to protect his family, he still felt 'a deep moral satisfaction' at having prevented the outbreak of civil war in the land. One thought predominated in his mind that night: that it was 'better to go into exile than to be responsible for bloodshed'.

Arriving at Cartagena at 4 a.m. next day he was received by Admiral Magar, and a company of marines rendered him royal honours for the last time. All of them, he noticed, seemed crestfallen at this sudden turn of events as they talked to him in hoarse whispers, some clearly breaking down with emotion. As he shook hands with them, he told them firmly that he had 'preserved his traditions intact', ending with a vigorous 'Long live Spain!' Later, he admitted sadly, it was 'harder to leave like that than in leading a squadron into a battle'.[10] Within a few minutes he was on board the battle-cruiser *Principe Alfonso*, where he was treated with courtesy for the most part, though he was forbidden to listen to the wireless while on the ship. When the commander asked him out of courtesy which ensign should be hoisted on the mast, the King tactfully suggested that it would be inadvisable to fly the royal standard, and in order to protect him from any vengeance on the part of the republican government, he recommended that the national flag of Spain would be best.

They reached Marseilles just before dawn on 16 April. It had been such a calm journey by sea that the French authorities were not expecting them until later in the day, and the port was so deserted that it took the King's valet some time to find a taxi. As he was about to drive away, a young man stepped out of the darkness and asked the sovereign for an interview. He told the man bluntly to 'try to be kind even if it hurts you and leave me alone'.[11]

Though he was not to know at the time, King Alfonso XIII would never again see the country over which he had reigned for almost forty-five years.

＊　　＊　　＊

Meanwhile Queen Ena and the children had been left in the Palacio Real, alone except for a few faithful retainers, servants and other members of the family. Memories of the imperial Russian family's fate at Ekaterinburg cannot have been far from their minds. Throughout the night the mob howled around outside, and at one stage they heard the noise increase to frightening proportions. Amidst the noise, shouts of '*Muera al Rey! Muera a la Reine!*' (Death to the King! Death to the Queen!) and '*Viva la Republica!*' could be heard. Only twenty-five guards outside and twenty-five guards inside were there to protect them from the mob. The Queen and her children saw a truck being driven repeatedly into one of the palace doors in an apparent attempt to break it down. Some youths had already made their way up the façade and attached a republican flag to the main balcony, but the family were saved by the guards who managed to disperse the mob. The Queen's children told her bravely that they were willing to take up arms in order to defend themselves if necessary.

At 5 a.m. the next day the Queen was told by an old friend of the King, Joaquin Santos Suárez, that the revolution had come. Instead of going to a station in Madrid, they would have to be driven by car to the Escorial station outside the city, where they could board an express train that would take them across the French frontier. She and the remaining members of the family gathered a few things together. While they were preparing to leave, a group approached the gates and insisted on being allowed in. The family's worst fears were not realised, as the newcomers were a company of nuns who had taught Infante Jaime to speak after his operation; they had come to offer to tell him what was happening, though like the others he could understand all too well.

A little later the family left by the garden entrance. Among those who travelled with the Queen and her children were her cousin

171

Beatrice, the Queen's sister-in-law, the Marchioness of Carisbrooke, and various members of the aristocracy, including her faithful friends the Leceras. As the crowds watched them go, a man produced a camera, and an Englishman started to walk towards him with a determined look in his eye. The Queen begged him to hold back, and not to provoke an incident. 'Ma'am, I would only kick him',[12] was the reply.

They drove to the Escorial, where they spent their last moments on Spanish soil praying at the grave of Queen Maria Cristina. As they went in, the Queen, her eyes swollen from weeping, told the others that the King had not abdicated or signed anything, and they did not know what was going to happen to them, 'but I feel sure it will turn out for the best'. An American reporter watched them depart, commenting that one curtain was raised on the train as it left the station, and a hand appeared through it. It was that of the Queen, 'her last farewell to a land that never learned affection for her'.[13] Her last action was to send a message to Infanta Isabel, her aunt by marriage. Now aged seventy-nine, Isabel was still recovering from a stroke and unable to leave her room.

The Prince of Asturias was still very weak and had to be carried aboard the train. Before they left he gave his valet all his money and asked him to distribute it to those who had served the royal family with loyalty. Isabel, who had always been popular in Spain, had been given permission by the Republicans to stay in Madrid, but she regarded this as insolence and declared she would leave with the rest of the family as soon as she was well enough to travel. Four days later she arrived in Paris from Madrid and was taken to the Convent of the Assumption at Auteuil in an ambulance. Having outlived the revolution by one week and survived just long enough to see her nephew King Alfonso welcome her and the rest of the family on foreign soil, she died peacefully on 23 April.

A few days later Robert Sencourt, the journalist and future biographer of King Alfonso XIII, arrived in Madrid to find out for himself why the monarchy had collapsed. After talking to diplomats, republican leaders, ministers and other journalists, he concluded that the people, or rather the ruling classes, did not find their

sovereign serious enough. He had no taste for philosophers or pro-
fessors, and 'no habitual communion' with the country's intellectual
leaders, caring more for polo than parliaments; his sons' ill-health
also tarnished his popularity. But the greatest cause of ill-feeling
against him was that after Primo's dictatorship was over, he still
remained on the throne, and was thus the obvious scapegoat for the
General's period of absolute power and his failings. The King fell
from grace, the writer considered, 'because neither among Spanish
Conservatives or Spanish Liberals was there yet the energy and
cohesion to group around Primo de Rivera . . . to adapt tradition to
new needs'.[14]

ELEVEN

'Always such a gentleman'

King Alfonso arrived in Paris later on 16 April to a hero's welcome, with large numbers mobbing him at the Gare de Lyon, shouting and waving enthusiastically as he made his way to the Hotel Meurice. A similar crowd awaited Queen Ena, who looked haggard and bemused when she joined him, but smiled bravely as she acknowledged those who had come to greet her with shouts of *'Vive la Reine!'* As they and their entourage went to the hotel, where they would occupy almost thirty rooms, there were enthusiastic acclamations, which prompted the King to go up to the balcony and acknowledge them. When the Queen joined him, the cheers became wilder still. Such scenes were repeated when the King crossed the Channel and arrived at Victoria station en route for Claridge's Hotel in London on 21 April, where he had gone to make arrangements for Don Juan to enter the Royal Navy as a cadet.

Now they were entering what they knew might be a lifetime of exile, and the French capital was to be their next home. Yet it could not be anything other than a temporary place of refuge, as the new Spanish government informed the French Foreign Office that it had no objection to the King keeping an office in Paris for 'private purposes', but wanted him to live outside the capital. Within a few weeks it was decided that the royal family should make their temporary home in a virtually private wing of the Hotel de Savoie in Fontainebleau.

The part of the hotel which they occupied was an annexe to the main building. It was in effect a virtually self-contained house which gave them plenty of privacy, with all their meals served in their own private dining room. At first the King did not move in himself, but

174

stayed on for a while at the Hotel Meurice, while accommodation was prepared for him and his retinue, including his private secretary and a legal adviser, at the Savoie. In the past a number of friends and confidantes of Queen Ena had also lived with them in the palace, but they had nothing in common with the King's friends and knew they would not be at ease in his company.

Among Ena's most faithful companions were the Duke and Duchess of Lecera. Unfortunately their marriage, like that of the King and Queen, had been in trouble for some time. The Duke, it was averred, was a little in love with the Queen, and so apparently was the Duchess. A number of the Duchess's maids and governesses had been dismissed from her service for reasons which could never be disclosed in the days when lesbianism was not a fit subject for general conversation. The Queen was worldly enough to be aware of these rumours but her behaviour was always circumspect, and there is no reason to suppose that she reciprocated in any way or was carrying on an affair with either. The Duchess had a habit of sitting on the floor and putting her head on the Queen's lap, but if the latter ever regarded this as anything more than innocent if slightly over-affectionate friendship, she kept her views to herself.

The Leceras were among the very few true friends she had at this low point in her life. On the day King Alfonso left the country, the Duchess turned up at the palace after playing golf and found the mob gathering outside, as a result of which she and the Duke hurried to the Queen's support, leaving the country with her and the children. After that they never left the Queen's side, and when the King decided to move, he went to Paris and asked her to choose between him and them. At this she lost her temper and said the words to her husband that she would regret as long as she lived: 'I choose them,' she shouted, 'and never want to see your ugly face again.'[1] The last King of Spain was not used to anybody, least of all his wife, speaking to him like that. Though they never divorced, in effect this marked the end of a marriage which had been dead in name for some time. Both of them realised that any possibility of a reasonably tranquil life together in future was over. Fontainebleau remained their nominal joint home for the sake of appearances, though they were rarely there at the same time. Husband and wife travelled much, mostly throughout Europe, and generally managed to avoid being in each other's company.

The King travelled to various European capitals, ostensibly in connection with 'work'. As there was obviously no work for a former King who was unwelcome in his own country to do, it was easy for others to see that the ever-restless Alfonso was just filling in time the best he could, especially as he was often seen with female company. Because Fontainebleau was a home in name only, he felt obliged to look for somewhere more permanent. Like some other European royals of his day he was interested in and moderately supportive of fascism, seeing it as a bulwark against bolshevism and communism. This, coupled with his respect for the regime of Mussolini, made Rome an obvious choice. He bought a villa just outside the city, but after a while he found it too expensive to maintain, and instead he moved into the Grand Hotel in Rome itself.

Feeling homesick for the country of her birth, Ena looked towards London and acquired a house at Porchester Terrace, off Bayswater Road in west London. She later decided to part from the Leceras, probably because they were eager to return to their house in Andalucia, and she felt guilty about taking their loyalty for granted.

Among Ena's visitors to Fontainebleau in the early years was one of the few senior surviving Romanovs who had witnessed some of the horrors of the Russian revolution. Grand Duke Alexander, 'Sandro', the estranged husband of Grand Duchess Xenia, sister of Tsar Nicholas II, was impressed to find how she had braved the unhappy events of the previous few months, and found her 'just as friendly and refreshing in the simplicity of her manner as in the old London days'. She told him of her experiences during the final days in Madrid, revealing how unexpected had been their swift change of fortune after her visit to her mother in England when she had been welcomed home with such enthusiasm. 'It came so suddenly, so unexpectedly. It seems I returned from London only a day before, not wishing to be absent from Madrid during the political crisis. And the crowds at the station that met my train! . . . How could a nation change its sympathies so abruptly?'[2]

While in London in April 1931 the King had given an interview to the Marquis Juan Ignacio Luca de Tena, proprietor-editor of the pro-monarchist journal *ABC*, which was published on 5 May. 'I am resolved, quite resolved, not to place the slightest difficulty in the path of the Republican Government, which, for me, above all else, is at the present moment identified with Spain,' he declared. 'During the last year of my reign all sorts of obstacles were placed in the path of my Government. Whatever others may do, I will never approve of the people being stirred up against the present authorities or their agents, nor agree to the misfortunes of Spain being used as a lever to decry the new regime. I forbid Monarchists to stir up military rebellion in my name. News has reached me that many officers were refusing to give the promise of fidelity to the Republic required of them. Those within my reach I asked to do so. The Monarchy ended in Spain by an adverse vote of the people, and if it ever returns it must be by the same path of the will of the people.'

He had declined offers made to him to remain and rule by force, and for Spain he made the greatest sacrifice of his life when he found that the country no longer wanted or needed him. While he accepted that he might sometimes have made mistakes, in doing so he had only thought of the welfare of Spain; and he accepted the dictatorship when it was a *fait accompli* as he sincerely thought it was the will of the majority in the country. It was 'demanded with cries and received with enthusiasm by the same people who, some years after, accused me of having betrayed the country. I substituted it for a Constitutional Government, seeing that the people spoke in favour of it in their meetings and that public opinion required it. And I have not hesitated to leave Spain, making for her the greatest sacrifice of my life, when I understood that Spain no longer loved me. It would be very sad if I did not hope that, one day, history will do me justice.'[3] This dignified statement must have gone a long way towards reassuring the government, if any reassurance was needed, that they had nothing to fear from him in the form of any efforts to regain his crown by force or by invasion.

Nevertheless the Cortes was still determined to put King Alfonso on trial *in absentia* later that year. Calvo Sotelo, the only Deputy who was not allowed to take his seat, was exiled in Portugal but sent the Cortes a strong protest against the indictment of their former sovereign. He alleged that in an interview in the house of Dr Maranon between Count Romanones, representing the King, and Alcalá Zamora, representing the provisional government, an agreement was made with King Alfonso by virtue of which he refrained from resistance and went away quietly. At that time the Republic considered dethronement sufficient, so it could not now impose additional penalties, such as confiscation of the King's property, without resuscitating the Bill of Attainder methods that had long since gone from what were referred to as 'civilised codes of justice'.

In addition to his exile and the confiscation of everything that he owned in Spain, an indictment laid before the Cortes on 19 November proposed that if King Alfonso ever returned to Spain, he should be seized and sentenced to life imprisonment. If he was to do anything to provoke armed rebellion, the death penalty would be imposed. It was also proposed that all his decorations, rights and titles would be taken from him, and that he would be forbidden to use them within or outside Spain. This sentence against him was to be posted up in every village throughout Spain, and communicated to all States and to the League of Nations. Those elements of the press which were traditionally sympathetic to the monarchy were silenced. Under a recently passed Law of Defence of the Republic, they could not say anything favourable about the monarchy without being subject to severe penalties.

After a sitting that lasted from early evening until about 4 a.m. on 20 November 1931, the Cortes passed a resolution that found the former King guilty of high treason, as one who 'utilised the executive powers conferred upon him to prejudice the Constitution of the State, violating in the most criminal manner the juridical order of his country'. As a result he was placed outside the pale of the law; the Republic would take possession of his property, and any Spanish citizen would be free to seize his person should he enter national territory.

Count Romanones, the former Prime Minister, spoke gallantly in the King's defence. He declared that the accusation against the King lacked the most elementary form of justice because it did not provide for the accused man to be heard. If the King was not in Spain it was certainly not the King's fault, and it was necessary that he should be allowed to appoint a defence. The terms of the accusation, he said, were full of vagaries, such as leanings towards absolutism, dictatorial inclinations, distributing titles and decorations to make himself loved, and so forth. Proofs were what should be produced but had not been produced. He appealed to former ministers in the house, among them Zamora, to ask if the King had ever attempted to make them sign a decree with which they did not agree. With regard to the dictatorship, it was well known that the Dictator had public opinion and the army on his side, so the King could hardly go against them. When public opinion failed the Dictator, the King interpreted the will of the nation as best he could by a return to constitutional rule, and in so doing had ironically convoked the elections which had resulted in bringing about a Spanish republic.

One or two other voices were raised, albeit less eloquently, arguing against the indictment, but the tide of opinion ran against the King and it was passed. Zamora accepted full responsibility for having urged the King to depart before nightfall on 14 April, as he intended that the republic should be in a position to prevent possible tragedies that might have stained the dawning of the new era red with blood. But the King had departed without an escort, the people had let him go, and as a result the great powers – even England, whose royal family was related to him so closely – had recognised the new republic immediately. The general view was that there could be no doubting the King's full responsibility for crimes committed against the Spanish nation, but a trial was pointless as the nation had already given its verdict, by expelling the dynasty without bloodshed.[4]

As ready to defend the King as ever, *ABC* attacked the proceedings as 'a rancorous and needless act of persecution'. They were 'vengeful and unnecessary', and would not make the republic any stronger, nor secure any advantage for the present regime. The Cortes fined the management 1,000 pesetas and ordered suspension of publication for three days, for having infringed the Defence of the Republic Act.

Further unequivocal championship of the former monarch and sympathy for him in his plight came from Winston Churchill, in a short but perceptive character study published six years later. 'To be born a king; never to have been anything else but a king; to have reigned for forty-six years [*sic*], and then to be dethroned!' the statesman wrote. 'To begin life again in middle age under novel and contracted conditions with a status and in a state of mind never before experienced, barred from the one calling to which a lifetime has been devoted!' It was indeed a 'harsh destiny' to be rejected by the nation which he had presided over during an age when it had grown in prosperity and reputation.[5]

His position was comparable with that of another contemporary former sovereign who had left his country and was now living in exile, the former German Emperor William. Yet while the latter had more or less accepted his dethronement and was living in relative contentment, the much younger King Alfonso still hoped that the sudden reversal of his fortunes might yet be overturned. Spain might not revert to monarchical rule within his own lifetime, he knew, but he may have had a presentiment that the pendulum would swing back. Yet his time had come and gone, and it would be up to a younger member of the Bourbon family to take on the mantle of sovereignty. 'I hope I shall not go back,' he declared, 'for that will only mean that the Spanish people are not prosperous and happy.'[6]

* * *

In July 1936 civil war broke out in Spain, with the monarchists joining the Falangists and nationalists under the banner of the nationalist leader General Franco. From his exile in Italy King Alfonso watched the course of events with intense interest, hoping for and expecting the Republican government to fall sooner rather than later. On his departure from his country, he had declared that he would have nothing to do with any attempt to unseat any Spanish government of any political complexion. It seemed ironic that the conflict which he had left his kingdom to avert had broken out within a little more than five years. However, any hopes he may have nursed of being recalled to the throne which he had not formally abdicated, slight though they were, were dashed once and for all in July 1937 when Franco asserted that 'should the moment for a restoration arrive the new monarchy would be very different from that of 1931, different in constitution and in the person who should reincarnate it'.[7]

Much as he might pay lip service to the institution of monarchy, Franco's expressions of contempt towards the Bourbons made plain his attitude as well as the fact that he was loath to relinquish power. King Alfonso donated one million pesetas to the nationalist cause, and soon afterwards wrote to Franco expressing concern at the restoration being seemingly low on his list of priorities. Franco replied on 4 December 1937, suggesting bluntly that the problems which had caused the Spanish Civil War were of the King's making; that there were urgent tasks to be carried out after the conflict, and that the former sovereign could not expect to play any part in the country's future destiny. The new Spain they were forging had so little in common with the liberal and constitutional Spain over which he had ruled that his training and 'old-fashioned political practices necessarily provoke the anxieties and resentments of Spaniards'. Franco's reply ended with a request to the former sovereign to look to the preparation of his heir instead.[8]

The Spaniards, it was observed, were 'tearing each other to pieces'. For all its faults, the era of King Alfonso XIII had perhaps been a golden age after all, or at least a reasonably contented one, compared to the period of bloodshed and dictatorship that was to follow it.

Though the outlook for a restoration seemed bleak, Don Juan remained his father's brightest hope, especially in view of the sad fate of his brothers. In 1933, while undergoing treatment at a clinic in Switzerland, the eldest son Alfonso, Prince of Asturias, fell in love with a Cuban woman, Edelmira Sampedro-Ocejo y Robato, who was a patient at the same institution, and told his family that he was going to marry her. She was neither rich nor socially acceptable, especially for the heir to a throne which was in abeyance but might perhaps be restored at any time, and King Alfonso refused to give them his blessing. The younger Alfonso replied that he was going to go through with the marriage anyway, and renounced his rights to the succession, being given the title Count of Covadonga. As he expected to have only a few years to live, and believed that his family's chances of regaining their throne were only slight, it was not much of a sacrifice.

Queen Ena and her daughters attended the wedding on 21 June 1933. She begged the King to show some family solidarity by coming to join them, especially as the bridegroom was their eldest child, but he refused, telling her that he had 'lost this son for ever'.[9] Relations between the King and Queen were particularly difficult at the time, partly as Alfonso still strongly resented her friendship with the Leceras, and partly as she was bitter about his bullying attitude towards their unfortunate son.

Nevertheless the Count of Covadonga was very much like his father in one way. Both had a roving eye, and the marriage did not long survive his infidelities. It was dissolved by the civil law of Cuba in May 1937, and he went to the altar a second time, with Martha Rocafort, that same summer. This union lasted a mere eight months and they were divorced by January 1938.

At the time of his elder brother's wedding, Don Jaime also renounced his rights to the throne of Spain and took the title Duke of Segovia. In March 1935 he married Emmanuella Dampierre Ruspoli, daughter of Viscount Roger de Dampierre, a Papal Duke, and the Roman Princess Victoria Ruspoli.

For the last few years the former King and Queen had done their best to avoid each other. One rare exception was when a hostess at Lausanne invited them both to a lunch party. They accepted with some reluctance, and found themselves in a party of twelve, sitting at opposite ends of the table. Recently there had been rumours of a romance between a prince of the Bonaparte family and their younger daughter Cristina, and Ena had telegraphed Alfonso about it. The matter had remained more or less confidential – and in fact never came to anything – so Ena was exasperated as well as thoroughly embarrassed when Alfonso proceeded to shout across the table at her, 'What a ridiculous telegram you sent me from Balmoral!'[10] Naturally this outburst made it an uncomfortable occasion for everyone present.

Both their daughters had been anxious that as probable carriers of haemophilia like their mother, they might be condemned to a life of spinsterhood. Remembering his bitter disappointments, King Alfonso felt morally obliged to warn any prospective suitors of the danger they might face. Happily any such fears proved unfounded. Beatrice married Alexander Torlonia, Prince of Civitella-Cesi, in January 1935, and Maria Cristina married Enrico Marone-Cinzano in June 1940. They were given the titles Count and Countess Marone. It had been a source of some amusement in the family that the word Marone meant Brown in English, and that the Infanta could therefore become Mrs Brown on marriage.

When his two elder brothers had renounced their rights to the succession, Don Juan became his father's heir and thus the new Prince of Asturias. After the family's departure from Spain he had had to leave the college at Cadiz and instead entered the Royal Naval College at Dartmouth. When he received his father's telegram informing him of his brothers' renunciations, he was a serving officer in the Royal Navy aboard HMS *Enterprise*, anchored in Bombay. As he knew that this new role, which might result in him being recalled to the throne at any time, would involve him leaving his beloved naval career, he accepted with some reluctance. In May 1934 he was promoted to sub-lieutenant, and in September he joined the battleship HMS *Iron Duke*. Ten months later he passed his examinations in naval gunnery and navigation, which would have enabled him to become a lieutenant and command a vessel. To do this, however, he would need to renounce his Spanish nationality, a step he did not wish to take. As a result his cousin King George V granted him the rank of honorary lieutenant.

A few months later Don Juan wanted to join the cruiser *Baleares*, but Franco forbade him to do so as he did not want a popular monarchist figurehead playing a prominent role in one of the armed forces. To allow him to join would pose an unacceptable threat to the head of state's personal standing. When the vessel was torpedoed on 6 March, Franco looked back on this decision with mixed feelings as he remarked wryly, 'And to think that Don Juan de Bourbon wanted to serve on board.'[11]

Unlike his elder brothers, Don Juan was to prove fortunate in his choice of wife. In January 1935, at a party in Rome given by the King and Queen of Italy on the eve of his sister Beatrice's marriage, he had met Doña Maria de las Mercedes Bourbon and Orleans. As she was descended from the royal families of Spain, Italy, Austria and France, she could hardly be more suitable as a prospective bride, and they were married in the capital on 12 October. Queen Ena did not attend the wedding but King Alfonso was there, and several thousand Spanish monarchists used the ceremony as an excuse for a demonstration against the Spanish republic. They settled at the Villa Saint Blaise, Cannes, and their eldest child, a daughter Maria del Pilar, was born on 30 July 1936.

Twelve days earlier the Spanish Civil War had broken out, initially through a revolt of military commanders in Morocco against the growing socialist and anti-clerical tendencies of the Popular Front Republican government of President Azana. The insurgents were led by General Sanjurjo and General Franco, who overthrew the government and the latter was proclaimed Chief of the Spanish State in October. The Republicans' power base was primarily urban and largely secular, while some other, more rural, regions also supported them. Their support was particularly strong in Madrid, Catalonia and the conservative Roman Catholic Basque country, partly because these regions were granted a strong autonomy during the Second Republic, while the ultimately successful *Nationals*, led by Franco, had a primarily rural, religious and conservative power base in favour of the centralisation of power.

At first the revolt in Morocco was welcomed by Don Juan and his father. They followed the progress of the rebels by radio, and a group of monarchist supporters thought it would be politically prudent for the former to be seen fighting on the nationalist side. Both the King and Queen supported this decision, and on 1 August he crossed the French border into Spain in a chauffeur-driven Bentley, ahead of a small convoy of cars carrying his followers. Despite their determination, the rebel commander in the north, General Emilio Mola, was thoroughly anti-monarchist, and without consulting the other generals he ordered the Civil Guard to ensure that Don Juan left

Spain immediately. As a result several pro-monarchist officers transferred their political loyalties from Mola to Franco.

After Don Juan's return to Cannes, the presence of important supporters of the Spanish military rebellion attracted the population of local leftists, and militant groups took to gathering outside the villa each evening shouting pro-Republican slogans. As Doña Maria was expecting their second child, Don Juan decided to move to Rome, partly as his father was already resident there and partly because the authorities would ensure that there would be no repeat of similar unpleasantness. At first they lived in the Hotel Eden, but later moved into a flat on the top floor of his sister Beatrice's home, the Palazzo Torlonia in Via Bocca di Leone.

On 5 January 1938 Don Juan Carlos, elder son of the Prince of Asturias, was born one month prematurely at the Anglo-American hospital. Having being assured that the baby's arrival was not imminent, Don Juan had gone hunting with friends. When he received the telegram announcing his son's arrival he set off in his Bentley, driving at such speed that he broke an axle spring. King Alfonso could not resist the temptation to play a trick on his son, and when he welcomed him he was holding a Chinese baby boy in his arms. The latter had been born at the same time in an adjoining room to the secretary at the Chinese Embassy. Though Don Juan was not taken in, when he saw his baby son the thought crossed his mind that he would almost have preferred the Chinese infant. Even Doña Maria was less than enamoured at first of her child, later recalling that he had 'big bulging eyes' and was 'as ugly as sin', but magnanimously she admitted that 'he soon sorted himself out'. He was christened at the chapel of the Knights of Malta by Cardinal Pacelli, later Pope Pius XII. Yet the earliest photographs of Juan Carlos were not taken until he had 'sorted himself out' and was aged about five months.[12]

Though the year 1938 had started well for the Bourbons, with the birth of the Prince who was destined to be the next King of Spain, tragedy was to follow. On the night of 6 September Alfonso was driving home from a nightclub in Miami with a cigarette girl, Mildred Gaydon, whom he was planning to make his third wife. He swerved to avoid an oncoming vehicle, struck a telephone pole and bled to death from internal injuries. King Alfonso was in Rome and Queen Ena on the Isle of Wight when they each received the news by telegram. Queen Ena took the first available steamer to New York but did not arrive until after his death. She and King Alfonso agreed that their son's funeral should take place in Florida with Catholic rites, and then he should be laid to rest in the Graceland Memorial Park cemetery.

This sudden if perhaps not totally unexpected death had mirrored that of his youngest brother and fellow haemophiliac Gonzalo, who had gone out for a drive in Switzerland with his sister Beatrice at the wheel in August 1934. They too had to swerve to avoid an oncoming bicycle, and crashed into a wall. Though neither was badly injured in the crash, it brought on a major attack of bleeding in Gonzalo's case, and he died two days later, aged nineteen.

Not long after Queen Ena's return to Europe, she became aware that there was a grave likelihood of conflict breaking out and involving much of Europe. Anthony Eden, the British Foreign Secretary, visited her at her London home to warn her that in the event of war, the British government could not guarantee her safety if she stayed in England. Technically she was no longer a member of the British royal family, and if she was trapped in London by the outbreak of hostilities there could be complications, not least financial ones. She had had no real home since leaving Spain, and though a part of her remained very much English, and though she wanted to remain near her mother who was now in her early eighties and very frail, she decided to go to Switzerland where she had various friends.

Her destination was L'Elysee, Lausanne, where she came as the guest of Mary, Marchioness of Craymayel, arriving in August 1939, a few days before the outbreak of the Second World War. King Alfonso's health was deteriorating, and though they had drifted too far apart for there to be any genuine chance of a reconciliation, she wanted to be near him. In the following year she left for Rome, though after Italy's entry into the war on Germany's side she realised that as an English-born Queen she could not stay there. However, with the King becoming progressively weaker and in increasing pain, she was reluctant to go too far away, and in the end she compromised by living just outside Rome itself.

On 15 January 1941 King Alfonso finally renounced his rights to the throne in favour of Don Juan. For the last two years Alfonso had been suffering from angina pectoris, the disease which had killed his mother, and he sensed that his own death could not be far away. He had clung to the hope that Franco intended to restore the monarchy, and was outraged that any such prospect was dwindling as republicanism became more firmly entrenched. A growing sense of bitterness darkened his last days, and to the end he remained angry about the man who had in effect supplanted him in Spain, telling the American journalist John T. Whitaker that he picked Franco out when he was a nobody. 'He has double-crossed and deceived me at every turn.'[13] When he asked repeatedly whether Franco had made any enquiries about his health, the family told him out of kindness that he had sent a telegram asking about his condition. In fact Franco expressed no concern whatsoever.

Though they had rarely seen each other since separating nearly ten years earlier, Ena was alarmed at the news she received of her husband's deteriorating condition. She was living in a villa in the hills overlooking Rome, while he was in the Grand Hotel. When she was finally shown into his room, she was horrified at the sight of him. He had just had a severe heart attack, and asked her to forgive him for not getting out of his chair to greet her, as he was 'suffering like mad'.[14]

Ena and the children moved into the hotel so she could be as close to her husband as possible. Though he was suffering multiple heart attacks and knew he was dying, he made it clear he did not particularly want to see her. Perhaps those words of ten years earlier still rankled. On one occasion she had to force her way into the sickroom when she thought the end was near. By the time his life was ebbing away and he was receiving the last rites from his Jesuit confessor, she was by his side, but he was drifting in and out of consciousness and was only vaguely aware that the wife whom he had loved all too briefly was with him. She slept in the sickroom on the last night and held his hands as he told her that it was 'all over'.[15] He died at 2 p.m. on 28 February 1941, aged fifty-four.

A funeral was held two weeks later at the Church of St Mary of the Angels in Rome, after which his body was given a provisional burial there. He had left a written request, and extracted a solemn promise from Don Juan, that one day he would be interred in the grave he had chosen for himself alongside that of his ancestor King Carlos V in the Escorial. Franco did not intend to declare a period of national mourning for the King, and was only grudgingly persuaded to change his mind when black bunting appeared from balconies in the streets of Madrid. With some reluctance he sent a red and gold wreath to the funeral.

The widowed Queen stayed in Rome for several months, living a discreet and secluded existence with her daughter Beatrice and her husband at the Palazzo Torlonia. During the summer she decided to leave Rome and return to Switzerland. She had only remained where she was to be near her children, but she now recognised that it was time to move on. In January 1942 she made her home at the Hotel Royal. It was the fourth time in eleven years that she had had to start life afresh in another country, as she noted in a letter to Queen Mary, and she found the effect rather unsettling. However, as one of the few neutral countries, Switzerland was one of the very few options open to her.

Time gradually softened her attitude towards the memory of her husband. Though theirs had been an unhappy marriage, she proved forgiving towards him. 'Poor, poor King,' she was heard to say some years after his death. 'Always such a gentleman and so good!'[16] With her positive, forward-looking nature, she strove to remember the good and blot out the bad. If not completely happy, at least she was free from his shadow, and now she could find some degree of contentment. She doted on her grandchildren, who in turn loved her and relished her visits. They were particularly glad that she sportingly pretended not to notice when they helped themselves quietly to second and even third helpings of their favourite chocolate cake which she invariably provided for them at tea.

TWELVE

'Better to be dumb than to stammer'

After the death of King Alfonso XIII, in the eyes of Spanish monarchists, Don Juan was now *de jure* King Juan III, and he took the title Conde de Barcelona, the prerogative of the King of Spain. However, Franco did not bring back the monarchy and some pro-monarchist conservatives were reluctant to risk their careers by supporting Juan too openly. As his mother was English and as he had served in the Royal Navy, he was keen to look to Britain for support, but his residency in Fascist Italy placed him in a difficult position, especially while the Axis Powers seemed in the ascendant. One of his advisers recommended he should consider seeking support from Berlin, or at least try to secure its benevolent neutrality towards monarchical restoration in Spain. Overtures were made to the Italian and German authorities, and Spanish generals suggested to Field-Marshal Goering in 1942 that he should help to place Don Juan on the Spanish throne in exchange for an undertaking that Spain should maintain her pro-Axis policy. Franco was unenthusiastic, and such approaches were soon abandoned.

After the Allied landings in North Africa Don Juan felt it prudent to distance himself from Franco in an effort to persuade the Allies that after the war monarchy could provide stability and national reconciliation. Franco was warned by General Alfredo Kindelan, the most senior general on active service and the Captain-General of Catalonia, that if he formally committed Spain to the Axis Powers, he would have to be replaced as head of state.[1] Franco denied any commitment to the Axis, implied he was anxious to relinquish power, and said he wanted Don Juan to be his successor. In November 1942 Don Juan published a declaration in the *Journal de*

Genève, to the effect that he was 'the legitimate depositary of the secular political inheritance of the Spanish monarchy', and that when the people decided the time had come for its restoration, he would not hesitate to put himself at their disposal. He had no intention of imposing on his own authority the forms and institutions of their national life; his highest ambition was 'to be King of a Spain in which all Spaniards finally reconciled to each other can live in common'.[2]

Franco refused to commit himself; in 1943 he stated that monarchy represented 'the final process of the unification and imperial expansion of Spain', and a few months later said the regime would one day take 'the form which Spain possessed in the days of her glory'. Despite persistent demands by monarchists among the Cortes, military and naval officials, demanding an immediate return to 'the traditional Catholic monarchy' as the only way of bringing political stability back to the country, Franco refused to commit himself. In March 1945 a frustrated and disillusioned Don Juan issued a manifesto from Lausanne, drawing attention to the fact that since the events of April 1931 Spain had 'passed through one of the most tragic periods of her history', and regretting that the nation was seeing herself dragged into a new fratricidal struggle and finding herself isolated in the world. It was only a traditional monarchy, he declared, 'that can be the instrument of peace and concord leading to reconciliation among Spaniards', as well as guarantee respect for the country abroad and 'call into being that harmonious combination of order and liberty, which forms the Christian concept of the State'.[3]

In March 1947 a Succession Law, *Ley de Sucesión*, was drafted, passed by the Cortes, and ratified by an overwhelming majority by plebiscite. The law proclaimed that Spain was 'a Catholic and social state, and is a kingdom in accordance with tradition'.[4] General Franco was confirmed as head of state until death or incapacity, after which he would be succeeded by a person of royal blood chosen by a combined council of the kingdom and government and accepted by two-thirds of the Cortes. To qualify he must be male, Spanish, Catholic and over 30 years of age, and he would have to swear to observe the fundamental laws of Spain. Don Juan attacked this on the grounds that it interfered with the principles of legitimacy, and his stand was supported by the leaders of both the liberal and traditional monarchists. Later that year he and Franco met, and they agreed that Don Juan's eldest son Juan Carlos, now aged 9, should be educated in Spain.

Queen Ena doted on this grandson, who may have been a very ugly baby during his first few months but had grown up to be a good-looking young man. Though she was not totally at ease with the idea of his being sent to Spain to be educated, she accepted the family's decision to do so without question. At the same time she had some misgivings about her son, whom she thought did not have sufficient strength of character and lacked the necessary qualities of leadership to become king in a restored Spanish monarchy. She had a presentiment that the future would lie with her grandson instead. Remembering how difficult she had found learning the Spanish language, she made a great effort to ensure that he would have as good an accent as possible. As he had been brought up in Italy and Switzerland, speaking French as much as Spanish, she taught him to roll the letter 'r' in the Spanish style, in preference to the French 'r' which everyone thought sounded comical to Spaniards.[5]

Even after the Succession Law was ratified, a monarchical restoration was by no means certain. Franco's coldness, if not outright hostility, to the Bourbons was evident, and this was the main reason why Queen Ena was uneasy about her grandson being educated in the country. The situation was further complicated in December 1949 when Don Juan's eldest surviving brother Don Jaime announced that he considered his renunciation of his rights to the throne in 1933 invalid. He had done so at that time because he considered that as a deaf-mute he could never become king. In 1947 he had divorced his first wife, and in August 1949 he married Charlotte Tiedemann, a nightclub singer from Königsberg, in East Prussia, whose first marriage had also broken down. This one fared little better as the domineering Charlotte, a heavy drinker, soon became notorious for making mischief within the family. She caused particular offence when she encouraged her daughter by her first marriage to call herself Helga de Bourbon, thus implying that she was a member of the Spanish royal family.

However, Charlotte's marriage to Don Jaime brought one positive result. She taught her husband to communicate verbally to some degree, succeeding where speech therapists and others had failed, and within a few months he felt cured of his affliction. Unfortunately for the rest of the family, he and Charlotte decided this qualified him to reassert his rights as his father's heir to the vacant throne of Spain. There were suspicions that Franco was behind the move, and that he had paid Don Jaime to make such an announcement, paying his debts and providing him with an allowance in order to do so. Don Jaime, Franco knew, would be far easier to manipulate.

In March 1952 it was announced by a spokesman for Don Juan that Don Jaime's marriage to Emanuela de Dampierre had never been officially dissolved according to Spanish law. A furious Don Jaime claimed it was strange that the question of his second marriage had never been raised until the moment when he began an action to claim his place as successor to his father. He owed everything, he declared, to his present wife, not least his health, at a time when everybody else had abandoned him. Nevertheless, his divorce was never recognised by the Roman Catholic Church in Spain.

* * *

In the summer of 1954 Juan Carlos joined a cruise of the Greek islands on board a destroyer, organised by Queen Frederica of Greece. Several other members of the younger generation of European royalty were also there, among them Queen Frederica's daughter Princess Sofia. Their first meeting was hardly promising, and some years later he recalled that she told him she was learning judo. He told her that such an accomplishment would be of little use to her, whereupon she asked him for his hand – and threw him to the floor.[6]

At around this time Franco and Don Juan discussed Juan Carlos' future education, the question of universities and military training. Don Juan wanted to send him to the university at Bologna, with its world-famous reputation, or to that at Louvain in Belgium before he returned to Spain to resume his studies at the Military Academy, Zaragoza, then at the Naval College, Marin. Franco disagreed, saying that in such a case Juan Carlos would be at least twenty-two by the time he returned to Spain. At that age it would be very difficult for him to fit into military life, surrounded by boys of seventeen and eighteen, and he would not feel at ease with fellow cadets so much younger than himself. He would do his military training first, and then go to one of the Spanish universities, as it was 'out of the question for a prince who is to reign over Spain some day to be brought up abroad'.[7] Despite his reservations, Don Juan had no choice but to agree.

In December 1955 Juan Carlos went to the Zaragoza academy for two years. He intended to get on with his life as an ordinary cadet, in spite of a campaign against Don Juan in the press, which was overwhelmingly on the side of the *Movimiento*.* It was hardly surprising that he was irritated, not to say provoked, by constant insinuations from his fellow cadets about his father. They told him to his face that Don Juan was a freemason, or a bad patriot, mainly because he had served in the British Royal Navy. Such comments occasionally led to secret fights in the stables at night, though they were probably relatively good-natured physical spats and never led to any serious injuries. Juan Carlos complained about attacks in the media to Franco, who answered dismissively that he had no control over an independent press. The Prince knew that he could do nothing but laugh at such a downright lie.

---

* Formed during the early years of Franco's rule, the *Movimiento Nacional* was a coalition of the Falangists, who wanted to set up a fascist republic, and the Alfonsine and Carlist monarchists. To ensure that their rivalries did not undermine the war effort and to assert his control over their activities, Franco, who emerged as Generalissimo or Commander-in-Chief of the rebel forces, fused all three into a single entity whose full name was *Falange Española Tradicionalista y de las Juntas de Ofensiva Nacional-Sindicalista* (FET de las JONS), or *Movimiento Nacional* for short. It was the only lawful political organisation in Spain until after Franco's death.

Though Don Juan and his children were free from the taint of haemophilia, another tragedy would shortly strike the family. In March 1956 Juan Carlos and his younger brother 'Alfonsito', aged fourteen, went to spend the Easter holidays with their parents and siblings at Estoril, 'the Portuguese Riviera'. Alfonsito, then at school in Madrid, was to become a cadet at the Spanish naval college near Pontevedra. Regarded as more intelligent and outgoing than his introspective elder brother, he was the family favourite, though with their common love of golf and sailing the brothers were always close.

On 29 March, Maundy Thursday, the entire family attended morning mass and took communion at the Church of San Antonio de Estoril. Later that day Don Juan and Juan Carlos accompanied Alfonsito to the Estoril golf club where he was taking part in a competition; he won the semi-final and was looking forward to playing in the final two days later. They then attended an early evening mass in the Church of San Antonio and finally returned home. While waiting for dinner the two brothers went for target practice with a .22 revolver, which ended in Alfonsito being accidentally shot dead. Exactly what happened has never been fully explained, though several scenarios have been advanced. It has been widely accepted that Juan Carlos' hand was on the trigger when the fatal shot was fired.[8] Don Juan and Doña Maria were summoned to find their younger son on the floor in a pool of blood, and though Don Juan tried to revive him he died in his arms. After the funeral on Saturday 31 March, Don Juan threw the pistol into the sea.

Juan Carlos was ordered back to the Zaragoza academy within two days of the accident. He was desolate at his brother's death, and a previously extrovert character became noticeably introspective and withdrawn, more morose and guarded in his speech and actions. It was rumoured that he was so overcome by grief that he was considering renouncing his rights to the throne and joining a friary as a penance. Relations with his father were never the same again. Don Juan blamed his wife even more than his son, as he had forbidden the boys to play with the gun after he caught them shooting at street lights for fun, but she gave in to their repeated requests to be allowed to play with it again. She fell into a profound depression, took to drinking heavily, and at length spent some time in a clinic near Frankfurt.

Don Jaime, the brother of Don Juan, was among those who sent a message of sympathy to the bereaved parents. However, the following month he told his secretary that he disagreed with the stance of his brother, who in order to prevent future speculation had neither demanded the opening of an official enquiry into the accident nor called for an autopsy on the body of his dead son, as was usual in such a case. These comments found their way into the French press. Regarding himself as head of the house of Bourbon, on the grounds that he was the eldest surviving son of the late King Alfonso XIII, Don Jaime wrote to Don Juan's secretary demanding that he request in his name a judicial enquiry in order to clarify officially the circumstances of his nephew Alfonso's death. He himself could not accept 'that someone who is incapable of accepting his own responsibilities should aspire to the throne of Spain.'[9] Fortunately for the sake of the rest of the family, the secretary did nothing to act on this unduly insensitive demand.

Franco's attitude towards the family had long been lukewarm at the best of times, and he was not slow to exploit the incident. At a meeting with Don Juan four years later, the Caudillo told him bluntly that the Bourbon family was doomed. His Highness had two brothers, another deaf and dumb, a blind daughter and one son shot dead. With so many disasters in one family, they could not possibly appeal to the Spanish people or expect to be called back to the throne.[10]

On 18 July 1957 Juan Carlos passed out as second-lieutenant at Zaragoza. He then went to Lausanne to pay his grandmother a short visit, and while in Switzerland he gave a press interview in which he confirmed that he regarded his father as King. This drew forth a riposte from Franco, who said that like his father, the Prince was badly advised and he should not speak so much. In August he entered the naval school at Marin in Galicia. He faced initial hostility from some of his fellow cadets, but once settled in, his ready affability and capacity for physical hardship won them over and helped him to make friends easily.

195

At the same time he had a ready eye for female company. For a while he was infatuated with a childhood friend, Princess Maria Gabriella of Savoy. As she was the daughter of the former King Umberto of Italy, an exile whose chances of regaining his throne were almost negligible, neither Don Juan nor Franco were enthusiastic about the relationship going any further.

A more promising one at first glance was that with Countess Olghina Nicolis di Robilant, an Italian aristocrat and minor film actress, whom he met in December 1956 during the Christmas holidays at Estoril. She was four years older than him, but their infatuation was instant and their affair lasted on and off for almost four years. However, he was well aware that his duties to his father and to Spain would prevent him from marrying her, and he admitted as much to her. Some years later a number of the letters that he wrote her were published in the Italian and then the Spanish press, and in interviews which Olghina gave as a result, she said that Don Juan had done everything he could to put obstacles in the way of their relationship. Nevertheless she had fond memories of a passionate and impulsive young man who adored fast cars and motor boats. At the same time he never forgot his position and was always aware of his destiny. He was 'serious albeit no saint', not shy but inclined to be puritanical, and disliked women who seemed calculating or immoral; very generous, even though he had little money at the time; and unlike General Franco he disliked hunting as he had no desire to kill animals.

For a while there was speculation in the press about the relationship between Juan Carlos and Maria Gabriella, culminating in a rumour that their engagement would be announced in October 1960 at the silver wedding celebrations of Don Juan and Doña Maria, but it was not to be. Both Don Juan and Franco were unenthusiastic about the prospect, partly as they thought he was not yet mature enough, and partly as they found her too frivolous. This was not the only conjecture about Juan Carlos at around this time. Added to Franco's persistently lukewarm attitude towards a restoration of the monarchy after his death was his growing feeling that Alfonso, Juan Carlos' cousin, should be 'cultivated' as the heir-in-waiting, in case the son appeared as unsatisfactory as his father.

In September 1958 Juan Carlos joined the Air Force academy of San Javier in Murcia. With him he took his pet monkey Fito, which he dressed in Air Force uniform, as well as teaching him to salute and shake hands. This was frowned upon by his superiors, who confined the Prince to barracks, and at length Don Juan persuaded him to part company with Fito. In the spring of 1959, while still a cadet at the academy, he took part in Franco's annual victory parade to celebrate the end of the civil war. At some points of the parade he was heartily applauded, but at others a group of Falangists booed and mocked him, calling out that they did not want 'idiot kings'. In December 1959 his military training came to an end, and he was given the rank of lieutenant in each of the three armed services. At one month short of his twenty-second birthday he had visibly matured during his time in the academies, and Franco was pleased with his progress. But he was increasingly disenchanted with Don Juan, whom he told a colleague was 'beyond redemption' and 'with every passing day . . . more untrustworthy', on the grounds that he was still set on the idea of a liberal monarchy, and too ready to go along with the last person to offer him advice.

Next Juan Carlos was to go to university, and on 19 October 1960 he entered the faculty of law of the University of Madrid, accompanied by a police escort. He took the brunt of jeering from some Carlist supporters, and afterwards the rector threatened to expel those responsible if such scenes were ever repeated. During his time at university he nevertheless had to endure a measure of Carlist hostility, part of a plan to disrupt the inevitability of his being named successor. Next year he graduated and went to live in the palace at Zarzuela, where he began to carry out official engagements.

Meanwhile, another important matter was about to be settled. Since their first meeting on the cruise of the Greek islands, the paths of Juan Carlos and Sofia of Greece crossed again, first in July 1958 when they were both present at the wedding of the daughter of the Duke of Württemberg at Althausen Castle near Stuttgart, and again in September 1960 when Sofia's brother, Crown Prince Constantine, was participating in the Greek Olympic sailing team. The Spanish and Greek royal families were both staying in the same hotel, and the young people saw much of each other. At the time Juan Carlos had a moustache, and Sofia told him she thought it looked horrible. When he told her he did not see what he could do about it, she took him by the hand to a bathroom, sat him down, put a towel around his neck and shaved it. Far from objecting, after he returned to Portugal he told a friend that he and the Greek princess had become devoted to each other.

They were together again in England the following year. On 8 June 1961 they were among guests at York Minster for the wedding of Queen Elizabeth II's cousin Edward, Duke of Kent, to Miss Katherine Worsley, and Juan Carlos was chosen to escort Sofia. Such an arrangement may have been less by accident and more by design, as it was thought that Queen Ena and Queen Frederica both asked Lord Mountbatten to bring his influence to bear on the matter. Later Juan Carlos said that they effectively became engaged in England. Perhaps appropriately, at this point the only common language they had was English, though hers was more fluent than his, as her father had lived in exile in England for eleven years (before she was born), she had been brought up partly by a Scottish nurse, and as a small girl she had spent most of the war with her family in South Africa. She also spoke German well, whereas the other languages in which he was fluent were French, Italian and Portuguese. Now she concentrated on learning Spanish while he made an effort to improve his English, and from then on they would speak to each other alternately in both languages.

There was something of an obstacle to their marriage in that Juan Carlos was not considered an ideal candidate. Sofia was the daughter of a reigning monarch, while he was merely the disputed heir to the empty throne of a country where the future of the monarchy was still in considerable doubt. Moreover there were religious differences to be overcome, in that he was Roman Catholic and she was Greek Orthodox. These aspects apart, she was an ideal future wife for him. As personalities they were thoroughly compatible. He was good-looking, fun to be with, and enjoyed 'larking about', though he could be taciturn and melancholy; as she realised, he was still deeply affected by the loss of his brother. He found her attractive, cultured and unassuming, and he also approved of what he saw as a puritanical streak as well. The first Queen Frederica knew of it was when Crown Prince Constantine rang her one night to tell her that there was 'something funny going on between Sophie and Juanito'.[11] When the news was confirmed, King Paul and Queen Frederica were delighted but greatly concerned about the religious issue, and agreed there would have to be some discussions on the subject. Nevertheless, they invited the young couple to spend the rest of the summer with the Greek royal family at Mon Repos in Corfu.

As yet, the engagement was still unofficial. Efforts were made to ensure that no news of their relationship should reach the Spanish embassy in Greece. Don Juan and his family returned to Estoril from Greece later that summer to be asked by Ibáñez Martin, the Spanish ambassador in Lisbon, about the rumours of a supposed idyll, and Don Juan told him that there was nothing in them. He wanted Franco to be among the last to know. In September Martin asked Don Juan a second time more directly, saying that it was important Franco should be kept informed; and, moreover, that according to the *Ley de Sucesión*, claimants to the throne had to seek permission of the Cortes in any marriage plans. Don Juan, who had never accepted the *Ley*, said that the relationship between his son and the Greek princess was in its early stages, and nobody was in a position to predict the outcome. As Juan Carlos' father, he had no objections to the relationship.

Next day Don Juan set off from Lisbon airport for Lausanne. Just before the plane took off, Martin asked him again for news of the engagement, to be told that it was pure fantasy. He did not reveal that he was going to meet the young couple, as well as King Paul and Queen Frederica, for a family dinner to be presided over by Queen Ena. At the dinner table that evening King Paul asked them to make an announcement of the engagement sooner or later. He wanted to put an end to the rumours and uncertainty, and he also wanted to boost the monarchist cause in Greece, where an election was due shortly. On 13 September the Greek and Portuguese newspapers carried news of the engagement on their front pages, with photographs of a beaming Sofia and a slightly apprehensive-looking Juan

Carlos. In Athens an official announcement was made by Crown Prince Constantine, acting as regent in his father's absence from the country, followed by a 21-gun salute from Mount Lycabettus.

At the time Franco was fishing on his yacht, and Don Juan contacted him on his ship-to-shore radio to tell him the news. As there was a large amount of interference, he had to shout to make himself heard. He explained over the radio as best he could that he had wanted to send a letter, but the King of Greece had asked for the news to be announced early. Once Franco realised the significance of what he was hearing, he asked Don Juan to wait, and disappeared for a few minutes so he could consider his reply and write it down. Don Juan waited but could hear nothing but dead air, so he handed the receiver to his private secretary and went to fetch a drink. When he returned he heard Franco reading out a stilted, lengthy message of congratulation. Nevertheless the Caudillo was irritated that he and the Cortes had been bypassed in this way. His intention was to show that the monarchy merely derived its legitimacy from his regime and not from dynastic continuity, which was precisely what Don Juan had not wanted to happen.

On the following day Juan Carlos, Sofia and Doña Maria went to Athens to begin preparations for the wedding, which would be held there with successive ceremonies in the Greek Orthodox and Roman Catholic rites.

In order to try to make amends with Franco, Don Juan wrote to him congratulating him on his twenty-five years as head of state, and offering the Caudillo the highest honour in the gift of the King of Spain, the Order of the Golden Fleece, on the occasion of the forthcoming wedding. It was to be an expression of recognition by the royal family of his great services to Spain as a soldier and statesman. Franco rejected the offer, replying patronisingly that Don Juan 'should request historical information on the subject' – in other words remind himself that only a king, and not a mere 'Pretender' could grant such an honour. It was beneath Franco's dignity to be reminded who was King of Spain, in theory if not in practice.

Monarchists in Spain were delighted by the news, and displeased that the *Movimiento* press went to such lengths to ignore the Spanish royal family in its coverage of the engagement. Franco was clearly still angry at not having been consulted first, and at Don Juan's having flouted the *Ley de Sucesión* in making the news public. At the same time he knew that a royal wedding would do nothing but intensify monarchist sentiment in Spain, something which had never been far below the surface. It was noticed that the press said much about the Greek royal family, but nothing about their Spanish counterparts. Some sections of the Falangist press even attacked the idea of a mixed wedding between a Catholic heir and a non-Catholic princess, implying that it would be unacceptable and that the Spanish people would never tolerate such a thing.

By November there were rumours in the press that Juan Carlos, then in Estoril, would not return to Madrid unless he was recognised as Prince of Asturias. There was some speculation as to where he would live after his wedding, and the British ambassador Sir George Labouchere reported that he was assured by some monarchists that they would rather Juan Carlos and his wife stayed in Estoril, as if they moved to Madrid there was a fear that he would take all the limelight from his father, thereby making it impossible for the latter to return to Spain and reign once Franco was dead. The Generalissimo, he was convinced, had turned against Don Juan, and it remained to be seen whether Juan Carlos had the right leadership qualities to become a worthy King of Spain when he reached the age of thirty, eight years hence.

With regard to the religious issues, Franco and the supporters of Don Juan expected Sofia to convert to Catholicism before the wedding, following the precedent set in the marriage of Princess Victoria Eugenia to King Alfonso XIII. This overlooked certain major differences, particularly the fact that Sofia was not marrying a reigning monarch. The Greek royal family was in a sense the senior monarchy, and therefore better placed to lay down certain conditions. Don Juan was not wealthy, and there could be no question of the wedding taking place in Estoril. As it would be in Athens, the Greek government and royal family would naturally expect a Greek princess marrying in the Greek capital to have a Greek Orthodox marriage ceremony. All they could hope for was the possibility of Sofia converting formally to the Catholic Church straight after the Orthodox ceremony so she could proceed to a second, Catholic, marriage service afterwards.

In January 1962 Juan Carlos and Sofia accompanied Don Juan to Rome, where they were received in audience by Pope John XXIII, and papal dispensation was granted for Orthodox and Catholic ceremonies. Franco was asked to the wedding, but in order to attend he needed an official invitation from the Greek government, and to be seen at the ceremonies would have been taken as an endorsement of Juan Carlos as heir, something he was loath to do. Moreover, by the time he received Don Juan's invitation, he was recovering from a shotgun injury sustained while out pigeon shooting. Tests on the weapon afterwards indicated that the gun was not faulty, and there was speculation that it had been tampered with, suggesting that there had been an attempt on the Caudillo's life.

On 1 March Juan Carlos visited Franco for the last time before his marriage, and personally invited him to the wedding to be held two months later. All three armed service ministers were also included in the invitation. Franco declined, on the grounds that he would be represented by Rear-Admiral Felipe Abárzuza Oliva, minister for the navy. However, Franco was evidently warming to his young guest, telling him that while he could not agree to Juan Carlos being styled Prince of Asturias, he assured him that he had more chance of being King of Spain than his father.

This was the clearest indication yet Juan Carlos had been given that his father was being sidelined if not eliminated as king of a restored monarchy. Rather embarrassed, he said he would inform his father of the conversation as it was his duty to do so. Franco also told Juan Carlos that he should stay in Spain after his marriage, so the people could get to know him better. The elder man was much impressed by him, telling a confidant afterwards that he was very intelligent, with a lively imagination, and very well informed as to what was going on in Spain.[12]

One small but unfortunate accident occurred shortly after Juan Carlos arrived in Athens to prepare for the wedding. On 20 April he was practising judo with Crown Prince Constantine, his future brother-in-law, when he broke his left collarbone. For the next three weeks he had his arm in a sling, and it was only removed on 12 May, just two days before the ceremony.

After the service at the Catholic cathedral, bride and groom returned to the palace in Athens, and after a brief break they set off again in procession to the Greek Orthodox Metropole, travelling in separate carriages. He travelled with his mother, while she went with her father in the state coach, drawn by six white horses with a military escort. Franco watched the proceedings on television and commented that the Prince, wearing the uniform of a lieutenant of the Spanish army, looked very military. Even so, he had ordered that the wedding should be given as little publicity as possible, and that the groom should not be seen in any of the published photographs. Nevertheless more than five thousand Spanish monarchists travelled to be part of the crowds who watched the procession, while the press and television coverage in Spain provided far more, and more positive, publicity than the Caudillo had wanted. Don Juan's participation was virtually excluded, and he complained that wags in Madrid were calling it the wedding of the little orphan, as his parents were nowhere to be seen.

In the following month a Congress of the European Movement was held at Munich. Among those present were monarchists and Falangists, meeting exiled Socialists and Basque and Catalan nationalists. Alarmed at the company they were keeping, Franco was convinced that it was a conspiracy to undermine his regime, staged by an unholy coalition of freemasons, Jews and Catholics. When one speaker, the liberal pro-royalist lawyer Joaquin Satrustegui, said he looked forward to a monarchy under Don Juan, he said that Juan Carlos' undying loyalty to his father could not be taken for granted. Such a comment did the likelihood of a restoration after the death of Franco no favours by implying disunity between royal father and son, and after the congress was over Franco had several of the delegates arrested and sent into exile for their role in what he described as the 'filthy Munich cohabitation'.

Later that year there were clearer signs that if and when Spain became a kingdom again on the death of Franco, Juan Carlos would be wearing the crown. The Greek papers reported that Queen Frederica had asked Queen Ena to encourage Don Juan to stand down from the succession in favour of her son. The Greek court issued a denial, but Queen Frederica had a reputation for getting her own way, and she undoubtedly looked forward to seeing her daughter on the Spanish throne. Everyone noticed that marriage had given Juan Carlos a new-found confidence in himself. Sofia encouraged him to seek a closer rapprochement with Franco, in order to pave his way towards the throne. She probably sensed – as he did himself – that if he did so, he would be pushing at an open door. Franco was becoming ever more disenchanted with Don Juan, whom he thought prided himself on being liberal and aligning himself with the regime's enemies. The Count of Barcelona, he predicted, would never become king because his way of thinking would open the way to a Communist revolution like the one which his forces had defeated in the civil war. If a king who would guarantee a continuation of the regime could not be found, a regent would need to be appointed, and it might be necessary to put the choice of his successor to a referendum.

Juan Carlos and Sofia were keen to move from Estoril to La Zarzuela. Don Juan wanted them to stay in Portugal, saying their marriage was no reason for them to move to Spain, but Franco wanted them to establish themselves in the capital. Aware that he was highly regarded by Franco, Juan Carlos was anxious not to antagonise him. However, he was shortly to offend the Caudillo, albeit inadvertently. In September 1962 some areas of Catalonia were devastated by floods, and Juan Carlos and Sofia immediately decided to visit the areas and meet some of those who had suffered. They made arrangements with members of Franco's government, and everywhere they went they were well received by those who were moved that the Prince and Princess cared enough to come. But Franco was offended that they had visited the region before he could do so himself.

Nevertheless the unintended slight was soon forgotten. King Paul of Greece encouraged Don Juan to let his son and daughter-in-law return to Spain, and in February 1963 Don Juan wrote to Franco, saying he was reluctant to let them settle in Madrid as he wanted to keep them away from the potentially harmful influence of high society in the capital. He also thought it would result in adverse public relations for them if they were seen to be living at La Zarzuela at state expense while not carrying out official functions. Franco replied that the Prince's education had barely started, and with regard to baneful society influences the situation would be far worse if they stayed in Portugal. It was agreed that the couple would return to Madrid, and by the end of the month they had settled at La Zarzuela. Their relations with Franco continued to improve, and he was very impressed. Whereas he had previously tried to belittle the heir, he now told his colleagues that there was no truth in the remarks put about by his enemies or rivals that Juan Carlos was unintelligent. On the contrary, he was evidently thinking for himself and not on the basis of what he was told by his family and friends. The Princess was also highly intelligent and charming, and spoke Spanish very well.

Nevertheless Franco's attitude towards them could not be trusted implicitly. Their first public appearance after returning to Spain was the annual funeral service for the kings at El Escorial on 28 February 1963, the twenty-second anniversary of the death of Alfonso XIII. Juan Carlos and Franco jointly shared the presidency of the occasion. When the royal couple watched the news coverage on television later that day, they saw with amazement that they were nowhere to be seen in the film, and their presence was not even mentioned. Juan Carlos' humiliation and anger at having been airbrushed from an event commemorating his grandfather and other ancestors can easily be imagined. Franco was clearly using him to give a monarchist veneer to his regime, while doing nothing to quell anti-monarchist hostility inside the *Movimiento*. Any suggestions that Juan Carlos was in Spain as his father's representative were dismissed by Franco's retort that Don Juan had no recognised right to the crown of Spain, though with his son it could be a different matter altogether. The Caudillo was obviously intent on keeping everyone guessing.

When Juan Carlos asked Franco to be allowed to spend more time with an army regiment or aboard a naval vessel, the Caudillo suggested cynically that his only reason for wanting to do so was to have plenty of time to play cards in the bar. Instead Juan Carlos was given a schedule enabling him to visit various ministries, learning about how they worked; he also visited major new construction projects and was given some insight into the workings of the civil service. His natural affability encouraged people to talk to him, and he proved a good listener.

On 20 December 1963 Juan Carlos and Sofia became parents with the birth of a daughter, Elena. Don Juan, Doña Maria and their daughters were allowed by Franco to come to Spain, the first time he had given them permission to do so, for the christening. Doña Maria and her husband's uncle Alfonso de Orleans Bourbon were the godparents. The Caudillo and his wife were also present at the ceremony, but any family fears of unpleasantness on the occasion proved to be unfounded. Eighteen months later, on 13 June 1965, a second child Cristina was born. Much to her parents' sadness, Don Juan did not attend this christening, having been persuaded by his Privy Council not to go.

Among Franco's entourage there were increasing fears for his failing health. His speech and walk were becoming more hesitant, he seemed frail, and he was often seen in public with a vacant, open-mouthed expression. Now in his early seventies, he was suffering from Parkinson's disease and possibly the early stages of dementia; he was on heavy medication and sometimes seemed unaware of what was going on around him. Yet still he would not name a preferred successor, be it a civilian prime minister or a member of the royal family whom he wished to wear the crown after the restoration of the monarchy. The wearer of the crown had to be at least thirty years old but Juan Carlos was still only in his twenties; it was thought that Franco would try to wait until he was thirty, in order to avoid having to choose Don Juan. All this depended on the ageing Franco's still being alive and with his mental faculties not yet severely impaired. Increasing pressure was being put on him to complete the constitutional scheme for the post-Franco succession, a document called *Ley Orgánica del Estado*, which would outline the powers of a future king.

Though Juan Carlos would have preferred to see his father on the throne in any restoration, he sensed that Franco did not see things the same way, and he was very careful not to provoke any kind of clash which would jeopardise the chances of the Bourbons wearing the crown of Spain again. Franco was encouraged by any sign that Juan Carlos might be wavering in his loyalty to his father. The Prince was invited to attend a lunch with Don Juan's Privy Council on 5 March 1966 at the Hotel Palacio in Estoril, commemorating the twenty-fifth anniversary of the death of King Alfonso XIII. It was to be made the occasion for Don Juan being declared heir to the Spanish crown, and if Juan Carlos was present, this would be taken as endorsement and a refusal to supplant his father. A few days beforehand Juan Carlos sent his apologies to his father, saying he would be unable to attend the meeting because of a stomach upset.

Franco was delighted that he did so, and was well enough to pay him a personal visit, during which Juan Carlos said he did not want to attend the meeting. Sofia had urged her husband not to go to Estoril, and instead he sent a telegram to be read out pledging his affection, loyalty and respect. When Juan Carlos telephoned to say he would not be coming, Don Juan shouted that princes had no right to be ill, and slammed the phone down. He told his privy councillors at the meeting that the Prince had rejected his authority and disobeyed orders. The policy that they had followed until this point had been based on an inviolable unity between his son and himself, a unity which had now been broken.

On 22 November 1966 Franco made a speech in the Cortes introducing the *Ley Orgánica*, or organic law. He looked so aged that his followers were quite shocked. In a speech read out in a halting voice, he made no mention of considering retirement; on the contrary, he seemed determined to remain in office until the end. During the last thirty years, he said, he had dedicated his life to the cause of Spain and accepted the great responsibility of governing the Spanish people. 'Whoever takes on such a responsibility can never be relieved nor rest, but must burn himself out in finishing the task.'[13] Whom he had in mind as his successor was not made clear, though the new legislation did facilitate the eventual nomination of a monarch. The law was to be put to the vote in a referendum on 12 December, but the opposition was silenced and a campaign was mounted in order to secure a positive vote. About 93 per cent of the electorate voted for the proposals.

At the end of the month Don Juan visited France, where he told the press that he would not renounce his rights of succession in favour of another candidate, whether chosen by Franco or the Cortes. It was believed that his refusal to renounce his rights to the throne could bring deadlock on the matter of the succession, and might lead to a regency as the only solution. Senior members of the regime still hoped he would renounce his rights in favour of Juan Carlos, who was regarded as the man under whom Franco's rule was more likely to endure.

Some of the *Movimiento* press seemed intent on putting forward Alfonso, Juan Carlos' cousin, as an equally plausible candidate for the crown, and shortly after the referendum the journal *Pueblo* featured interviews with both men. By the end of 1966 Alfonso was courting Maria del Carmen Martinez-Bordiu, Franco's eldest grand-daughter. If a prince were to marry a descendant of the Caudillo, this would give the impression that Franco was trying to found a new dynasty, and the couple became engaged in December 1971. Juan Carlos found himself in a difficult position, especially when he and Sofia went on a private visit to the United States in January 1967 as part of a programme to raise their profile, and at a press conference he was asked by a reporter from the *New York Times* to accept that the Spanish monarchy's future would depend on rapid democratisation. If he made any public announcements to this effect, they would get back to Franco and his circle at once, and reduce his chances of being chosen as successor; if he did not, it would damage his image with the democratic forces in Spain. It was safer to comply with the former, and he said that any restoration of the monarchy could only consolidate itself if it was established as the continuation of the *Movimiento* and of the regime. Too hasty a transition to democracy could mean the end of the monarchy in Spain, and it was vital to proceed with caution.

In private Franco spoke approvingly of Juan Carlos and Sofia, praising them for showing maturity, being very intelligent, serious and sensitive. When their day arrived, he said, they would serve Spain with the greatest patriotism. 'Anyone who speaks ill of them just does not know their noble qualities and the life of sacrifice that they lead.'[14] He saw to it that the Prince was given a chance to start learning about the workings of his ministry and various government departments. When his Minister of Finance, Juan José Espinosa San Martin, suggested to Franco that the Prince should be allowed to take on more responsible jobs than merely opening exhibitions, visiting charities and being 'a dumb Prince', the Caudillo replied that everything would come to pass; the Prince should not be in too much of a hurry, as it was 'better to be dumb than to stammer'.[15]

Ironically, the family was about to suffer a blow which weakened the cause of contemporary monarchy, and reminded them that nothing could be taken for granted. Sofia's father, King Paul of the Hellenes, had died from cancer in September 1964, and was succeeded by Crown Prince Constantine as King. In April 1967 a coup aimed at forestalling an election victory by the socialist leader Andreas Papandreou was hatched between the palace and the colonels. After an unsuccessful counter-coup by the almost powerless King Constantine in December 1967, he went into exile and the Greek throne was in abeyance. In 1973 the monarchy was abolished and a referendum in December 1974 confirmed the matter.

Such lessons would not be lost on Juan Carlos at a crucial time in his life some years hence.

THIRTEEN

The last days of the republic

On 5 January 1968 Juan Carlos celebrated his thirtieth birthday, the age at which the *Ley de Sucesión* made him eligible to succeed to the throne. Some newspapers, particularly the *Movimiento* journal *Pueblo*, which was committed to a Falangist future, were eager to exploit the uncertain situation and attempted to drive a wedge between him and his father by asking him what he would do if the law provided for his nomination as Franco's successor as head of state. To this question, Juan Carlos tactfully answered that his reaction would be whatever was in the best interests of the country at the time. Pressed further as to whether his father could renounce his place in the succession or not, Juan Carlos replied sagely that his father 'obviously has the ability to do so'.[1]

Some three weeks later, on 30 January, Sofia gave birth to a son, whose arrival seemed adequate proof in Franco's eyes that Juan Carlos was the best candidate for the succession. Before confirming the date of the infant's baptism, Juan Carlos consulted Franco to ensure that their choice, 8 February, would be suitable for the Caudillo. Even though he and Sofia had already settled on the name Felipe, he went through a show of allowing Franco to make suggestions. Fortunately the men agreed on the matter.

The birth of an eventual heir-in-waiting also came as excellent news to another member of the elder generation. While she did not live long enough to be certain that her grandson would be the next King of Spain, Queen Ena had a presentiment that this would probably be the case, and from her home in Switzerland she watched his progress with great interest. It was unlikely that she felt more than a twinge of disappointment at seeing Don Juan being sidelined, as she

210

had long since decided that he did not have the makings of a future king, and he would find the transition extremely difficult if he was to ascend a vacant throne at his time of life. In any case, she was delighted to see her grandson taking such a visible role in public. Her daughter Beatrice told her that she was convinced Don Juan would willingly make the sacrifice of ceding his rights to Juan Carlos, if indeed it could be regarded as a sacrifice. Now he was fifty-four, he probably felt he would be too old to be king when Franco died, and it would be best for the crown to skip a generation.

The Queen had completed her eightieth year in good health, and in October 1967 her birthday was celebrated with a large reunion of family and friends at Lausanne. Three months later, while she was staying with friends at Monte Carlo, she was told about the birth of Felipe and was invited to be his godmother, if Franco would let her go to Madrid for the baptism. He agreed on condition that it would be regarded strictly as a private visit. Don Juan particularly wanted to go to Monte Carlo and accompany her back to Spain, but she advised against his coming, on the grounds that with matters very much in the balance, it would be too political a move that could be easily misconstrued. Likewise, when Juan Carlos asked Franco if he would go to the airport to meet his grandmother on her arrival, Franco declined for the reason that he could not compromise the state with his presence there. Privately he did not want to attend an occasion which might be used by Spanish monarchists as an excuse for a pro-Don Juan demonstration.

When the Queen arrived for a four-day visit at Barajas airport, Madrid, on 7 February, and set foot on Spanish soil for the first time since her departure in April 1931, she was astonished to be greeted by a crowd of thousands as if she were still a reigning monarch. Though Franco was not present to meet her, he had sent General José Lacalle Larraga, his Minister of Aviation, and Antonio Maria Oriol, his Minister of Justice, who was responsible for the government's relations with the royal family. To Franco's annoyance, three other ministers also went to the airport without seeking his permission first. The monarchist press dwelt enthusiastically on Ena's reception and the popular demonstrations of warmth and respect that had greeted Don Juan on his progress through Madrid on his way to La Zarzuela, in stark contrast to the perfunctory seventeen-second report broadcast on Spanish television that evening.

At the christening in the chapel at Zarzuela Palace on 8 February Ena was the guest of honour, holding her great-grandson as he was baptised. Franco was also present, and Infanta Sofia, the baby's mother, standing near him, noticed how emotional he became when he saw the former Queen. After the ceremony she met Franco, and it was said – though maybe not too accurately – that she had taken advantage of the situation by telling him bluntly that she was confronting him on the future of the dynasty; he had all three Bourbons in front of him, and he must decide. It would surely be the last time, she told him, that they would ever see each other. She acknowledged that he had done so much for their country, and it was up to him to finish the job by naming the next King of Spain. If he did not do so while he was alive, there would probably be no king. Non-committally, he told her that everything would be 'as Your Majesty wishes'.

Afterwards he claimed that she had implicitly acknowledged the need to sacrifice Don Juan for the sake of the dynasty, and allow Juan Carlos to ascend the throne on the Generalissimo's death.[2] He also said she would accept his choice of successor, as long as he nominated a descendant of King Alfonso XIII. Despite his indications that she particularly favoured her grandson as the next king, it was noticed that she had bowed to Don Juan when he met her at the airport, greeting him as if he were the reigning sovereign.

While in Spain she visited the headquarters of her beloved Red Cross, where she was moved to see a large portrait of herself dressed in a nurse's uniform. It was ample testimony to the fact that she was still remembered for her work in years past.

When she returned to the airport at Madrid on 11 February she was accompanied by Don Juan, Prince Juan Carlos and Princess Sofia, and several thousand Spaniards came to wave goodbye. It had been an emotional occasion, and she knew that she had probably seen the country for the last time. Moved and elated beyond measure, she murmured that now she could die happily.[3] Her reception had been so enthusiastic that Emilio Romero, editor of *Pueblo*, warned monarchists in an article of the need for caution; the reaction she encountered 'does not guarantee the permanence of the monarchy'.[4]

The next few months were marked by some friction between Juan Carlos and his father. In May Don Juan asked him to come back to Estoril until the autumn. Juan Carlos declined, saying that to be in La Zarzuela meant being near Franco, and in the last few years he himself had done nothing to damage either his father or the monarchy. He could not insult Franco by leaving Spain for five months.

As yet Franco was reluctant to name Juan Carlos as his successor, dithering as he told those around him that he had to wait for 'the right psychological moment'. He seemed worried by continued opposition to the Prince from within the *Movimiento*. Juan Carlos was subjected to certain petty humiliations, such as when he travelled in Iberia, normally going tourist class in order to save money. If the captain or purser of the aircraft recognised him and invited him to move into the first-class seats, Falangist pilots would quickly overrule this by coming into the passenger cabin and ordering him back to his original seat.

Juan Carlos suffered from the uncertainty of the situation, and in July he met Franco to discuss the problems he was having regarding his uncertain status and also his relations with his father. Franco told him he was doing the right thing, and advised him to be patient. When Juan Carlos said his position was not clear and begged him to name his successor, the Caudillo replied that he had to wait for the right moment, and test the mood of the new Cortes first.

Perturbed by the close relationship between his son and Franco, Don Juan was still keen for him to return to Estoril. Doña Maria was particularly concerned at the growing estrangement between father and son, and did her best to reconcile them both. Some of Franco's ministers were keen to try to undermine their master's progress towards nominating Juan Carlos, and in October 1968 they asked Don Juan to write to his son. He did so with reluctance, asking him not to get involved in 'dynastic upheaval', saying that if he accepted nomination as Franco's successor, he would be laying himself open to accusations of filial disloyalty, and would give the impression that the royal family was divided. Being thirty did not absolve him of his obligations to, and discipline from, his father as the head of the family, and it was the young man's duty to see a solution for the future that combined legitimacy and legality. In short, he had to play his part in ensuring the nomination of Don Juan, *de jure* King of Spain, as Franco's successor.

This apparently served as a catalyst for two of Franco's inner circle to expedite a solution to the Caudillo's hesitation about the succession. Towards the end of the month they prepared a lengthy memorandum aiming to convince him that a restored monarchy would guarantee the continuation of his regime. At the same time Juan Carlos' secretariat at La Zarzuela prepared a document giving details of his education and training, aimed at proving to Franco that Juan Carlos identified totally with the regime. Carrero Blanco, one of Franco's key advisers, took both documents to El Pardo and went through them carefully with Franco. He also took a copy of Don Juan's letter to his son, recommending that Juan Carlos should be nominated and that it should come as a surprise, in order to pre-empt any possibility of Don Juan's supporters from mounting a hostile publicity campaign against such a move at home or abroad. This would need the prior agreement of Juan Carlos in order to maintain absolute secrecy. After the meeting Carrero Blanco asked López Rodó to prepare a draft of the Prince's acceptance speech of his nomination as successor. All that was needed now was a date for the occasion.

Before this could be done, there were further problems to contend with from a zealous and none-too-accurate press. On 22 November *Point de Vue*, a French journal noted for its obsession with society gossip, published an interview with Juan Carlos and Sofia, asking whether he was uncomfortable with being Franco's designated heir while he was also son of the legitimate heir. He replied unequivocally that he was not, all the more so as there could be no problems between his father and himself. Dynastic law existed and could not be changed by anybody; he would never agree to rule while his father lived, as he was the King, and if he, Juan Carlos, was living in Madrid, it was to ensure there would be a representative of the Spanish dynasty there while his father was in Portugal.

Juan Carlos and his staff were startled to read this, as they had been led to believe that the journalist was merely going to produce an uncontroversial article about the family, devoid of any political content or speculation about the dynastic issue. He categorically denied having made any such statement to Françoise Laot, the journalist involved. As he had been quoted making an identical comment in *Time* magazine about three years earlier, and it had subsequently been repeated in an article in *ABC*, it was believed that the new article had taken this as a source. A member of the royal household telephoned Laot, who admitted that the offending phrase was not strictly true, but had been inserted on the recommendation of 'friends'. Further so-called interviews appeared in other journals over the next few weeks, culminating in Juan Carlos' statement to his father that he would prefer him to be named successor, but the most important thing was the future of the monarchy. If Franco nominated the younger man, then he would have to accept.

By this time Queen Ena's health was failing. Her liver had been deteriorating for some time, and the family knew she did not have long to live. Some years later one of her daughters remarked how strange it was that her mother and Queen Marie of Roumania had both died largely as a result of liver trouble, yet neither of them ever drank a drop of alcohol.[5] Prince Juan Carlos and Princess Sofia visited Lausanne regularly to be with her in the spring of 1969 as she lay in her bed, slipping in and out of consciousness. Three times she fell into a coma, only to rally.

On 15 April she was given the last rites by the priest assigned to the Spanish Mission in Lausanne, and she died just before midnight. It was thirty-eight years to the day since she had left Spain on the fall of the monarchy. An hour after her death her body was moved to a clinic for embalming. She had left a request that her body should lie in state in the chapel, dressed in a blue gown given to her by her granddaughter Maria del Pilar, eldest child of Don Juan. Her body was wrapped in the Spanish flag, and her head was covered in a mantilla of white silk.

Her death made the front pages of all the Spanish papers. Franco sent his condolences to the family and three days of official mourning were declared. An official mission was sent to the funeral at the Church of the Sacred Heart at Ouchy, Lausanne, on 18 April, headed by the Foreign Minister, Fernando Castiella. Juan Carlos and Don Juan both went to Switzerland for the funeral. While there father and son had a disagreement on the succession issue, and Don Juan took him to task for some of the things he had said in interviews, accusing him of trying to take his place. Once again, it took the efforts of Doña Maria to prevent a major rupture between them.

Some of Franco's more pro-monarchist entourage tried to take advantage of the increasingly royalist mood that followed the Queen's death to expedite nomination of the Prince as his successor. After a few weeks of prevarication, during which Juan Carlos was alarmed as to what his father's reaction might be, on 15 July Franco received him and told him that he was to be formally named as his successor. With this nomination he intended to guarantee the stability of his own regime.

Though he had been expecting the news for some time, Juan Carlos was a little surprised by its suddenness, but did not hesitate to accept. If he declined, he knew, Franco would not turn to his father, but probably to another candidate altogether, such as his cousin Alfonso. Juan Carlos said that he must inform his father at once, but Franco asked him not to do so, and showed him a formal letter he had written to Don Juan telling him the news. Juan Carlos was keen to write his own letter of explanation, asking for his father's blessing and hoping to deflect any irritation he might feel. Doña Maria telephoned and spoke to the Marques de Mondéjar, head of the Prince's household, to say she was really pleased for her son, and to let him know that she would ensure 'nothing silly happens here'.[6] However, as expected Don Juan was disappointed if not surprised at being passed over, and refused to take any calls from his son that evening, believing that he had betrayed him.

Nevertheless, official arrangements had to be made to clarify the matter. On 22 July the Cortes approved the measure, with 491 votes in favour, 19 against (mostly by supporters of Don Juan or the Carlist rival, Prince Carlos Hugo), and 9 abstentions. The event, it was recorded, went largely unnoticed by most of the population, who were not so much indifferent as more interested in a televised film of the first moonwalk by the astronauts of Apollo XI, two days earlier. There was a marked absence of crowds outside the Cortes, and only small republican demonstrations in working-class areas of the large cities. On 23 July Juan Carlos took the oath of his accept-ance as successor at a private acceptance ceremony in La Zarzuela. In his speech he paid a glowing tribute to the Caudillo, saying that he had witnessed step by step the important achievements that had been attained under Franco's rule, and that he swore to ensure that the principles of the *Movimiento* and the fundamental laws would be scrupulously observed. Only a select few, the future king among them, were aware that these laws could easily be amended.

At the same time, in order to give him a proper rank in Spain, Franco raised Juan Carlos to the hitherto non-existent dignity of Prince of Spain, a title which he would continue to use for the next six years. As Franco had not recognised the Count of Barcelona as King Juan, Juan Carlos had been careful not to use the title Prince of Asturias in Spain, though in effect he had been entitled to – and indeed regarded himself as such – since the death of his grandfather in 1941.

Don Juan let it be known that on the day his son took the oath, he would not be interrupting his normal routine, but planned to be at sea in his yacht. However, when the time came he anchored at a small village on the Portuguese coast so he could watch the pro-ceedings on a television in a fishermen's bar. After his son finished speaking, he remarked, 'Nicely read, Juanito, nicely read.'[7]

Relations between Juan Carlos and his father were strained for some months, the latter feeling that he had been betrayed, and neither was on normal speaking terms with the other. In England Lord Mountbatten, a distant cousin, was concerned by the volatile situation between them, and the effect it might have on the restor-ation of the crown in Spain. When Don Juan attended the funeral of Mountbatten's sister Princess Andrew of Greece at Windsor in December 1969, he was invited to the family home, Broadlands, where his host discussed the matter in some detail. Afterwards he wrote to Juan Carlos, reporting that he had urged his father 'to execute a legal Instrument of Abdication to be issued by him on the evening before you became King so that the world can see you are the legal King in your own right and not the puppet of a dictator'.[8]

A little later father and son met at Lausanne. Since the age of eight, Juan Carlos said bitterly, he had been 'nothing more than a minion', and only ever did what his father ordered him to. When told to go and study in Spain, when told to leave Spain afterwards as a direct consequence of Don Juan falling out with Franco, then being sent back to Spain after both elder men had made up again, he obeyed. Franco and Don Juan had planned his whole life for him, without ever asking what he wanted or did not want. That he, Juan Carlos, had been named as 'successor with the title of king' was purely because his father had put him in Spain, and he had never had any choice in the matter. Still obsessed with the idea that he had been deceived, Don Juan was dismissive of his son's comments. Juan Carlos warned him that Franco could still change his mind, and as father and son they still needed each other. He, Juan Carlos, was being surrounded and watched all the time, and therefore prevented from having any real contact with the opposition. Only Don Juan could do so, and only in this way could Juan Carlos help to make a democratic monarchy for all Spaniards, 'irrespective of the way that they think'.[9] At length they embraced, but deep down inside the tensions between them were not yet fully resolved.

Now that he had accepted Franco's nomination, Juan Carlos was under suspicion from the majority of the democratic opposition, especially his father's supporters. At the same time he intended to carry out democratic reforms when the time came. Though he kept his thoughts to himself, the regime suspected as much and there was some hostility towards the young man chosen to be King.

Years of silent appearances next to Franco on public and cere-monial occasions had created the impression that Juan Carlos lacked intelligence and courage. While awaiting Franco's decision as to his royal successor, he had been obliged to keep quiet. Now he had been nominated as successor, he hoped to go travelling around Spain and to speak with greater authority. He had learnt from the experience of his brother-in-law, the former King Constantine of Greece, who had lamented his own inability to make himself better known to ordinary Greeks while he was heir to the throne. Now Juan Carlos was becoming frustrated as he found that cabinet ministers were reluctant to let him make the journeys around the country which he wanted to and which he knew were necessary for a future sovereign. While he knew that the economic achievements of Franco's regime had to be safeguarded, he was aware that the political system which had emerged from the Civil War needed to change to meet the needs of the modern society and economy that he had come to know. It also irritated him that he seemed unable to speak as freely as he wished on foreign trips, presumably as the ministers feared he would reveal too much about the stagnating political system in the country and his intention to modernise things when he had the chance.

Any fears by the government and ministers that he did not intend to be cowed by their expectations of him were demonstrated in an article published in the *New York Times* in February 1970. Written by the paper's Madrid correspondent, Richard Eder, it revealed that Juan Carlos had told his acquaintances that he did not accept the role apparently chosen for him, that of 'docile successor', and that he had privately admitted he had 'no intention of presiding over a dictatorship'. He was Franco's heir, but he was Spain's heir as well, and he had a duty towards the people. Only under some form of democracy would he have any real chance of remaining Spain's King.[10]

When the article was published, Juan Carlos felt that he might have gone a little too far in revealing his personal thoughts and intentions. As a result for some months he kept more or less silent in public, though in private he was more forthcoming. In a long conversation with the British ambassador Sir John Russell that same month, he said he was beginning to get more of a feel for the job, and he had recently stopped asking Franco every time he wanted to go somewhere or do something. Instead, he would make his own arrangements and then inform the Caudillo. However, he was clearly discomfited by the consequences of the *New York Times* feature, and realised it would be as well not to be seen publicly to reveal plans for the future which suggested any sort of discrepancy, let alone an outright break, with the present regime. Franco and his closest associates continued to silence even moderate opposition, making it clear that they would not countenance any political reform or liberalisation of the regime.

Nevertheless some sections of the press were becoming more forthright. In March *ABC* published an article, '*La via española a la democracia*' (The Spanish road to democracy), pointing out that the integration of Spain into Europe was unlikely to be fulfilled until Spain embraced real democracy with all political parties legitimately recognised. The Catholic daily, *Ya*, followed suit by calling for full democratisation of life in Spain. Demands for change would come soon enough.

At the time Juan Carlos said he hoped that the handing over of power would not come too soon. In his view he would like at least another two and a half years to prepare himself by learning the job and establishing his own position. He still had no idea as to whether Franco, now ageing rapidly, would resign during his lifetime – perhaps on the occasion of his eightieth birthday in 1972 – or cling to power until his death.

As Juan Carlos had told others, Franco could still change his mind and nothing could be taken for granted. He was very concerned in December 1971 when his uncle Don Jaime announced the engagement of his son Alfonso to Maria del Carmen Martinez-Bordiu y Franco, eldest granddaughter of the Caudillo. It looked suspiciously as if Franco might be trying to subvert the succession by bringing royal blood into his family. Suspicions deepened in March 1972 when Don Jaime gave Franco the *Toisón de Oro*, an order which Franco had declined when Don Juan had offered it to him just before the wedding of Juan Carlos and Sofia ten years earlier, on the grounds that it could be conferred only by the King of Spain. Although Franco's acting Prime Minister Louis Carrero Blanco successfully prevailed on him not to wear the insignia, it began to look as if Franco's appointment of Juan Carlos as his successor had become decidedly uncertain. The Prince's adviser, Pedro Sainz Rodriguez, even feared that the Prince might soon be eliminated in a 'mysterious accident'.

At the wedding on 18 March 1972 at El Pardo, a beaming Doña Carmen, Franco's wife, entered the chapel on the arm of Juan Carlos. Her demeanour was in stark contrast to that of her husband, a pathetic, trembling figure as he gave the bride away. When the bride and groom returned from their honeymoon, Doña Carmen made a point of curtseying to her granddaughter as if she were a princess.

After a daughter was born to them, she issued instructions to her guests and servants that the baby was to be called 'Your Highness'. It was a reminder to everyone that this infant, and the brother who followed soon afterwards, were not only General Franco's great-grandsons, but also the great-grandsons of King Alfonso XIII. She supported Alfonso's aspirations for a title equivalent to that granted to Juan Carlos, preferably those of Prince of Bourbon and Royal Highness. Don Juan, who was still head of the family, opposed this on the grounds that only the first son of the King had the right to be called a prince, and Alfonso's father had been neither king nor prince. At length a compromise was reached and Juan Carlos persuaded Don Juan to give Alfonso the title of Duke of Cadiz, with the right to be styled 'Royal Highness'. Nevertheless, relations between both families remained distant, and Juan Carlos never ceased to fear that Franco might consider reversing his nomination as successor. For his part, Alfonso pressed Carrero Blanco repeatedly to use his influence with Franco to have him named as second in line to the throne after Juan Carlos, but the minister proved obdurate to such appeals.

Franco celebrated his eightieth birthday on 4 December 1972. He was increasingly showing his age, often saying nothing in cabinet meetings and nodding off at the table. Juan Carlos and others wondered again whether the Caudillo would hand over power while he was still alive, and by early 1973 he was giving serious thought to the men whom he hoped would serve in his first government. While he did not intend to make Carrero Blanco, then Vice-President of the State Council, his Prime Minister, he knew that the transition from Franco's last government to his first would proceed more smoothly if it was handled by conservative figures known to be loyal to the

Caudillo. Such a government, he assumed, would probably last for only six months, certainly no longer than two years. After this he would be free to name a government of younger men more in line with his own way of thinking, and thus pave the way for more thoroughgoing democratic reform. He told Torcuato Fernández-Miranda, his old tutor and adviser, that the new Spanish monarchy had to be democratic, and could not be built on what he called 'the present excessively partisan institutions'. This was the only way in which it could be accepted by Europe and by the world, and the only way in which it could survive.

During the next few months there was an atmosphere of major unrest in Spain. In April police killed a striking worker near Barcelona, and in the following month a policeman was stabbed to death during a May Day demonstration, to which the police responded with mass arrests of leftists on the grounds of subversion. In June Franco officially appointed Carrero Blanco, now seventy years of age, his Prime Minister, remaining only as head of the country and as commander-in-chief of the military forces. His appointment lasted only six months and came to a violent end on 20 December when his car was blown up by explosives planted beneath it as he returned from daily mass. He was killed instantly. A squad of ETA (*Euzkadi Ta Azkatsuna*) activists, agitating for Basque independence, claimed responsibility. Franco was too ill to attend the funeral and Juan Carlos represented him, wearing the uniform of a rear-admiral and walking alone at the head of the procession behind the gun carriage carrying the coffin. Despite ETA warnings of a further attack, he refused to wear a bulletproof vest.

On 2 January 1974 Carlos Arias Navarro was sworn in as the new Prime Minister, though he knew that he was helping to preside over a regime whose days were numbered. Suffering severely from phlebitis in the right leg and regular attacks of internal bleeding as well as Parkinson's disease, Franco was clinging to life. In July 1974 he was admitted to hospital for what he believed would be a life-threatening operation. Thinking he had only days to live, he asked Arias Navarro and Alejandro Rodriguez Valcárcel, President of the Cortes, to prepare the decree that would permit Juan Carlos to take over as interim Head of State, yet without being proclaimed King. Spain's international prestige had been tarnished particularly by two events in March, a couple of executions by strangulation of a common criminal and a Catalan anarchist, and the expulsion from the country of the Bishop of Bilbao for allowing the publication of a pamphlet in defence of ethnic minorities. Juan Carlos was reluctant to take over the position, as he did not intend to be tarnished by the actions of such a regressive government which never consulted him. Arias Navarro and several other members of the cabinet wanted to make him accept, in order to safeguard the continuity of the regime, maintaining that if he did not want to, he would have to be forced to.

Against all expectations, Franco had recovered by the end of July. Though still infirm, he appeared much improved; he was given exercise therapy and a new, more varied diet. His family and ministers warned him that plans were being made to have him declared incapable, and whispered to him of a conspiracy between Juan Carlos and Don Juan, saying that the former was planning to recall the latter as King. Franco angrily declared that he had no intention of giving up power. His medical team decided that he was restored to full health by the end of August, and on 2 September he decided to resume his full powers.

At least one other cause of dissension was about to be removed, for by this time Don Jaime had long since given up any claim on the throne. Though his second marriage had endured, it had not become any happier. His sons took him to court, accusing him of squandering his fortune and of being mentally unbalanced since his second marriage. The case was rejected, but the family estrangement lingered until the end. In March 1975 Don Jaime and Charlotte had a violent argument, during which he fell over and banged his head. The doctors prescribed complete rest, but she insisted that he accompany her by car to St Gallen Hospital in Switzerland where she was going for treatment for her drink problem. It was a long and exhausting drive, and afterwards he went to bed to recover. Within a few hours he had a stroke and died.

Meanwhile, as Franco's health continued to deteriorate, he toyed with the idea of standing down and proclaiming Juan Carlos as his immediate successor, but repeatedly changed his mind. On 1 October 1975, the 39th anniversary of his elevation to the headship of state, he made what would be his last public appearance, before a large crowd on the balcony at the Palacio de Oriente. He was accompanied by a solemn-looking Prince Juan Carlos and Princess Sofia. Before taking his leave of the crowds he gave the Fascist salute, though it was observed that the Prince and Princess pointedly refrained from following suit.

From the middle of October Franco suffered a series of heart attacks, and by the end of the month he was showing symptoms of peritonitis. Despite several operations it was soon clear that not even dependence on complex life-support machinery could prolong his existence indefinitely, and his daughter Carmen asked that he should be allowed to die in peace. When he knew he was dying, Franco dictated a political testament to her. It was handed to Arias Navarro, who read it out in a voice broken with emotion on television at 10 a.m. that day. In it, he asked the people of Spain to show the same affection and loyalty to Don Juan Carlos de Bourbon as they had shown to him. Early on the morning of 20 November 1975 he was given further resuscitation and a final heart massage, but his life was ebbing away. At 5.25 a.m. he was officially pronounced dead as a result of heart failure brought on by peritonitis. Ironically it was Dr Pozuelo, Franco's personal physician, who took the trouble to let Prince Juan Carlos know. Neither Arias Navarro nor Rodriguez Valcárcel, who became interim Head of State, had thought fit to inform him.

On the last couple of occasions that Juan Carlos had seen Franco, during the final week of the latter's life, Franco had impressed on the young sovereign-to-be that the most important thing he could do was maintain the unity of Spain. Franco's last coherent words to him were concerned with the subject. What struck Juan Carlos more than anything else was the force of Franco's hands pressing his, as the old man told him that all he asked was that when he became King, he would preserve the unity of the nation.[11]

FOURTEEN

'We are all monarchists now'

For several hours on 20 November 1975 Juan Carlos and Sofia joined Franco's family in their mourning. The man who had just become King assured Franco's widow that she could remain at El Pardo for the rest of her life, though in the end she stayed for less than three months.

Once he had paid his due respects to the man he had so long looked up to, yet was determined to succeed in a very different manner, Juan Carlos' first priority was to make a fitting start in the role for which he had waited so long. On his proclamation as King by the Cortes on 22 November 1975, he swore fidelity to the fundamental laws and the principles of the *Movimiento*, and at the same time he paid a respectful yet cautious tribute to Franco for his period of office and conduct of government of the state.

Then he announced that a new stage was starting in the history of Spain, one which had 'its starting point in peace, in work and in prosperity; the fruit of a common and collective will and strength'. The monarchy, he said, in a speech which he had prepared well in advance for the occasion, would be 'the faithful guardian of this inheritance and will attempt at all moments to maintain the closest relationship with the people'.[1] A coronation mass, the first real public celebration of the reign, was held at the Church of Los Jerónimos, Madrid, on 27 November. Among the foreign dignitaries attending were Prince Philip, Duke of Edinburgh, Valéry Giscard d'Estaing, President of France, and Walter Scheel, President of the German Federal Republic. It was vital, the King recognised, to secure the symbolic presence of leaders and representatives of the main democratic powers from the start, in recognition of a new era which would come, despite the ingrained opposition of Franco's acolytes.

For the last few days Juan Carlos had been anxious about how his father would react to the situation. He had recently seen a draft version of a declaration that Don Juan intended to publish on Franco's death. In it he claimed that he maintained 'his well-known and permanent political position, as son and heir of Alfonso XIII and as the repository of a secular treasure whose duties he holds to be unrenounceable'. For the monarchy to be useful, it had to overcome the legacy of the civil war, establish 'profound social justice which will eliminate corruption', introduce multi-party democracy and seek full integration into the European Economic Community.[2] When it referred to Juan Carlos as 'his son and heir', Juan Carlos himself felt that it implied that Don Juan did not recognise him as King, and would not do so until he had completely dismantled Franco's regime. The declaration was published in Paris and Madrid on 21 November, much to the fury of the *Movimiento*. Only on 28 November did Don Juan set his son's mind at rest by sending an emissary to La Zarzuela with a message that he did indeed accept his son as King and head of the dynasty. He would also abdicate formally as soon as it was clear that satisfactory progress had been made towards full democracy. As it happened, this would take eighteen months to achieve.

Those who had seen the King as merely the successor to Franco's restrictive regime would soon be proved wrong. His dismantling of the old order was set in motion largely by a new Law of Political Reform, voted by the Cortes to bring about its own substitution by a genuine parliament based on universal suffrage. To enable this, the King chose Torquato Fernández-Miranda from the Francoite National Movement to carry out the task, and appointed him President of the Cortes. For seven months he bided his time by retaining Franco's last Prime Minister, Carlos Arias Navarro. The latter had regarded Fernández-Miranda as his rival for the premiership, and despite his reservations on political and personal grounds, was therefore content to see him given the other post instead.

In May 1976 the government passed legislation in the Cortes which permitted the holding of meetings and demonstrations. One month later another law, legalising political parties, was similarly approved. Hours later the legislation needed to put the bill into effect was thrown out, but was eventually rescued. Believing he would be incapable of leading the country to democracy, and aware that the King shared his reservations, in July Arias Navarro tendered his resignation. To succeed him the King appointed Adolfo Suárez, the youngest member of the outgoing government. It would be his responsibility to lead Spain peacefully towards a democratic, parliamentary monarchy without annoying the powerful conservative factions, particularly among the military.

As the fate of the monarchy hinged on Suárez's success or failure, he warned the King that he was in effect gambling the crown on his appointment. The consequence of the process of reform, the politician told him candidly, would be to leave the monarchy stripped of political power, something which the King knew well and was prepared to accept. On 14 July the legislation permitting political parties went back to the Cortes and was passed. Suárez's programme recognised that sovereignty lay with the people, proclaimed the government's determination to introduce a democratic system and promised a referendum on political reform and elections within the next twelve months.

On 14 May 1977 Don Juan formally renounced his claim to the throne at a modest ceremony at La Zarzuela, and Juan Carlos thanked him by confirming the title of Count of Barcelona that Juan had assumed in exile. The verdict of historian John Hooper was that Don Juan would probably go down as 'one of the tragic figures of the twentieth century – the King who never was, a simple man who always said that his happiest years were spent as an ordinary naval officer', who was caught between his distaste for Franco and his responsibility for the survival of the Bourbon dynasty.[3]

The pace of democratic reforms was quickening, much to the great displeasure of conservative elements, especially in the military, who had expected the King to maintain the authoritarian state. On 20 May 1977 future president and leader of the only recently legalised Spanish Socialist Workers' Party (PSOE) Felipe González, accompanied by Javier Solana, visited Juan Carlos in the Zarzuela Palace. This historic meeting was followed on 15 June 1977 by the first democratic elections of the post-Franco era. When asked by the press what he most wanted the King to do, González admitted that as a matter of principle he was a republican, but it was not for him to call for the abolition of the monarchy in Spain: 'It should be the Spanish people who decide.'[4] The result of the elections was victory for Suárez, the first democratically elected Prime Minister of modern Spain, and his Democratic Centre Union (Unión de Centro Democrático, UCD). With this, according to the King's biographer Paul Preston, the Franco regime was laid to rest.[5]

On 22 July the King addressed the recently elected Cortes, telling them that 'the different ideologies' represented were 'nothing more than different ways of understanding peace, justice, freedom and the historic reality of Spain. In their diversity, they respond to the same ideal – understanding and comprehension for all – and they are motivated by the same impulse: love of Spain.' Though he pointed out that he was non-partisan, he had no hesitation in identifying himself with the sweeping process of democratic reform in Spain since Franco's death. The crown, he said, was very satisfied with the recent elections for the legislature, 'about the manner in which the aims which it formulated not so long ago are being achieved'.[6]

Suárez formed a minority government, and general agreement among the leading parties led to the passage of the new constitution in 1978, acknowledging Juan Carlos as rightful heir of the dynasty and King. It established a constitutional monarchy, separated Church and State, and provided for the creation of seventeen autonomous communities throughout Spain. Juan Carlos thus relinquished absolute power and became a reigning but non-governing monarch, and the move was approved in a referendum on 6 December 1978.

On the accession of Juan Carlos, the Communist leader Santiago Carrillo had led the chorus of those who nicknamed him 'Juan Carlos the Brief', predicting that the monarchy would not last long. Within two years, during debates on the powers of the crown, Carrillo was acknowledging Juan Carlos' contribution to the establishment of democracy, praising him and his role during the transition as 'the hinge between the apparatus of the State and the authentic democratic aspirations of civil society'. As long as the monarchy respected the constitution and popular sovereignty, he said, the Communists would respect the monarchy.[7]

How and why, the King was asked some years later, did he manage to change Spain so rapidly after forty years of dictatorship? It was no mystery to him, he said; when he ascended the throne, he had two trump cards up his sleeve. First, he had the full support of the army. In the first few days after Franco's death, it could have done just as it liked, but it obeyed him, as sovereign, as he had been nominated King by Franco, and even after the latter's death his word was still law. Secondly, he gave full credit to the wisdom of the Spanish people, who admitted that they did not know Juan Carlos as a person, but their attitude was one of 'let's give him some time to explain himself before we accept or reject him'.[8] Fernández-Miranda had told him that much would depend on his first speech, the purpose of which was to tell the Spanish people what he wanted to do and how he planned to do it. When his speech made clear that he wanted to be 'King of all the Spanish people', his objectives were beyond doubt and his future as good as assured.

* * *

Two years later his grandfather was able to return home. King Juan Carlos had bided his time to make sure that the restored monarchy was secure, and after four years he decided the moment had come. Now, at last, the body of King Alfonso XIII could be disinterred from its temporary resting place in Rome, and brought back by a Spanish frigate to Spain, then to the Escorial by helicopter. Don Juan, King Juan Carlos, Queen Sofia and their children were present at a ceremony on 20 January 1980 as the coffin was escorted by a guard of honour through icy streets, lined by several thousand loyal spectators, for a requiem Mass in the Escorial. Five years later, in April 1985, the body of Queen Ena was brought back from Switzerland and laid beside that of her husband.

Any lingering doubts that may have been entertained about the stability of the monarchy were soon dispelled. A few disgruntled right-wing elements in the armed forces yearned for an end to democracy and a return to Franco's regime. On 23 February 1981 about two hundred civil guards, led by Colonel Jerjero Molina, stormed the Cortes, firing automatic weapons, and ordering all members present, numbering about three hundred and fifty, to lie down. For a brief moment it looked as if Spain's experiment with political reform was hanging in the balance.

Visibly strained, the King appeared on television in the early hours of the following day, denouncing the military takeover in no uncertain terms and calling for unambiguous support for the legitimate democratic government. Spain, he said, could not 'tolerate in any form actions by persons who attempted to interrupt by force the democratic process and the constitution voted by the Spanish people through a referendum'.[9] In the hours before his speech he had personally called many senior military figures to tell them that he was opposed to the coup, and that they must take all necessary measures to maintain constitutional order under the law. He would neither abdicate nor abandon Spain, he told them, and warned that if anyone rebelled they would be responsible for starting a new civil war.

It was a remarkable reversal of the role once played by his grandfather, Lord Kilmarnock noted in a letter to *The Times* of London, pointing out that by endorsing a coup d'état in 1923 King Alfonso XIII had sided with the generals against the politicians. Now, just over half a century later, the King had managed to hold the generals firm on the side of the politicians.[10] He had also doubtless reflected on the fate of his brother-in-law, King Constantine of Greece, who had lost his throne after a comparable intervention by the generals in 1967.

After the collapse of the coup Carrillo told television viewers 'God Save the King'. Public support for the monarchy among democrats and left wingers before 1981 had been muted. After his courage and level-headed dealing with the crisis, there could be no doubt of his commitment to democracy. Even the most radical Spanish politicians could affirm that 'we are all monarchists now'.

On the night of the coup, it was said, King Juan Carlos ceased, for millions of Spaniards, to be merely the man who had been General Franco's successor as head of state, and became King of Spain in his own right. Only then did the Spanish people discover for themselves that their sovereign possessed the three specific virtues of the Bourbons of Spain, namely common sense, a long memory and courage – 'a calm courage in which boldness and patience were united'.[11] He also had the courage of his convictions that he was doing the right thing.

*   *   *

In 1985 the Count and Countess of Barcelona celebrated their golden wedding. Among the guests was Leandro Alfonso, son of King Alfonso XIII by Carmen Ruiz Moragas. Don Juan had first met him in 1968 when he drove unexpectedly to Estoril, and his half-brother told him he did not need to introduce himself as he was 'so much like Papa'. He was reluctant to recognise him officially until after the death of Queen Ena the following year, but Leandro was later introduced to the rest of the family, including King Juan Carlos and Queen Sofia. After he published his autobiography in 2002 the Queen saw it at a book fair in Madrid. 'Oh, this is my uncle's book,' she said eagerly. 'I will have it.'[12] His half-sister Cristina, Countess Marone, often invited him to her flat in Madrid, referring to him as her brother 'of the left hand', in contrast to her sister Beatrice, who could not forget how much her father's infidelities had upset her mother, and firmly refused to meet him.

The Count of Barcelona made his last public appearance on 18 January 1993, when the King presented him with the Gold Medal of Navarre in recognition of his efforts on behalf of democracy in Spain. By this time he was seriously ill with cancer and was unable to make his acceptance speech, which had to be read out by his grandson Prince Felipe. He had less than three months to live, and died at Pamplona Hospital on 1 April, aged seventy-nine. A chapel of repose was set up in the palace, and many thousands of ordinary Spaniards came to pay their last respects. At La Zarzuela over four thousand telegrams of condolence were received from all over the world. Two days after his death he was buried with full state honours in the Escorial as if he had been a reigning King of Spain.

King Juan Carlos undoubtedly regretted the fact that relations with his father had been strained at times because of the peculiar positions in which destiny had placed them. Yet during the last few years tensions between them had eased, and he was visibly moved by the many messages of sympathy and affection he received.

* * *

Having established himself securely on the throne by his skilful consolidation of democracy, King Juan Carlos could at length afford to unbend a little and relax. He was fascinated by sports and speed, and enjoyed the more conventional sports of skiing, squash and tennis, as well as driving fast cars and motorcycles, piloting helicopters and aeroplanes, and racing yachts. His enthusiastic participation in such activities sometimes resulted in accidents and injuries, and once as he was removed carefully from an aircraft by stretcher, it was remarked that a king should be seen in such a state only on his return from the Crusades. This passion for such hazardous pastimes was criticised by those who thought it unseemly for a monarch to risk his life in some way, while praised by those who felt he had earned the right to make up his own mind on such matters and saluted his personal courage.

If the King took a long time to acquire the ability to deliver a prepared speech with confidence and without awkwardness, he was at his best in the more informal atmosphere of audiences and receptions. He soon acquired two of the essential attributes of a democratic King – an evident, self-effacing sense of humour, and an excellent memory for names and faces. Informality was the keyword, he maintained. He told the author José Luis de Vilallonga that what had impressed Queen Sofia most when she first arrived in Spain as his wife was the discovery that people of their rank could lead an almost normal life, going out to the cinema or the restaurant and to dine with friends with the minimum of ceremony. Such things were simply not done in Athens. When Vaclav Havel, President of the Czech Republic, came to visit the King in Mallorca, he was taken out one morning to a bar where everyone greeted the sovereign as if he were an old acquaintance. Havel was amazed, even more so when he saw the King cheerfully decline the barman's offer to serve their drinks on the house, put his hand in his pocket and pay for them like any other customer.[13]

In an interview broadcast by Spanish state television in November 2000 on the 25th anniversary of his accession, the King spoke candidly of his fears for the country and the burden that had been placed on him during the transition to democracy after Franco's death. From the beginning of his reign, he admitted, he knew that the monarchy could not be anything other than democratic if it was to survive, but the problem for him was how to bring it about. It was Franco who had passed on to him the powers over the armed forces, something which gave him 'a huge responsibility, but it made my task easier in the end'. Because of their association with Franco's repressive rule, the armed forces had not been held in high esteem by many at the time, but now they were liked and respected. He also said how important it was for the crown to be approachable. Since his accession, he had 'always wanted the monarchy to be open and close to the people, for many people to be able to reach the King, the Queen – in short, for them to be able to see us, to be able to talk to us, to be able to speak to us. Because the truth is that before being King, one of the things I learnt and which is still of great use to me is to listen.'[14]

The Spanish monarchy was rarely closer to the people than on 11 March 2004, when the Madrid train bombings left 192 dead and over 2,000 wounded. That afternoon the King, Queen, their heir Felipe, Prince of Asturias and his fiancée Letizia Ortiz visited survivors, mostly injured commuters, in a hospital in central Madrid. In a televised address to the nation, Juan Carlos spoke movingly of 'terrorist barbarity' that had 'plunged Spain into the deepest grief in the face of which we must stand united and strong'. He would like, he continued, 'to tightly hold everybody in an embrace filled with consolation and sadness. We will always be with you, with all those who suffer the consequences of a macabre madness with no possible justification.'[15]

Two months later, on 22 May 2004, the Prince of Asturias married Letizia Ortiz, a former newscaster. Though she was a divorcée, the Roman Catholic Church did not oppose her remarriage to the heir to the throne as the original wedding had not been held in a church. On 31 October 2005 the Princess gave birth to a daughter, Leonor, the seventh grandchild of King Juan Carlos and Queen Sofia, and a distant descendant of Kings Louis XIV and Henri IV of France. At the time the socialist administration of Jose Luis Rodriguez Zapatero was advocating constitutional reform which would lead to giving women equal rights to the royal succession, and this would apply to the next generation, that of Leonor, and not that of her father.

The news that Leonor might one day be Spain's first queen regnant since her great-great-great-grandmother Queen Isabel coincided with the thirtieth anniversary of King Juan Carlos' accession to the throne. In a speech to mark the occasion he said that consensus, harmony and reconciliation were the very basis of the 1978 constitution, which was the key to understanding how much they had achieved in three decades of parliamentary monarchy.[16]

The Spanish politicians could not have agreed more. In an interview earlier that year Zapatero had called the King 'fairly republican', someone who 'defends institutions, democratic values, who defends public life and who respects the principles of a free citizenship and so in that sense we are very calm and at ease'.[17] There could have perhaps been no better tribute to the man who had inherited the throne under somewhat awkward circumstances, and had made the institution of monarchy virtually unchallenged in an age when certain elements found it all too easy to question or deride the very existence of royalty.

Notes

Abbreviations: BL – British Library; PROL – Public Record Office, London; PRONI – Public Record Office, Northern Ireland; RA – Royal Archives, Windsor

1: A child queen (pp. 1–16)
1. Polnay, *Queen of Spain*, p. 54
2. Aronson, *Royal Vendetta*, p. 37
3. Polnay, *Queen of Spain*, p. 56
4. Sencourt, *Spain's Uncertain Crown*, p. 183
5. *The Times*, 18.11.1843
6. Polnay, *Queen of Spain*, p. 89
7. Polnay, *Queen of Spain*, pp. 79–80
8. Connell, *Regina v. Palmerston*, p. 38, Queen Victoria to Lord Palmerston, 10.9.1846
9. Woodham-Smith, *Queen Victoria*, p. 254, Queen Victoria to King Leopold, 14.9.1846
10. Victoria, *Letters 1837–1861*, vol. II, p. 108, Queen Victoria to King Leopold, 17.11.1846
11. Polnay, *Queen of Spain*, p. 119
12. *The Times*, 12.10.1846

2: 'Destitute of honest and able friends' (pp. 17–33)
1. Sencourt, *Spain's Uncertain Crown*, p. 208; Irving, *Letters from Spain*, p. 75
2. *The Times*, 19.4.1847
3. Polnay, *Queen of Spain*, p. 120
4. *The Times*, 3.5.1847
5. *The Times*, 26.5.1847
6. Polnay, *Queen of Spain*, p. 124
7. *La Presse*, quoted in *The Times*, 2.6.1847

8. *The Times*, 12.8.1847
9. *The Times*, 12.8.1847
10. Polnay, *Queen of Spain*, p. 126; Sencourt, *Spain's Uncertain Crown*, p. 213
11. *The Times*, 24.8.1847
12. *The Times*, 24.8.1847
13. Polnay, *Queen of Spain*, p. 129
14. Polnay, *Queen of Spain*, p. 130
15. Connell, *Regina v. Palmerston*, p. 62, Lord Palmerston to Queen Victoria, 24.10.1847
16. *The Times*, 20.11.1847

3: Revolution (pp. 34–57)
1. Polnay, *Queen of Spain*, p. 141
2. Aronson, *Royal Vendetta*, p. 70
3. *The Times*, 20.7.1850
4. *The Times*, 7.2.1852
5. Polnay, *Queen of Spain*, p. 148
6. *The Times*, 14.2.1852
7. *The Times*, 25.1.1854
8. Polnay, *Queen of Spain*, p. 168
9. *The Times*, 25.7.1854
10. *The Times*, 28.8.1854
11. Sencourt, *Spain's Uncertain Crown*, p. 221
12. *The Times*, 11.11.1854
13. Polnay, *Queen of Spain*, p. 179
14. PROL, Sir John Crampton to Lord Palmerston, 3.2.1863
15. PROL, Sir John Crampton to Lord Palmerston, 23.1.1863

16. PROL, Sir John Crampton to Lord Palmerston, 7.2.1863
17. PROL, Sir John Crampton to Lord John Russell, 17.11.1863
18. PROL, Sir John Crampton to Lord John Russell, 29.12.1863
19. PROL, Sir John Crampton to Lord John Russell, 8.2.1864
20. Ludwig Ferdinand, *Through Four Revolutions*, p. 37
21. Carr, *Spain 1808–1975*, pp. 291–2
22. Polnay, *Queen of Spain*, p. 185
23. *The Times*, 24.4.1868

4: 'King Macaroni' (pp. 58–71)
1. Victoria, *Your Dear Letter*, pp. 208–9, Queen Victoria to Crown Princess of Prussia, 1.10. 1868, 10.10.1868
2. *The Times*, 29.6.1870, Queen Isabel's farewell manifesto, Paris, 28.6.1870
3. Aronson, *Royal Vendetta*, p. 106
4 Aronson, *Royal Vendetta*, p. 107
5. Carr, *Spain 1808–1975*, p. 318
6. Hume, *Modern Spain*, p. 470
7. *The Times*, 6.12.1870
8. Challice, *Secret History*, p. 226
9. Petrie, *Spanish Royal House*, p. 194
10. Challice, *Secret History*, p. 225
11. Challice, *Secret History*, p. 235
12. Hume, *Modern Spain*, p. 501
13. Ludwig Ferdinand, *Through Four Revolutions*, p. 29
14. Eulalia, *Court Life*, p. 49
15. *The Times*, 18.2.1873, King Amedeo's farewell manifesto, Madrid, 11.2.1873
16. *The Times*, 27.2.1873

5: 'A young and unprejudiced monarch' (pp. 72–87)
1. Sencourt, *Spain's Uncertain Crown*, p. 241
2. Petrie, *King Alfonso XIII*, p. 35
3. Ludwig Ferdinand, *Through Four Revolutions*, p. 45
4. Ludwig Ferdinand, *Through Four Revolutions*, p. 45
5. Pilar and Chapman-Huston, *Don Alfonso XIII*, p. 37
6. Petrie, *Spanish Royal House*, p. 206
7. Eulalia, *Court Life*, p. 52
8. Eulalia, *Court Life*, p. 58

9. Eulalia, *Court Life*, p. 60
10. Ludwig Ferdinand, *Through Four Revolutions*, p. 52
11. Eulalia, *Court Life*, p. 20
12. Hardinge, *Diplomatist in Europe*, p. 73
13. Ludwig Ferdinand, *Through Four Revolutions*, p. 57, diary, 27.8.1877
14. Aronson, *Royal Vendetta*, p. 122
15. Ludwig Ferdinand, *Through Four Revolutions*, p. 62, diary, 25.1.1878
16. Ludwig Ferdinand, *Through Four Revolutions*, p. 64, diary, 29.1.1878
17. Ludwig Ferdinand, *Through Four Revolutions*, p. 62, Queen Isabel to Pilar 18.1.1878
18. Ludwig Ferdinand, *Through Four Revolutions*, p. 70, diary, 18.6.1878
19. Eulalia, *Court Life*, p. 89
20. Ludwig Ferdinand, *Through Four Revolutions*, p. 71, diary, 28.6.1878
21. *The Times*, 3.7.1878
22. Eulalia, *Court Life*, pp. 89–90
23. Graham, *Life Story of King Alfonso XIII*, p. 31
24. Ludwig Ferdinand, *Through Four Revolutions*, p. 72, diary, 24.8.1878
25. Ludwig Ferdinand, *Through Four Revolutions*, p. 74, diary, 29.10.1878

6: 'He had so longed for a son' (pp. 88–101)
1. Ludwig Ferdinand, *Through Four Revolutions*, p. 80, diary, 1.9.1879
2. Aronson, *Royal Vendetta*, p. 127
3. Ludwig Ferdinand, *Through Four Revolutions*, p. 81, diary, 16.10.1879
4. Ludwig Ferdinand, *Through Four Revolutions*, p. 84, diary, 7.12.1879
5. Ludwig Ferdinand, *Through Four Revolutions*, p. 80, diary, 10.12.1879
6. Petrie, *Royal House*, p. 213
7. *The Times*, 14.4.1879
8. Eulalia, *Court Life*, p. 92
9. Frederick, *Diaries*, p. 264
10. Frederick, *Diaries*, p. 276, 22.11.1883
11. Frederick, *Diaries*, p. 363, 14.12.1883
12. Pilar and Chapman-Huston, *Don Alfonso XIII*, pp. 32–3, King Alfonso XII to Infanta Paz, 20.3.1885

13. Sencourt, *Spain's Uncertain Crown*, p. 252
14. *The Times*, 25.11.1885
15. Aronson, *Royal Vendetta*, p. 142
16. Victoria, Letters 1862–1885, vol. III, p. 706, journal, 25.11.1885
17. Ludwig Ferdinand, *Through Four Revolutions*, p. 159, diary, 25.5.1886
18. Pilar and Chapman-Huston, *Don Alfonso XIII*, p. 44
19. Aronson, *Royal Vendetta*, p. 147

7: 'The smallest quantity of King' (pp. 102–16)
1. Aronson, *Royal Vendetta*, p. 148
2. Sencourt, *Spain's Uncertain Crown*, p. 256
3. *The Times*, 18.5.1886
4. Petrie, *King Alfonso XIII*, p. 46
5. Pilar and Chapman-Huston, *Don Alfonso XIII*, p. 47
6. Aronson, *Royal Vendetta*, p. 151
7. Pilar and Chapman-Huston, *Don Alfonso XIII*, p. 52, Queen Isabel to Infanta Paz, 21.1.1890
8. Ludwig Ferdinand, *Through Four Revolutions*, p. 196, Paz to Queen Isabel, 20.1.1890
9. Pilar and Chapman-Huston, *Don Alfonso XIII*, p. 54
10. Pilar and Chapman-Huston, *Don Alfonso XIII*, p. 61
11. Aronson, *Royal Vendetta*, p. 154
12. Pilar and Chapman-Huston, *Don Alfonso XIII*, p. 61
13. Graham, *King Alfonso XIII*, p. 51
14. Graham, *King Alfonso XIII*, p. 54
15. Sencourt, *Spain's Uncertain Crown*, p. 274
16. Sencourt, *Spain's Uncertain Crown*, p. 274
17. Sencourt, *Spain's Uncertain Crown*, p. 277
18. Erskine, *Twenty-nine Years*, p. 37
19. Vacaresco, *Kings and Queens*, p. 229
20. Graham, *King Alfonso XIII*, p. 61
21. Wells, *Last King*, p. 42
22. Pilar and Chapman-Huston, *Don Alfonso XIII*, p. 59
23. Graham, *King Alfonso XIII*, p. 72

24. Aronson, *Royal Vendetta*, p. 156
25. Eulalia, *Court Life*, p. 18
26. Eulalia, *Court Life*, p. 190
27. *The Times*, 11.4.1904
28. Polnay, *Queen of Spain*, p. 206

8: 'An awful danger' (pp. 117–34)
1. Graham, *King Alfonso XIII*, p. 171
2. *The Times*, 2.6.1905
3. Gelardi, *Born to Rule*, p. 131
4. Noel, *Ena*, p. 53
5. Gelardi, *Born to Rule*, p. 133
6. Graham, *King Alfonso XIII*, p. 171
7. PRO NI, MSS D/4091/B/3/1/5, Princess Beatrice to Louisa, Lady Antrim, 16.2.1906
8. Lee, *King Edward VII*, vol. II, p. 514
9. Aronson, *Royal Vendetta*, p. 179
10. Argyll Etkin, King Edward VII to Arthur, Duke of Connaught, 16.2.1906
11. Brook-Shepherd, *Uncle of Europe*, p. 107
12. Pope-Hennessy, *Queen Mary*, p. 401
13. Gore, *King George V*, p. 212
14. Gore, *King George V*, p. 212, Prince of Wales journal, 31.5.1906
15. Pope-Hennessy, *Queen Mary*, p. 407
16. BL, Add. MSS 43830, Queen Ena to Lady Paget, 22 June 1906
17. Lee, *King Edward VII*, vol. II, p. 535
18. Lee, *King Edward VII*, vol. II, p. 536
19. Lee, *King Edward VII*, vol. II, p. 537
20. Petrie, *King Alfonso XIII*, p. 92
21. Gelardi, *Born to Rule*, p. 158
22. BL, Add. MSS 46721/178, Princess Beatrice to Bishop of Ripon, 23.12.1907
23. Pilar and Chapman-Huston, *Don Alfonso XIII*, p. 138
24. Erskine, *Twenty-nine Years*, p. 153
25. Graham, *King Alfonso XIII*, pp. 223–4

9: 'Neutrality was a murderous risk' (pp. 135–55)
1. Sencourt, *Spain's Uncertain Crown*, p. 315
2. RA GV CC45/475, Queen Ena to Crown Princess Margaret of Sweden, 21.2.1915

3. Noel, *Ena*, pp. 154–5
4. Sencourt, *Spain's Uncertain Crown*, p. 315
5. Churchill, *Great Contemporaries*, p. 162
6. Ibañez, *Alfonso XIII Unmasked*, pp. 28–9
7. Pilar and Chapman-Huston, *Don Alfonso XIII*, p. 160
8. *The Times*, 9.9.1915
9. RA GV AA43/288, Queen Ena to Queen Mary, 17.11.1918
10. *The Times*, 24.12.1918
11. Petrie, *King Alfonso XIII*, p. 161
12. Petrie, *King Alfonso XIII*, p. 161
13. Carr, *Spain 1808–1975*, p. 523
14. Noel, *Ena*, p. 159
15. Medrano, 'The Others'
16. Noel, *Ena*, p. 205
17. Pakula, *Last Romantic*, p. 373
18. Gelardi, *Born to Rule*, p. 330
19. *The Times*, 16.4.1969
20. Breese, *Hutch*, p. 29
21. RA GV CC45/697, Queen Ena to Queen Mary, 25.7.1926

10: 'He tires of everything' (pp. 156–73)
1. Sencourt, *Spain's Uncertain Crown*, pp. 337–9
2. Carr, *Spain 1808–1975*, p. 582
3. RA GV CC45/799, Ena to Queen Mary, 9.10.1930
4. Sencourt, *King Alfonso*, p. 216
5. *The Times*, 18.3.1918
6. Sencourt, *Spain's Uncertain Crown*, p. 350
7. Wells, *Last King*, p. 233
8. Sencourt, *Spain's Uncertain Crown*, p. 355
9. Pilar and Chapman-Huston, *Don Alfonso XIII*, p. 384; *The Times*, 16.4.1931
10. Sencourt, *King Alfonso*, p. 231
11. Alexander, *Twilight of Royalty*, p. 18
12. *The Times*, 16.4.1931
13. *New York Times*, 16.4.1931
14. Sencourt, *King Alfonso* (article)

11: 'Always such a gentleman' (pp. 174–88)
1. Noel, *Ena*, p. 240

2. Alexander, *Twilight of Royalty*, pp. 21–3
3. Erskine, *Twenty-nine Years*, p. 248, Petrie, *King Alfonso XIII*, p. 229, *The Times*, 6.5.1931
4. *The Times*, 21.11.1931
5. Churchill, *Great Contemporaries*, p. 159
6. Churchill, *Great Contemporaries*, p. 168
7. Petrie, *Spanish Royal House*, p. 257
8. Preston, *Juan Carlos*, p. 12
9. Gelardi, *Born to Rule*, p. 386
10. Noel, *Ena*, p. 249
11. Preston, *Juan Carlos*, p. 10
12. Preston, *Juan Carlos*, pp. 7–8
13. Whitaker, *We Cannot Escape History*, p. 106
14. Noel, *Ena*, p. 260
15. Noel, *Ena*, p. 262
16. Gonzalez-Doria, *Las Reinas de Espana*, p. 604

12: 'Better to be dumb than to stammer' (pp. 189–209)
1. Preston, *Juan Carlos*, p. 17–19
2. Petrie, *Spanish Royal House*, pp. 257–8
3. Petrie, *Spanish Royal House*, pp. 260–1
4. Petrie, *Spanish Royal House*, p. 262
5. Noel, *Ena*, pp. 66–8; Preston, *Juan Carlos*, p. 34
6. Preston, *Juan Carlos*, p. 76
7. Vilallonga, *The King*, p. 65
8. Powell, *Juan Carlos*, p. 17; Preston, *Juan Carlos*, p. 101
9. Preston, *Juan Carlos*, p. 105
10. Salmador, *Don Juan*, p. 82
11. Hourmouzios, *No Ordinary Crown*, p. 321
12. Preston, *Juan Carlos*, p. 167
13. Preston, *Juan Carlos*, p. 202
14. Preston, *Juan Carlos*, p. 209
15. Preston, *Juan Carlos*, p. 213

13: The Last Days of the Republic (pp. 210–24)
1. Preston, *Juan Carlos*, p. 215
2. Gelardi, *Born to Rule*, p. 395
3. Noel, *Ena*, p. 296
4. *The Times*, 12.2.1968

Notes

5. Private information
6. Preston, *Juan Carlos*, p. 237
7. *Independent*, 2.4.1993
8. Ziegler, *Mountbatten*, p. 678, Earl Mountbatten to Juan Carlos, 14.12.1969
9. Preston, *Juan Carlos*, p. 248
10. Preston, *Juan Carlos*, p. 255
11. Vilallonga, *The King*, p. 175

14: 'We are all monarchists now'
(pp. 225–34)
1. *The Times*, 24.11.1975
2. Preston, *Juan Carlos*, p. 321, *The Times*, 25.11.1975

3. Hooper, *New Spaniards*, p. 96
4. *The Times*, 21.11.1985
5. Preston, *Juan Carlos*, p. 393
6. *The Times*, 23.7.1977
7. Preston, *Juan Carlos*, p. 416
8. Vilallonga, *The King*, pp. 176–7
9. *The Times*, 24.2.1981
10. *The Times*, 27.2.1981
11. Vilallonga, *The King*, p. 112
12. Medrano, 'The Others'
13. Vilallonga, *The King*, p. 150
14. BBC internet news, 20.11.2000
15. *Daily Telegraph*, 12.3.2004
16. *Spain Herald*, internet, 23.11.2005
17. *Expatica*, internet, 14.4.2005

239

Bibliography

LETTERS

British Library, London: letters of Queen Victoria Eugenie to Mrs Paget, and Princess Beatrice to Revd William Boyd Carpenter, Bishop of Ripon

Public Record Office, London, letters of Sir John Crampton to Lord Palmerston and Lord John Russell

Public Record Office, Northern Ireland, letters of Princess Beatrice and Louisa, Lady Antrim

Royal Archives, Windsor, letters of Queen Victoria Eugenie to Queen Mary

Argyll Etkin, London, letter of Edward VII to Arthur, Duke of Connaught

BOOKS

The place of publication is London unless otherwise stated

Alexander, Grand Duke, *Twilight of Royalty* (New York, Ray Long & Richard R. Smith, 1932)

Aronson, Theo, *Grandmama of Europe: The Crowned Descendants of Queen Victoria* (Cassell, 1973)

——, *Royal Vendetta: The Crown of Spain 1829–1965* (Oldbourne, 1966)

Breese, Charlotte, *Hutch* (Bloomsbury, 1999)

Brook-Shepherd, Gordon, *Royal Sunset: The Dynasties of Europe and the Great War* (Weidenfeld & Nicolson, 1987)

——, *Uncle of Europe: The Social and Diplomatic Life of Edward VII* (Collins, 1975)

Carr, Raymond, *Spain 1808–1975*, 2nd edn (Oxford, Clarendon, 1982)

Challice, Rachel, *Secret History of the Court of Spain during the Last Century* (John Long, 1909)

Churchill, Winston, *Great Contemporaries* (Odhams, 1947)

Connell, Brian, *Regina v. Palmerston: The Correspondence between Queen Victoria and Her Foreign and Prime Minister 1837–1865* (Evans Bros, 1962)

Duff, David, *The Shy Princess: The Life of HRH Princess Beatrice, the Youngest Daughter and Constant Companion of Queen Victoria* (Evans, 1958)

Erskine, Mrs Steuart, *Twenty-nine Years: The Reign of King Alfonso XIII of Spain* (Hutchinson, 1931)

Eulalia, HRH The Infanta Eulalia of Spain, *Court Life from Within* (Cassell, 1915)

Frederick, Emperor, *Diaries of the Emperor Frederick*, ed. Margarethe von Poschinger, trans. Frances A. Welby (Chapman & Hall, 1902)

Galiano, Alvaro Alcala, *The Fall of a Throne* (Butterworth, 1933)

240

Gelardi, Julia P., *Born to Rule: Granddaughters of Victoria, Queens of Europe* (Headline, 2005)

Gonzalez-Doria, Fernando, *Las Reinas de España* (Madrid, Editorial Bitacora, 1989)

Gore, John, *King George V: A Personal Memoir* (John Murray, 1941)

Graham, Evelyn, *The Life Story of King Alfonso XIII* (Herbert Jenkins, 1930)

Hardinge, Sir Alexander, *A Diplomatist in Europe* (Jonathan Cape, 1927)

Haslip, Joan, *Imperial Adventurer: Emperor Maximilian of Mexico and His Empress* (Weidenfeld & Nicolson, 1971)

Hooper, John, *The New Spaniards* (Penguin, 1995)

Hourmouzios, Stelio, *No Ordinary Crown: A Biography of King Paul of the Hellenes* (Weidenfeld & Nicolson, 1972)

Hume, Martin, *Modern Spain, 1788–1898* (T. Fisher Unwin, 1907)

Ibañez, Vicente Blasco, *Alfonso XIII Unmasked: The Military Terror in Spain* (Eveleigh, Nash & Grayson, 1925)

Irving, Washington, *Letters from Sunnyside and Spain* (New Haven, CT, Yale University Press, 1928)

Judd, Denis, *Eclipse of Kings: European Monarchies in the Twentieth Century* (Macdonald & Jane, 1976)

Lee, Sir Sidney, *King Edward VII*, 2 vols (John Murray, 1925–7)

Ludwig Ferdinand of Bavaria, Infanta of Spain, Princess, *Through Four Revolutions, 1862–1933* (John Murray, 1933)

Mack Smith, Denis, *Italy and its Monarchy* (Yale University Press, 1988)

Noel, Gerard, Ena, *Spain's English Queen* (Constable, 1984)

Pakula, Hannah, *The Last Romantic: A Biography of Queen Marie of Roumania* (Weidenfeld & Nicolson, 1985)

Parry, E. Jones, *The Spanish Marriages 1841–1846* (Macmillan, 1936)

Petrie, Sir Charles, *King Alfonso XIII and His Age* (Chapman & Hall, 1963)

——, *The Spanish Royal House* (Geoffrey Bles, 1962)

Pilar of Bavaria, Princess, and Chapman-Huston, Desmond, *Don Alfonso XIII: A Study of Monarchy* (John Murray, 1931)

Polnay, Peter de, *A Queen of Spain: Isabel II* (Hollis & Carter, 1962)

Pope-Hennessy, James, *Queen Mary, 1867–1953* (Allen & Unwin, 1959)

Powell, Charles T., *Juan Carlos: Un rey para la democracia* (Barcelona, 1995)

Preston, Paul, *Franco: A Biography* (HarperCollins, 1993)

——, *Juan Carlos: A People's King* (HarperCollins, 2004)

Salmador, Victor, *Don Juan. Los Secretos de un Rey Sin Trono* (Madrid, 1993)

Sencourt, Robert, *King Alfonso: a Biography* (Faber, 1942)

——, *Spain's Uncertain Crown: the Story of the Spanish Sovereigns 1808–1931* (Ernest Benn, 1932)

Vacaresco, Hélène, *Kings and Queens I Have Known* (Harper, 1904)

Van der Kiste, John, *Crowns in a Changing World: The British and European Monarchies 1901–36* (Stroud, Sutton, 1993)

Victoria, Queen, *The Letters of Queen Victoria: a Selection from Her Majesty's Correspondence Between the Years 1837 and 1861*, ed. A.C. Benson and Viscount Esher, 3 vols (John Murray, 1907)

——, *The Letters of Queen Victoria, 2nd Series: a Selection from Her Majesty's Correspondence and Journal Between the Years 1862 and 1885*, ed. George Earle Buckle, 3 vols (John Murray, 1926–8)

——, *Your Dear Letter: Private Correspondence of Queen Victoria and the Crown Princess of Prussia, 1865–1871*, ed. Roger Fulford (Evans Bros, 1971)

Bibliography

Vilallonga, José Luis de, *The King: A Life of King Juan Carlos of Spain* (Weidenfeld & Nicolson, 1994)

Wells, Warre Bradley, *The Last King: Don Alfonso XIII of Spain* (Frederick Muller, 1934)

Whitaker, John T., *We Cannot Escape History* (New York, Macmillan, 1943)

Woodham-Smith, Cecil, *Queen Victoria, Her Life and Times: Volume One, 1819–1861* (Hamish Hamilton, 1972)

Ziegler, Philip, *Mountbatten: The Official Biography* (Collins, 1985)

ARTICLES

Aronson, Theo, 'Spain's Flamboyant Monarch, Queen Isabel II', in *Royalty Digest* I, April 1992

Beéche, Arturo E., 'Infantas of Spain', in *European Royal History Journal* XXXI–XXXII, February–April 2003

Bunford, Stephen, 'Spanish Prince, French King or Victim?' (Don Jaime), in *Royalty Digest* VII, April 1998

Medrano, Ricardo Mateos Sainz de, 'The Others: the Illegitimate Children of Kings Alfonso XII and Alfonso XIII', in *Royalty Digest* XII, November 2002

——, 'The Lovers of Isabel II', in *Royalty Digest* III, March 1994

Nash, Michael, 'A Sovereign for Spain' (Amedeo), in *Royalty Digest* X, July 2000

Sencourt, Robert, 'King Alfonso', in *Royalty Digest* V, August 1995 (reprinted from *Contemporary Review*, 1941)

PERIODICALS

Daily Telegraph
European Royal History Journal
The Independent
New York Times
Royalty Digest
The Times

Index

243

Index

Index

Index